FRENCH COOKING

FRENCH COOKING

Eileen Reece

Bloomsbury Books
London

PENGUIN BOOKS

Published by the Penguin Group
Penguin Books Ltd, 27 Wrights Lane, London W8 5TZ, England
Penguin Books USA Inc., 375 Hudson Street, New York, New York 10014, USA
Penguin Books Australia Ltd, Ringwood, Victoria, Australia
Penguin Books Canada Ltd, 10 Alcorn Avenue, Toronto, Ontario, Canada M4V 3B2
Penguin Books (NZ) Ltd, 182–190 Wairau Road, Auckland 10, New Zealand

Penguin Books Ltd, Registered Offices: Harmondsworth, Middlesex, England

First published 1978
This edition published by Bloomsbury Books, an imprint of
Godfrey Cave Associates, 42 Bloomsbury Street, London WC1B 3QJ,
under licence from Penguin Books Ltd, 1992

ISBN 1 854 71056 7

Editors: Mary Anne Sanders and Fiona Roxburgh
Designers: Yvonne Dedman and Gail Engert
Series designer: Rod Springett Associates
Photographer: Paul Kemp
Props research: Penny Markham
Diagrams: Marion Appleton
Production: Georgina Ewer

Printed in Hong Kong by Imago

Contents

WEIGHTS AND MEASURES

Imperial	US
$2\frac{1}{2}$ oz Allbran	1 cup
1 lb apples (diced)	4 cups
2 oz bacon, streaky	3 slices fatty bacon
2 oz bean sprouts	1 cup
4 oz black or redcurrants, blueberries	1 cup
4 oz breadcrumbs (fine dried)	1 cup
2 oz breadcrumbs (fresh soft), cake crumbs	1 cup
8 oz butter, margarine, lard, dripping	1 cup butter, margarine, shortening, drippings
3-4 oz button mushrooms	1 cup
8 oz cabbage (finely chopped)	3 cups
12 oz clear honey, golden syrup, molasses, black treacle	1 cup (1 lb $=1\frac{1}{3}$ cups) honey, maple syrup, molasses, black treacle
1 oz cooking chocolate	1 square baking chocolate
$4\frac{1}{2}$ oz cornflour	1 cup cornstarch
8 oz cottage, cream cheese	1 cup
$\frac{1}{4}$ pint single, double cream	$\frac{1}{2}$ cup + 2 tablespoons ($\frac{2}{3}$ cup) light, heavy cream
2 oz curry powder	$\frac{1}{2}$ cup
3 oz desiccated coconut	1 cup shredded coconut
4 oz digestive biscuits (8 biscuits)	1 cup Graham crackers
7 oz dried chick peas, haricot beans	1 cup garbanzos, navy beans
4 oz flour, plain or self-raising	2 tablespoons all-purpose or self-rising flour
$\frac{1}{2}$ oz gelatine (1 tablespoon sets 2 cups liquid)	2 envelopes
3 oz preserved ginger (chopped)	$\frac{1}{3}$ cup
8 oz glacé cherries	1 cup candied cherries
$3\frac{1}{2}$ lbs gooseberries	9 cups
4 oz grated cheese, Cheddar type, Parmesan	1 cup
4 oz ground almonds	1 cup
7 oz long-grain rice	1 cup
4 oz macaroni, raw	1 cup
8 oz mashed potato	1 cup
8 oz minced raw meat	1 cup ground raw meat, firmly packed
4 oz nuts (chopped)	1 cup
2 oz onion (chopped)	$\frac{1}{2}$ cup
2 oz parsley (chopped)	$1\frac{1}{2}$ cups
6 oz pickled beetroot (chopped)	1 cup
6 oz peeled prawns	1 cup peeled shrimp
5-6 oz raisins, currants, sultanas (chopped), candied peel	1 cup (1 lb =3 cups)
5 oz raspberries	1 cup
$3\frac{1}{2}$ oz rolled oats	1 cup
8 oz sausagemeat	1 cup
5 oz strawberries, whole	1 cup
8 oz sugar, castor or granulated	1 cup, firmly packed
4 oz sugar, icing (sieved)	1 cup sifted confectioner's sugar
8 oz tomatoes (chopped)	1 cup
$2\frac{3}{4}$ oz (smallest can) tomato purée	$\frac{1}{4}$ cup
4 teaspoons dried yeast	4 teaspoons active dry yeast
$\frac{1}{4}$ pint yoghurt	$\frac{1}{2}$ cup + 2 tablespoons ($\frac{2}{3}$ cup)

Liquid Measurements

20 fluid oz =1 Imperial pint	16 fluid oz =1 American pint
10 fluid oz $=\frac{1}{2}$ Imperial pint	8 fluid oz =1 American cup

Introduction

The French take their food seriously. Cooking they regard as an art. The traditions of French cooking are guarded by two committees of experts. *L'Académie Culinaire de France* through the expertise of its members, all brilliant chefs of repute, not only trains those aspirants to its ranks whose natural talent they consider worthy, they also safeguard the authenticity of the country's traditional recipes.

When, for example, doubts arise in any circumstance as to the exact ingredients and preparation of any national dish, theirs is the last word. Acting in concert with them *L'Académie des Gastronomes*, practised gastronomers of lifelong standing, undertake the task of co-ordinating the preparatory studies for the training of chefs and collecting and testing those recipes which merit the description of classic. In addition they determine the exact character of the well-known regional dishes and the vast numbers of lesser-known country recipes in order to present their findings to the general public in various publications.

This joint protection is given not only to the fine flower of *haute cuisine*, it is applied just as intently to the traditional dishes that every housewife and mother prepares for her family. Her interest is to please their palate, prepare food beneficial to their health and also to find in her cooking an expression of that artistic ability inherent in all people, whatever form it takes.

The Frenchwoman, characteristically thrifty, displays her skill with pleasure. It begins with the choice of ingredients. Potatoes are chosen as carefully as peaches, value for money demanded, and good quality insisted upon in every cut of beef and bunch of radishes.

The use of wine, cream and butter in French cooking is not foreign extravagance as judged by our Edwardian forefathers. The French family uses butter in cooking, not on its bread, cream goes into the sauce not over the fruit, and the bottle of wine for the table leaves a glassful in the kitchen to flavour the casserole.

Recourse to these seemingly luxurious ingredients persists from the times when lack of communications in the largest country in Europe made each region dependent on its own products. In Normandy, an area of lush pastures bordered by apple trees, eggs, cream and apple brandy were everyday ingredients for local inhabitants, and the Burgundian naturally cooked his game in red wine. But in southern France where good quality wine is not generally produced, the Provençal has always cooked his exotic vegetables in olive oil and the wild herbs that cover the mountain sides.

In France food snobberies give way to appreciation of quality. Guests will be presented with Strasbourg black puddings, perfect mashed potatoes and pungent apple purée as assuredly as the same hostess will serve roast duck cooked with muscat grapes on another occasion.

Care, attention to detail and patience are as important in French cooking as the ingredients. These qualities, and the interest shown by those who savour it as keenly as by those who cook it, are the secrets of their art.

Kitchen equipment

The utensils used in French family kitchens are notable for their quality, not for their number or their decorative effect.

The metals used to make them, for example the cast-iron *pot-au-feu* and the cast-iron enamel-lined *cocotte* with domed lid, are high in heat conductivity and form miniature ovens when used on top of the cooker. This effects considerable saving not only of fuel but in the ingredients themselves. A joint cooked by this classic French method suffers much less shrinkage than when cooked in the oven; a casserole can be started on top of the cooker and then transferred to the oven when the ingredients are simmering. All these pans perform best over a very low heat, thereby quickly recuperating in fuel economy their not inconsiderable cost. They do, however, last for generations.

The cast-iron, enamel-lined utensils made by Le Creuset and the other equipment mentioned are obtainable at all kitchen equipment shops, and from the kitchen departments of large department stores.

The following items are planned to cater for a family of 4–6 people.

1. Mouli-légumes – this metal vegetable mill replaces an electric blender at much less cost and produces various textures.
2. Pot roaster or *Doufeu* with indented lid, 24 cm ($9\frac{3}{4}$ in) diameter for soups, *pot-au-feu*, and roasting joints. When the indented lid is kept filled with hot water during cooking, condensation is created inside the casserole. This bastes the meat automatically, keeps it moist and considerably reduces shrinkage.
3. Oval earthenware game casserole with domed lid, also for cooking pâté.
4. Round cocotte for vegetables.
5. Birch whisk. This avoids scratching enamelled surfaces.
6. Small heavy saucepan with pouring lip, 14 cm ($5\frac{1}{2}$ in) diameter and 10 cm (4 in) deep. This pan must be small enough to place in a larger pan of hot water to form a *bain-marie* when making sauces (*see page* 14). This is more practical than using an English double-boiler where the heat of the water cannot be judged visually. In an emergency, a baking tin half-filled with hot water replaces a *bain-marie* for use in the oven.
7. *Bain-marie* stand. For resting a saucepan in a larger one of hot water.
8. *Sauté* pan with lid, 25 cm (10 in) diameter. This shallow wide-based pan takes a whole cut chicken, vegetables and liquids. When the ingredients are browned and liquids added, they can be left to cook without further supervision.
9. Oval metal gratin dish 30 cm (12 in) long, 20 cm (8 in) wide. Use also for soufflé omelettes and flambé dishes.
10. Iron frying pans, one 25 cm (10 in) and one 16 cm ($6\frac{1}{2}$ in) diameter. The larger pan is for large omelettes and sealing; the smaller one is for *sauté* preparations.
11. Oval earthenware gratin dishes, 28 cm (11 in), 24 cm ($9\frac{1}{2}$ in), 23 cm (9 in) and 21 cm (8 in) length.
12. Soufflé dishes, 18 cm ($7\frac{1}{4}$ in), 16 cm ($6\frac{1}{2}$ in), and 22 cm ($8\frac{3}{4}$ in) diameter.
13. Charlotte mould.
14. Brioche mould.
15. Shallow wide-topped mixing bowl.
16. Large and small whisk.
17. Baking sheet.
18. Square-ended wooden spatula.
19. Pastry brush.
20. *Gras-maigre* sauceboat. This separates the fat from the juices.
21. Large pestle and mortar.
22. Long-pronged cooking fork.
23. Carving knife with 30 cm ($11\frac{3}{4}$ in) blade.
24. Pair of game scissors.
25. Small pointed vegetable knife with 10 cm (4 in) blade.
26. Cook's knife with 20 cm ($7\frac{3}{4}$ in) blade.
27. Boning knife with 13 cm (5 in) blade.
28. Larding needle (*see page* 97).
29. Trussing pins and skewers (*see page* 43).
30. Chrome soup ladle.
31. Chrome skimmer.
32. Wire sieve.
33. Conical sieve or *chinois* for sieving sauces directly on to a finished dish.

2
3
4
8
9
10
13
15
17
18
19
7
16
12
33
14
32
31
30
29
23
24
25
26
27
28

Stocks and sauces

More good sauces have been invented by the French than by any other nation. They range from the simple but delicious *jus* – for meat juice it is and cannot be called gravy – that is served with roast meat or bird in every home, to the professional sauces of *haute cuisine* that require ingredients such as wine and herbs which, in medieval times, acted as preserving agents to keep meat edible and make it tender for future consumption. The ever-thrifty and logical Gauls then cooked the meat in its marinade, and through long slow cooking the liquid reduced and thickened, a technique perfected through the ages to become the same one used today in French cooking, for it is still true that a good sauce should always be reduced by simmering to intensify both consistency and flavour.

The basic ingredient of a good sauce is a good stock; but nowadays few home cooks have the time to make it. They used instead the leftover *bouillon* of *Pot-au-feu* and *Poule-au-pot* (*see page* 42–3). When none is available they use *bouillon* powder or cubes instead, but these substitutes have an over-riding flavour and are to be avoided when there is the carcass of a roast bird, either poultry or game, left in the larder with which stock can be simply made.

Stocks

Chicken carcass bouillon

White stock

INGREDIENTS

- 1 chicken carcass, skin and debris
- 1 large carrot
- 2 stalks celery
- 1 medium-sized onion
- 1 clove
- salt
- 6 peppercorns
- 1.4 litres ($2\frac{1}{2}$ pints) water

This chicken *bouillon* is an excellent basis for sauces and casseroles.

First brown the carcass (broken into pieces) in the bottom of the oven while it is in use for other cooking. This improves the colour and flavour of the stock. Trim and peel the vegetables and cut them into small pieces, but leave the onion whole and stick the clove into it. Put the vegetables, carcass, and skin, 1 rounded teaspoon salt and the peppercorns into a large pan with the water. Cover the pan and set it over a low heat. When the water boils remove any scum that has collected on the surface with a slotted spoon. To hasten this process add half a cup of cold water or an ice cube once or twice. Simmer until the liquid is reduced by half the original amount – that is, another 30–40 minutes.

Strain off the stock into a wide-topped bowl and leave to cool, then place it in the refrigerator until the fat has solidified on top.

If time is short and the fat must be removed while the stock is still hot, strain it through a sieve into a wide-topped bowl. Remove the excess fat with a large metal spoon and then trail bands of kitchen paper over the surface, using one side only before discarding it. Three or four bands about 8 cm (3 in) wide will clear the stock completely.

Rich beef bouillon

Brown stock

INGREDIENTS

- 40 g ($1\frac{1}{2}$ oz) butter or beef dripping
- 1 kg (2 lb) beef bones, chopped small
- 1 large onion
- 2 medium-sized carrots
- 1 stalk celery
- salt and 8 black peppercorns
- 450 g (1 lb) shin beef, cut into small pieces
- 2.3 litres (4 pints) cold water

Melt the butter or dripping in a large soup pot or braising pan over medium high heat, and in it brown the bones on all sides. Trim and peel the vegetables and cut into medium-sized pieces. Sauté them in the butter until lightly coloured. Then add 2 tablespoons salt, the lightly crushed peppercorns, meat, and the cold water. Bring slowly to boiling point, skim off any froth that rises, adding half a cup of cold water or an ice cube once or twice until the surface is clear. Then reduce the heat, cover and simmer slowly for 2 hours. Uncover the pan and reduce the stock by rapid simmering for a further 20 minutes. Strain and remove the fat first with a large metal spoon and then with bands of kitchen paper.

As meat stock requires long slow cooking, it can be made in advance by starting it on top of the cooker in a metal soup pot and after skimming put into the bottom of the oven when in use for other cooking.

Crêpes aux champignons with a sauce velouté made from rich veal stock

Rich veal stock

INGREDIENTS
1 medium-sized onion
1 large carrot
450 g (1 lb) pie veal (or veal trimmings)
25 g (1 oz) butter
40 g ($1\frac{1}{2}$ oz) flour
150 ml ($\frac{1}{4}$ pint) white wine
425 ml ($\frac{3}{4}$ pint) chicken *bouillon (page 12)*
salt and 4 white peppercorns
bouquet garni

For special recipes such as *sauce velouté* (*see page* 17), concentrated veal stock is sometimes necessary.

Peel the vegetables and chop into small pieces. Cut the veal or trimmings also into small pieces. Melt the butter in a heavy-based saucepan over a medium heat and sauté the meat and vegetables in it. As they begin to colour sprinkle with flour and let it colour until golden brown while stirring with a wooden spoon. Add the wine and allow to reduce by rapid simmering for a few minutes. Add the chicken *bouillon*, the peppercorns and salt to taste and the bouquet garni tied to the handle of the pan. Bring to boiling point and skim off any froth that rises.

Cover and simmer slowly for 1 hour over a low heat, then remove the lid and reduce the stock for 5 minutes by rapid simmering over an increased heat. Strain through a fine sieve and when cold remove the fat first with a large metal spoon and then with bands of kitchen paper. Refrigerate until required. This gives a strong veal stock of good quality.

Fish stock

INGREDIENTS
25 g (1 oz) butter
1 kg (2 lb) white fish trimmings and bones
1 cod's head
1 large onion, peeled and chopped
3 sprigs parsley
725 ml ($1\frac{1}{4}$ pints) cold water
275 ml ($\frac{1}{2}$ pint) dry white wine
1 bayleaf
1 teaspoon salt
$\frac{1}{2}$ teaspoon white pepper

Melt the butter in a large heavy pan over a medium to high heat. Before it begins to colour, add the fish trimmings, bones and the cod's head with the peeled and chopped onion and parsley. Mix well and cook for about 10 minutes until opaque, then add the water, white wine, bayleaf, salt and pepper.

Cook this mixture over a medium heat and when boiling reduce the heat and simmer, uncovered, for 30 minutes skimming the surface when necessary. Strain and remove the fat first with a large metal spoon and then with bands of kitchen paper. Store cooled stock in the refrigerator.

Sauces

There are four methods of thickening a sauce in French cooking:

1. with a starch binding *(liaison)* of plain flour, potato flour, rice, or occasionally with arrowroot (i.e. *sauce béchamel* and *velouté*). This is based on a *roux* or mixture of butter and flour cooked together to various degrees of colour before the liquids are added. These degrees are:

   (i) white – when the butter and flour are cooked without colouring, then milk, white wine or stock is added. Made with milk this is *sauce béchamel* used as a basis for many other sauces. When the *roux* is coloured to pale blonde, strong veal or chicken stock added and the resulting sauce reduced by simmering to at least half, *velouté* is obtained.

   (ii) blonde – when the butter is allowed to colour before the flour is added and they are then cooked together to a golden tone. When beef *bouillon* and/or wine vinegar is added with solid ingredients, a *sauce piquante* is obtained.

   (iii) brown – when the butter is brought to nut colour and the mixture cooked to golden brown. When red wine is added *sauce matelote* is obtained; with Madeira added instead, *sauce madère* is the result. A teaspoon of finely chopped onion browned in the butter before flour is added will give these sauces a good colour.

   To avoid lumps in a starch-bound sauce add the liquid all at once and beat vigorously with a birch whisk. A wire whisk tends to scratch the pan.

2. with a binding of egg yolks and/or cream (i.e. rich *sauce poulette*).
3. with softened butter (i.e. *sauce hollandaise*).
4. with oil (i.e. *sauce mayonnaise*).

1. Sauces bound with starch *(roux)*

Sauce béchamel

TO SERVE SIX

INGREDIENTS
50 g (2 oz) butter
40 g ($1\frac{1}{2}$ oz) flour
425 ml ($\frac{3}{4}$ pint) milk
salt and white pepper

Melt the butter over a medium heat, work in the flour with a wooden spoon and when the mixture froths remove the pan from the heat and add the milk all at once, stirring steadily, to avoid lumps forming. When the sauce is smooth return the pan to the heat and bring to simmering point. Season with salt and pepper to taste and continue cooking for 10 minutes. Add a little more milk if the sauce thickens too much.

There is a second method of adding the liquid to a *roux*: warm the milk and add it little by little, stirring continually and not removing the pan from the heat.

An extra teaspoon of butter cut into little flecks and beaten in one at a time will give the sauce a glossy finish.

If the *béchamel* is made in advance press a piece of buttered paper down on to the surface to prevent a skin forming. To keep hot stand the saucepan on a trivet or upturned saucer in a *bain-marie* or another large pan half-filled with hot water kept at simmering point.

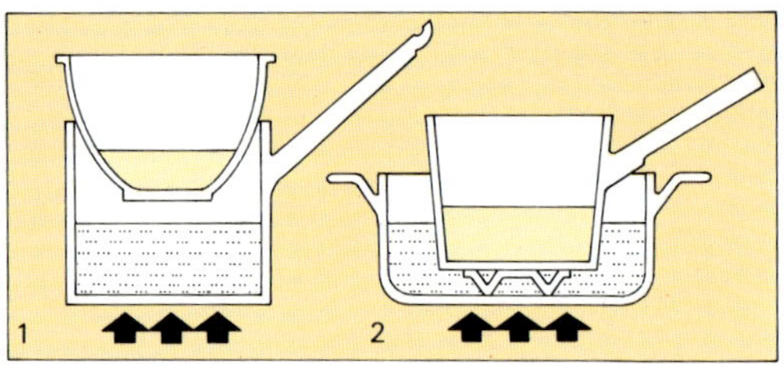

Use of the bain-marie: (1) for making delicate sauces; (2) for making sturdier sauces – note use of trivet

Sauce diable

TO SERVE SIX

INGREDIENTS
450 g (1 lb) shallots
salt and black pepper
425 ml ($\frac{3}{4}$ pint) white wine
15 g ($\frac{1}{2}$ oz) flour
75 g (3 oz) butter
1 tablespoon chervil

Peel and chop the shallots finely, add salt and pepper, and cook them with the white wine over a medium heat until a soft purée is formed. Work the flour into the butter with the fingers until well incorporated, this makes a *beurre manié*. Stir it into the purée and continue stirring until it is dissolved and the sauce starts to simmer and thicken. Continue cooking for 10–15 minutes depending on the thickness desired. Just before serving add the finely chopped chervil. Use parsley if chervil is not available.

Serve with grilled meat of all kinds and with some vegetables, e.g. *Epinards en gâteau* (*see page* 157).

Sauce douce on roast veal

Sauce douce

TO SERVE SIX

INGREDIENTS
50 g (2 oz) butter
150 g (5 oz) onions
25 g (1 oz) flour
425 ml (¾ pint) dry white wine
salt and black pepper
40 g (1½ oz) sugar
25 g (1 oz) blanched almonds
50 g (2 oz) seedless raisins

Melt the butter over a medium heat, add the finely chopped onions and colour them slightly, stirring frequently. Add the flour, and cook to the blonde stage. Season to taste, then pour the wine into the pan all at once. Stir briskly with a birch whisk until smooth and reduce the heat so that the sauce simmers very gently. Meanwhile put the sugar into another small pan with a teaspoon of water. Let it dissolve and when it bubbles and starts to turn golden brown, tip the pan to swirl the sugar around and remove it from the heat so that the caramel will not turn too dark a colour. Dissolve this caramel by adding a ladleful of sauce and stirring vigorously. Return the mixture to the larger pan, add the finely sliced almonds and the raisins. Lower the heat and allow the sauce to simmer briskly and reduce to the consistency desired.

Serve with boiled ox tongue, roast veal or baked ham.

Sauce hachée

TO SERVE SIX

INGREDIENTS
225 g (8 oz) onions
100 g (4 oz) shallots
100 g (4 oz) mushrooms
40 g (1½ oz) tinned anchovy fillets
40 g (1½ oz) capers
1 tablespoon parsley
50 g (2 oz) butter
salt and black pepper
15 g (½ oz) flour
a few tablespoons white wine or *bouillon*

Peel and trim the onions, shallots and mushrooms, drain the anchovies and pat them dry on kitchen paper, add the capers and parsley and chop them all together very finely. Put this mixture into a saucepan, add the butter, salt and pepper to taste, mix well and leave over low heat to cook for 20 minutes, stirring occasionally. Remove the pan from the heat and allow to cool a little before working in the flour very thoroughly. Return the pan to the heat and when the sauce starts to simmer, cook for 5–10 minutes, stirring constantly. If the sauce thickens too much add two or three tablespoons of white wine or *bouillon* and simmer for a further 3 minutes. This sauce is excellent served with grilled steak or fish.

Sauce ivoire

TO SERVE SIX

INGREDIENTS
425 ml ($\frac{3}{4}$ pint) *sauce béchamel* (*page* 14)
1 litre ($1\frac{3}{4}$ pints) strong chicken *bouillon* (*page* 12)
salt and pepper

Heat the *sauce béchamel* in a heavy saucepan and beat it well before adding the heated chicken *bouillon* to it little by little, beating it in with a birch whisk. Continue simmering briskly and stirring until the sauce is reduced to a medium thick *béchamel*, that is, by about a half. Test for seasoning before serving. Whatever the quantity of *béchamel* used the quantity of *bouillon* should be about double.

This is the classic sauce to serve with *Poule au pot* (*see page* 43). It is made with the strong chicken and vegetable *bouillon* produced in cooking the chicken.

Sauce mornay

TO SERVE SIX

INGREDIENTS
425 ml ($\frac{3}{4}$ pint) *sauce béchamel* (*page* 14)
grated nutmeg
salt and black pepper
100 g (4 oz) grated *gruyère* and Parmesan mixed together
1 teaspoon butter

Flavour the *sauce béchamel* with grated nutmeg and season with salt and pepper to taste and when thick and still bubbling, draw the pan away from the heat and beat in the grated cheese until melted, and the butter cut into little flecks. This will make the sauce glossy. Do not allow the sauce to boil in the pan once the cheese has been added as this causes the cheese to toughen. Serve with fish, eggs and vegetables.

When cooked vegetables or other ingredients are mixed with this sauce, scattered with fine baked breadcrumbs and a little more cheese, then browned under the grill, the crisp crust it forms is called a *gratin*.

Sauce piquante
(white)

TO SERVE SIX

INGREDIENTS
175 g (6 oz) onion
50 g (2 oz) butter
1 peeled clove garlic
2 tablespoons mixed chopped parsley and chives
1 sprig each of tarragon and savory
1 bayleaf
25 g (1 oz) flour
225 ml (8 fl oz) white wine
225 ml (8 fl oz) fish stock (*page* 13)
1 teaspoon wine vinegar
salt and pepper
juice of $\frac{1}{2}$ a lemon

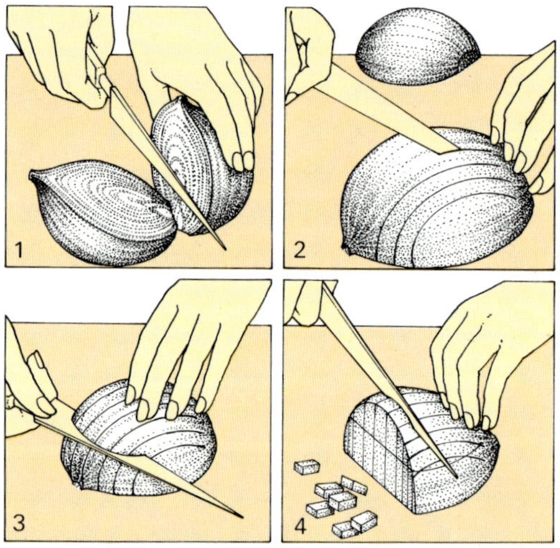

(1) Cut onion in half. (2) Slice lengthways, stopping just before the root. (3) Make one horizontal cut. (4) Chop downwards

Peel and finely chop the onion. Melt the butter over a medium heat and in it sauté the onion and garlic to the blonde stage. Add the mixed parsley and chives and the tarragon, savory and bayleaf tied together. Mix well with a wooden spoon, sprinkle with flour and work it in completely before adding the wine all at once. Stir until smooth and then add the fish stock and vinegar. Season with salt and pepper and cook until thickened. Add lemon juice to taste and continue simmering and reducing, skimming off any froth that rises to the surface. Cook for about 15 minutes after the sauce starts simmering, then test for seasoning and add a few more drops of lemon juice if necessary. Strain into a heated sauceboat.

Serve with poached halibut or other white fish.

Sauce poulette

TO SERVE SIX

INGREDIENTS
425 ml ($\frac{3}{4}$ pint) *sauce béchamel* (*page* 14)
2 tablespoons chopped parsley
2 egg yolks
juice of $\frac{1}{2}$ a lemon
salt and black pepper

When the *sauce béchamel* is smooth and starts to thicken during cooking, add half the parsley, stir it in well and continue cooking for 10 minutes. Meanwhile put the egg yolks into a small basin and beat in half the lemon juice. When the *béchamel* has been reduced for a further 5 minutes and is ready to serve add a little of it to the egg yolks, beat this mixture together and return it to the saucepan. Add the rest of the parsley, salt, pepper and more lemon juice if necessary and reheat but do not let it boil again.

Serve with broad beans, steamed chicken or grilled fish.

Sauce soubise

Onion sauce

TO SERVE SIX

INGREDIENTS

225 g (8 oz) peeled onions
25 g (1 oz) rice
275 ml ($\frac{1}{2}$ pint) cold water
salt and white pepper
grated nutmeg
25 g (1 oz) butter
100 g (4 oz) double cream

Chop the onions. Put them into a saucepan with the rice and cover generously with cold water. Add salt, pepper and a generous pinch of grated nutmeg. Cover the pan and place it over a medium heat until boiling point is reached, then reduce the heat to very low and simmer until the rice and onions are quite soft – about 20 minutes. Liquidize this mixture in the electric blender or pass it through a mouli-légumes. Return it to the pan but not to the heat and beat in the butter cut into small pieces.

Now add the cream little by little and test for seasoning, adding more pepper and/or nutmeg if necessary. Reheat very gently over a very low heat but do not allow the sauce to boil. Cook in an enamel-lined pan to prevent the onions discolouring.

Serve with roast lamb and haricot beans (*see page* 102) or with soft-boiled eggs (*see Oeufs soubise page* 70).

Sauce velouté

TO SERVE SIX

INGREDIENTS

50 g (2 oz) butter
40 g ($1\frac{1}{2}$ oz) flour
1 litre ($1\frac{3}{4}$ pints) rich veal stock (*page* 13) or rich chicken broth
salt and white pepper

Melt the butter in a heavy saucepan over a medium heat, allow to froth and work in the flour with a wooden spoon. Allow to colour to very pale blonde and add the stock or broth by the method preferred: either draw the pan away from the heat and add the cold stock all at once, then heat and whisk until smooth; or add hot stock little by little. Add the salt and white pepper. When smooth, bring to boiling point, reduce the heat and simmer slowly for 30 minutes, stirring frequently until the sauce has reduced by half. Skim the surface of any foam that rises, and strain before serving. Serve with *Crêpes aux champignons* (*see pages* 13 and 52).

Sauce piquante

(brown)

TO SERVE SIX

INGREDIENTS

1 shallot
75 ml (3 fl oz) wine vinegar
3 lumps sugar
50 g (2 oz) butter
40 g ($1\frac{1}{2}$ oz) flour
300 ml (just over $\frac{1}{2}$ pint) beef *bouillon* (*page* 12)
salt and black pepper
2 small pickled gherkins

Peel the shallot and chop finely. Put it into a small saucepan over a low heat with the vinegar and sugar. Mix well and reduce to half by simmering, but watch it closely as vinegar evaporates rapidly. In another saucepan make a brown *roux* by melting the butter to nut colour before working in the flour and cooking till golden brown. Add the *bouillon,* salt and pepper, then add the reduced vinegar and shallot. Bring to boiling point and then simmer gently for 10 minutes or until the desired consistency is reached. This sauce should not be too thick.

When required, dice the gherkins, strain the sauce into a heated sauceboat, add the gherkins, mix well and serve immediately. Never boil the sauce after the gherkins are added. If it is to be kept hot or reheated, place the sauceboat in a *bain-marie.*

Serve with boiled gammon, ox tongue, or with grilled trout (*see page* 83).

Sauce poivrade

TO SERVE SIX

INGREDIENTS

2 tablespoons oil
100 g (4 oz) carrot
100 g (4 oz) onion
1 large sprig parsley, 1 small sprig thyme, 1 bayleaf
75 ml (3 fl oz) wine vinegar
300 ml (just over $\frac{1}{2}$ pint) marinade (*page* 96)
75 g (3 oz) butter
50 g (2 oz) flour
425 ml ($\frac{3}{4}$ pint) beef *bouillon* (*page* 12)
salt and 8 black peppercorns

This sauce is made when a marinade is left over (*see Daube de gardiens, page* 96).

Heat the oil in a saucepan. Peel and coarsely chop the carrot and onion and mix in the oil. Add the herbs tied together and stir over a medium heat until the vegetables start to colour, then add the wine vinegar and half the marinade. When the mixture starts to simmer, stir well and allow to reduce to about a third.

In a second pan melt half the butter, work in the flour with a wooden spoon and when frothy cook to the blonde stage, then add the boiling hot *bouillon,* whip together with a birch whisk and add to the vegetables and marinade. Simmer gently for 30 minutes, then add salt to taste and the coarsely crushed peppercorns. Cook for a further 10 minutes. Strain the sauce through a nylon sieve into a clean pan. Add the rest of the marinade and leave to simmer for a further 30 minutes. Just before serving remove the pan from the heat and whip in the rest of the butter cut into small pieces. This sauce is served with marinated meat of any kind, or with fish cooked in *court-bouillon* (*see page* 74).

Sauce tomate provençale

Fresh tomato sauce

TO SERVE SIX

INGREDIENTS
350 g (¾ lb) onions
1 kg (2 lb) ripe tomatoes (Mediterranean variety if possible)
3 tablespoons olive oil
1 sprig rosemary, 1 sprig thyme, 1 bayleaf
salt and black pepper
2 lumps sugar

Peel and coarsely chop the onions and cut up the unpeeled tomatoes. Heat the oil in a heavy pan over a medium heat and put the vegetables into it. Tie the herbs together with thin string and put them into the pan, tying the loose end to the handle. Season with salt and freshly ground black pepper, add the sugar and when boiling point is reached reduce the heat, cover the pan and simmer for 1 hour. Then simmer uncovered until a thick purée is obtained. Remove the herbs and sieve the purée working it with a wooden spoon to pass through as much of the pulp as possible. Leave until cold. Store in closed jars in the refrigerator or preserve in bottles by your approved method. This sauce can be deep-frozen.

The following method can be used when tomatoes are expensive. After simmering the vegetables and herbs for 1 hour, remove from the heat and sieve. Thicken the purée with a blonde *roux* (*see page* 14) made with 25 g (1 oz) flour, 25 g (1 oz) butter and 425 ml (¾ pint) cooked sieved mixture. Serve with egg, meat, fish and vegetable dishes.

Sauce madère

TO SERVE SIX

INGREDIENTS
75 g (3 oz) butter
50 g (2 oz) flour
275 ml (½ pint) beef *bouillon* (*page* 12)
150 ml (¼ pint) Madeira
salt and pepper
15 g (½ oz) butter

Melt the butter over a medium heat to the golden brown stage. Do not let it colour too deeply. Add the flour and work it in before pouring in the *bouillon* little by little, stirring constantly with a wire whisk. Add the Madeira gradually, season to taste and continue cooking and stirring until the sauce has reduced and thickened. Should it become too thick add a little more *bouillon*. It should be the consistency of single cream. Add a small piece of butter cut into little flecks just before serving. Always cook this sauce over a medium heat.

Serve with gammon, grilled kidneys and roast red meats.

Sauce matelote

Red wine sauce

TO SERVE SIX

INGREDIENTS
4 large open mushrooms
2 shallots
½ litre (¾ pint) red wine
75 g (3 oz) butter
salt
40 g (1½ oz) flour
black pepper

Wipe the mushrooms with a damp cloth, trim and chop coarsely. Skins from mushrooms used in other dishes may also be added to give a good dark colour to the sauce. Peel and finely chop the shallots.

Put the wine to warm in a lined pan over gentle heat. Melt half the butter in a saucepan over a medium heat and when it froths add the mushrooms and a little salt to extract their juices, cover with a tight lid and cook for about 5 minutes until the mushrooms have rendered their dark brown essence. Pour into a bowl and set aside.

Wash and dry the pan, melt the rest of the butter in it and sauté the shallots until well coloured. Sprinkle with flour and work it in with a wooden spoon, add the warm wine, stir until smooth, and then add the mushrooms and juice. Season with a little more salt and plenty of black pepper and cook over a medium heat. Reduce this to low when the sauce starts to simmer and cook for 10 minutes stirring occasionally, until the sauce has thickened and reduced.

Sauce matelote should never be boiled fast. To reheat, place in a *bain-marie*. Serve with eggs or fish.

2. Sauces bound with egg yolks and/or cream

Sauce à l'oseille

Sorrel sauce

TO SERVE SIX

INGREDIENTS
450 g (1 lb) sorrel
40 g (1½ oz) butter
75 ml (3 fl oz) chicken *bouillon* (*page* 12)
15 g (½ oz) sugar
salt and black pepper
2 egg yolks (size 2)
25 g (1 oz) double cream (optional)

Wash the sorrel in several changes of water and tear out the coarse centre ribs, then wilt the leaves in butter over a medium heat. When they are quite soft and have turned yellow, add the *bouillon*, heat again to boiling point and then pass the mixture through a mouli-légumes or blend. Return to the pan and add the sugar, salt and pepper to taste and simmer over a low heat until reduced to a thin purée. Remove the pan from the heat. Beat the egg yolks in a basin and add a ladleful of purée little by little to the eggs, stirring constantly with a wooden spoon, then gradually return this mixture to the hot purée and continue stirring until the sauce is thick. It should not be heated again after the egg mixture is incorporated. A spoonful of cream can be beaten in, but this is not essential.

Serve with roast veal or grilled fish, bream in particular.

Sauce poulette

Parsley cream sauce

TO SERVE SIX

INGREDIENTS
2 large sprigs parsley
175 g (6 oz) button mushrooms
juice of 1 lemon
75 g (3 oz) butter
275 ml ($\frac{1}{2}$ pint) strong chicken *bouillon* or veal stock (*pages* 12–13)
3 egg yolks (size 2)
100 g (4 oz) double cream
salt and black pepper

Put the parsley into a colander and pour boiling water over it. Dry and chop finely. Peel and chop the mushrooms coarsely, sprinkle with lemon juice to prevent them from discolouring, and cook them in an open pan in 15 g ($\frac{1}{2}$ oz) butter until tender.

In a heavy saucepan standing in a *bain-marie,* melt the remaining butter with the chicken or veal stock. When warm add the beaten egg yolks gradually and stir with a birch whisk until the mixture thickens. Do this carefully over water that is kept at slow simmering point. Add the chopped parsley, the mushrooms and the cream little by little. Season with salt and pepper and add a few drops of lemon juice to taste. This sauce must never boil.

Serve with grilled trout, or with sheep's or pigs' trotters (*see page* 113).

Sauce poulette on grilled trout showing the use of a birch whisk

Sauce aux anchois

Anchovy sauce

TO SERVE SIX

INGREDIENTS
2 shallots
100 g (4 oz) butter
3 black pimento corns (or allspice)
2 black peppercorns
50 g (2 oz) anchovies
2 egg yolks (size 2)
150 ml ($\frac{1}{4}$ pint) port

Peel and thinly slice the shallots. Melt the butter in a small heavy saucepan over a low heat, add the shallots and cook very slowly for 10 minutes, stirring occasionally. Hang the pimento and peppercorns in the pan in a muslin bag tied with string to the pan handle. Add the port and when boiling point is reached reduce the heat and continue simmering for 10 minutes until the liquid is reduced by half. Meanwhile drain and dry the anchovies, chop them coarsely and pound with the egg yolks until thick and smooth. Take the pan from the heat, allow to cool a little, and remove the pimento and peppercorns. Beat half the port and butter mixture into the eggs a little at a time, and when incorporated beat this into the remainder of the butter in the pan, and stand it in a *bain-marie* over a medium heat. Beat until frothy and the consistency of thin cream. Pour into a warm sauceboat, and leave in the *bain-marie* until required. Serve with roast veal or escalopes of veal.

Beurre blanc

White butter

TO SERVE SIX

INGREDIENTS
200 g (7 oz) unsalted butter
2 shallots
2 tablespoons wine vinegar
1 tablespoon cold water
salt and black pepper

Cut the butter into small pieces and leave to soften. Peel and finely chop the shallots. Put the vinegar, cold water, shallots and a little salt and pepper into a small heavy saucepan and cook over brisk heat until reduced to one tablespoon of liquid. Place the saucepan in a *bain-marie* or a larger pan half-filled with hot water and set over a very low heat. Beat in the butter with a birch whisk, a little at a time, making sure that the temperature of the water does not increase – to maintain a constant temperature the *bain-marie* can be placed on an asbestos mat. This is always advisable when cooking over gas-jets which are difficult to control.

When the sauce is thick, white, and a little frothy, serve at once. It is always served tepid. If it is allowed to heat too much the butter turns to oil.

Serve with any poached white fish of fine quality, turbot, halibut or sole.

Sauce hollandaise

TO SERVE SIX

INGREDIENTS
225 g (8 oz) unsalted softened butter
4 egg yolks (size 2) at room temperature
1 tablespoon cold water
salt and black pepper
juice of $\frac{1}{2}$ a lemon

Sauce mousseline
sauce hollandaise
150 ml ($\frac{1}{4}$ pint) double cream
salt and pepper

Divide the softened butter into small pieces and set aside. Choose a small heavy saucepan, put the egg yolks into it, add 1 tablespoon cold water and beat well with a birch whisk. Place the pan in a *bain-marie* and set over a low heat so that the water simmers very gently. Add the butter to the eggs, a little at a time, and beat until the sauce is thick. Add salt, pepper and drops of lemon juice to taste. The water in the *bain-marie* must remain at a constant temperature so that the sauce never heats rapidly. Serve with asparagus, broccoli and with poached salmon.

Sauce mousseline
Heat the *sauce hollandaise* in a *bain-marie*. Heat the cream slowly in a *bain-marie*. Beat the cream into the *hollandaise* a little at a time with a birch whisk. Season to taste. Serve with fish or vegetables, especially asparagus or broccoli.

Sauce hollandaise on broccoli

Sauce béarnaise

TO SERVE SIX

INGREDIENTS
100 g (4 oz) unsalted butter
3 shallots
4 tablespoons tarragon vinegar
6 black peppercorns
2 sprigs tarragon, 10 cm (4 in) long
3 egg yolks (size 2)
salt
1 teaspoon lemon juice
1 tablespoon chopped tarragon

Put the butter in a warm place to soften. Peel and very finely chop the shallots and mix with the vinegar, peppercorns, and the tarragon cut into pieces. Reduce over brisk heat to 1 tablespoonful. Set aside to cool.

Put the egg yolks into a small heavy saucepan and stand it in a *bain-marie*. The water should reach half-way up the sides of the saucepan. Place over a low heat. Mix the egg yolks thoroughly with a birch whisk but do not beat.

Add the softened butter, a small piece at a time, stirring it in slowly until the mixture is thick. Do not stop stirring until all the butter is incorporated. Strain in the reduced vinegar drop by drop stirring constantly. Add a little salt and sharpen the flavour with a few drops of lemon juice. Mix in the chopped tarragon and serve immediately in a warm sauceboat. If the sauce is to be kept warm, place it in a *bain-marie* away from direct heat.

Should the sauce separate owing to the water in the *bain-marie* being too hot, remove the saucepan from the heat and, beating briskly, add iced water a teaspoonful at a time until it thickens again.

Serve with grilled meat and fish of all kinds.

Sauce mousseuse

TO SERVE SIX

INGREDIENTS
150 ml ($\frac{1}{4}$ pint) cold water
100 g (4 oz) butter
salt and white pepper
3 large egg yolks
juice of $\frac{1}{2}$ a lemon

Put the cold water and butter in a small heavy saucepan and stand this over a very gentle heat. Use an asbestos mat to ensure a low even temperature. Add the salt and pepper and beat the mixture constantly with a hand whisk until the butter melts. Add the egg yolks one at a time and beat constantly until the sauce becomes frothy and thick. Add one or two drops of lemon juice with each egg yolk. Remove the pan from the heat and set it aside for half an hour before serving. Serve tepid.

Mousseuse is much less rich than the other butter-bound sauces and much more economical, but is just as good to serve with artichokes, asparagus, broccoli or cauliflower.

4. Sauces incorporating oil

Sauce mayonnaise

TO SERVE SIX

INGREDIENTS
2 egg yolks (size 2) at room temperature
1 teaspoon wine vinegar
275 ml ($\frac{1}{2}$ pint) olive oil (room temperature)
salt and pepper
1 teaspoon lemon juice

The best known of the oil-based sauces is, of course, mayonnaise. For its preparation olive oil is necessary which, with its very special flavour, only requires the addition of a few drops of lemon juice or wine vinegar. But given the present high cost of this oil it is possible to make an excellent mayonnaise with good corn oil when a stronger flavouring is used, as in *sauce verte* (*see page* 22).

Put the egg yolks in a wide shallow bowl, add 2 or 3 drops of wine vinegar, and mix well with a wire whisk. Then start to add the oil drop by drop, constantly stirring. When the mixture is thick and creamy add the oil in a thin slow trickle, still stirring, until it turns paler in colour. If the mayonnaise becomes too thick before all the oil is stirred in, add a couple of drops of vinegar, one at a time, and continue until the oil is used up. Season with salt and pepper and sharpen with a few drops of lemon juice to taste. Serve with shellfish, cold chicken, vegetables and salads.

Mayonnaise is the most unpredictable of all sauces, so simple and sometimes so temperamental. If it separates, put another egg yolk into a clean bowl and add the separated mixture drop by drop stirring constantly. When this yolk thickens, continue adding the first mixture drop by drop until it is quite clear that it has homogenized again.

Mayonnaise au vin blanc

TO SERVE SIX

INGREDIENTS
275 ml ($\frac{1}{2}$ pint) mayonnaise
2 shallots
75 ml (3 fl oz) white wine
salt and black pepper
1 tablespoon chopped chives
cayenne pepper

When making the mayonnaise keep it very thick. Peel and chop the shallots finely and cook them with the wine in a heavy-based saucepan over a medium heat until the wine is reduced by half. Leave to cool. When quite cold, season with salt and pepper and beat into the mayonnaise adding the finely chopped chives at the same time. Stir in a big pinch of cayenne and taste for seasoning, adding more if necessary – it should be highly seasoned. Serve with cold meats of all kinds.

Sauce tartare

TO SERVE SIX

INGREDIENTS
- 275 ml (½ pint) mayonnaise (*page* 21)
- 1 teaspoon chopped pickled gherkins
- 1 teaspoon chopped capers
- 1 tablespoon mild French mustard
- 1 teaspoon chopped parsley
- 1 teaspoon chopped chives

When making the mayonnaise keep it thick. Slice the gherkins and capers very finely, add the mustard and then the chopped herbs. Add this mixture a little at a time to the mayonnaise. Serve with fried or grilled fish.

Sauce verte

Green mayonnaise

TO SERVE SIX

INGREDIENTS
- 275 ml (½ pint) mayonnaise (*page* 21)
- 1 tablespoon chopped tarragon
- 1 tablespoon chopped chervil
- 1 tablespoon chopped watercress or parsley
- 1 tablespoon chopped spinach
- salt and black pepper

When making the mayonnaise keep it very thick. Take a small handful of each of the herbs and wash and pick them over. When shaken dry and the leaves taken from the stalks, this will give approximately the required amount.

Put all the leaves into a colander, pour boiling water over them, then cold water, pat dry in kitchen paper and pound in a mortar. Force through a fine sieve and add the purée to the mayonnaise. Serve with cold salmon and salmon trout.

Aïoli

Garlic mayonnaise

TO SERVE SIX

INGREDIENTS
- 4 cloves garlic
- 2 egg yolks (size 2) at room temperature
- 275 ml (½ pint) corn oil (room temperature)
- salt and pepper
- 1 dessertspoon wine vinegar

Peel the cloves of garlic and crush them in a mortar to a smooth paste with salt and a pinch of pepper. Then drop in the egg yolks one at a time mixing them into the garlic with a wire whisk. Add the oil drop by drop at first and then, when the yolks and oil have thickened, add it in a fine steady stream. Do not stop stirring until all the oil is worked in. Add a few drops of wine vinegar to sharpen the taste.

Serve with cold rare roast lamb, or with cooked or raw vegetables, or also with salads.

Aïoli with cold roast lamb

Vinaigrette

French dressing

TO SERVE SIX

INGREDIENTS
- 2 large pinches salt
- black pepper
- 1 tablespoon wine vinegar
- 3 tablespoons oil

Vinaigrette (for salads, raw and cooked cold vegetables) can be of several kinds. Different qualities of oil, olive, groundnut or corn oil, may be used but the proportions of oil to vinegar and the method of preparation remain the same.

Put the salt into the salad bowl and use two twists of the pepper mill, then stir in the vinegar with a wooden spoon and keep on stirring until the salt has dissolved. Salt will not dissolve in oil. Then add the oil a spoonful at a time, beating the mixture until it is cloudy. This incorporates the vinegar and makes the *vinaigrette* agreeably piquant without being sharp.

Vinaigrette à la moutarde

After mixing the salt and vinegar add 1 teaspoon mild French mustard before beating in the oil.

Vinaigrette à la crème

Substitute 3 tablespoons of double cream instead of oil. This is very good for dressing a watercress salad.

Vinaigrette à l'oeuf

Mix a raw egg yolk with a teaspoon of mild French mustard and a big pinch of salt. Then add the vinegar, keep stirring until the salt has dissolved. Then add the oil.

Aillade

TO SERVE SIX

INGREDIENTS
3 cloves garlic
75 g (3 oz) fresh shelled walnuts
salt
75 ml (3 fl oz) olive oil

This is a kind of aïoli that is little known. It is eaten mainly in certain parts of la Dordogne where walnuts are grown as a commercial crop. Fresh damp walnuts are the most important ingredient in this recipe.

Peel the garlic, and crush it in a mortar with a little salt. With a small pointed vegetable knife, peel off the bitter yellow skin from the walnuts. Pound them in with the garlic and salt until smooth and then with a wire whisk stir in the oil drop by drop as for mayonnaise, until a thick sauce is obtained.

Serve this as an hors d'oeuvre with fresh hard-crusted bread and raw celery. Do not serve butter with the bread.

Sauce gribiche

TO SERVE SIX

INGREDIENTS
1 teaspoon salt
2 tablespoons wine vinegar
1 dessertspoon mild French mustard
6 tablespoons oil
1 tablespoon chopped chives (or spring onion)
1 tablespoon chopped capers
1 tablespoon chopped pickled gherkin
black pepper
1 tablespoon chopped parsley
2 hard-boiled eggs

Put the salt in the bottom of a bowl, pour the vinegar over it and stir with a wooden spoon until dissolved. Work in the mustard, then add the oil a spoonful at a time, beating continually until the sauce is smooth. Add the chopped chives, capers, gherkins, and pepper to taste. When ready to serve mix in the chopped parsley and the finely chopped hard-boiled eggs. If the eggs are added too soon they will discolour the green herbs. Serve with cold poached fish (*see page* 75).

Sauce rémoulade

TO SERVE SIX

INGREDIENTS
2 hard-boiled eggs
1 tablespoon mild French mustard
2 small pickled gherkins
1 teaspoon chopped capers
salt and black pepper
275 ml (½ pint) oil

Crush the hard-boiled egg yolks in a bowl with a fork, mix in the mustard with a wire whisk working the mixture until smooth, add the finely chopped gherkins and capers, a little salt and pepper and then add the oil as for mayonnaise, a drop at a time at first and then in a thin steady stream, stirring constantly. Add more seasoning if necessary. Serve with eggs or with raw vegetable salads as an appetizer (*see page* 46).

For these sauces in which the yolks of hard-boiled eggs are used, it is advisable to plunge the eggs into boiling water and leave them over a low to medium heat for exactly 10 minutes. Boiled any longer the yolks toughen. Plunge them at once into cold water to make them easier to peel.

Vinaigrette aux fines herbes
Wash and dry 3 tablespoons of herbs using fennel, chervil or parsley, tarragon, chives and 6 leaves marjoram. Use only a little marjoram as this herb is very pungent. Pick off the leaves and chop finely.

Pour 1 tablespoon of lemon juice into the bowl, and stir in 1 teaspoon of salt until dissolved. Beat in 3 tablespoons of oil until all the mixture turns cloudy, add a little pepper and mix well before adding the herbs.

Breakfast

Breakfast in France is a special treat. The crisp yet tender-crusted bread, soft *croissants* and strong, fresh coffee represent perfection; and to a gourmet this light yet stimulating meal is the ideal start to the day when the important events of lunch and dinner are still to come.

Coffee

TO SERVE TWO–FOUR

INGREDIENTS
25 g (1 oz) coffee beans, sufficient for 4 rounded tablespoons
425 ml ($\frac{3}{4}$ pint) water

Coffee is always bought in the bean and ground as it is required. In this way it goes further and loses nothing of its flavour as it does when pre-ground. The choice of coffee bean is a matter of personal taste. Mocha Mysore has a good full flavour, but for those who prefer a darker roast, Colombian beans are recommended.

In many homes the beans are warmed through before being ground, which brings out the aroma and further enhances their quality of making more coffee with fewer beans.

To heat coffee beans
Measure out the required amount of beans. 25 g (1 oz) of beans should give 4 tablespoons of ground coffee. Put them on to an enamelled plate or other heatproof dish and place it over a very low heat – very low indeed or the coffee will burn and be useless. Shake the plate to and fro to make the beans jump about while heating through. When the beans feel warm to the palm of the hand, empty them into the coffee grinder and grind to a fairly fine consistency. This will give the strongest essence.

Coffee pots and method of making
The traditional French coffee pot is made of brown earthenware in two parts. The upper part is shaped like a wide cylinder with small holes pierced in the bottom through which the coffee drips into the pot, the lower part is like a small teapot. While it is being made, the whole coffee pot stands in a saucepan half full of simmering water to keep the coffee hot. It must never come into contact with metal, not if it is to be perfect, and of course French coffee must never boil.

Modern coffee-making apparatus comes in too many kinds to be mentioned, but the one which approaches nearest to the traditional coffee pot is the Melita method. Its plastic funnel furnished with a filter paper replaces the porcelain cylinder of the old-fashioned type. The pot into which the coffee drips must also stand in a *bain-marie* as described above to keep the coffee hot while being filtered.

This method makes the best possible coffee, strong and aromatic, for drinking either black as after-dinner coffee or for breakfast, when it is served, in France, with hot milk.

Made with these precautions and in the following way, the best, both in quality and quantity, is obtained.

To make French coffee
Prepare the coffee beans and grind them to a fine but not powdery consistency. This should provide 4 tablespoons of coffee. Put the ground coffee into the filter-lined funnel if the Melita method is being used, otherwise put it directly into the cylinder of the porcelain pot. Stand the pot in a *bain-marie* of simmering water placed over gentle heat.

Pour 4 tablespoons of boiling water over the coffee and leave for 8–10 minutes. This causes the coffee to swell and absorb the hot water so that the rest of the water poured over it will draw out its full strength and aroma. After 10 minutes pour over just enough hot water to cover. To avoid further loss of aroma, this water must have boiled again and be left to go just off the boil. Continue until all the water has passed through the coffee. The water will, of course, reduce by boiling and evaporation, but the strong black coffee made will serve four people after dinner or two when served with hot milk for breakfast. Brown sugar used in coffee effects its flavour but white sugar does not.

Chocolate

TO SERVE ONE

INGREDIENTS
40 g ($1\frac{1}{2}$ oz) dark bitter-sweet chocolate
275 ml ($\frac{1}{2}$ pint) hot milk or half water, half milk mixed together

Chocolate as a drink has become a convenience powder sold in tins under various trade names like cocoa, but it is still a popular breakfast drink with French children. The real thing is another matter entirely. To savour its full strength and aroma it should be made the night before and reheated in an earthenware pot in a *bain-marie*. It should never boil.

These are the rules according to Brillat-Savarin, the eighteenth-century philosopher of gastronomy. They were given to him, with the following recipe, by the Mother Superior of the Convent of the Visitation at Belley, the town in southeast France where he was born.

Break up the chocolate into small pieces and place in a saucepan over gentle heat. Pour over it 3 tablespoons of hot milk, or milk and water, cover the pan and allow the chocolate to soften. Remove the pan from the heat and whip the contents into a smooth paste with a whisk. Add a little more hot milk to dilute it and then add the rest of the liquid, which must be boiling, stirring constantly. Do not return the chocolate to the heat once it is diluted.

It is quite exceptional for the French housewife to bake bread at home, and why should she with perfect *ficelles, baguettes* and *bâtards* sold warm from the oven three times a day at the baker's shop that stands on every neighbourhood street corner. This white bread, however, does go stale rapidly and in consequence, French families expect fresh bread at least once a day.

French bread, exactly as it is in France, is virtually impossible to reproduce in England. This difficulty is partly due to the difference in the qualities of the flour produced in the two countries, and according to some authorities even the type of water used in the baking has its influence, just as water has its influence on the flavour of tea.

In place of bread, however, home-made *brioche* is more than a good substitute, it is a treat, especially for breakfast.

Madame Legout's cramique

TO SERVE FOUR-FIVE

INGREDIENTS
- a 25 cm (10 in) diameter baking tin
- *brioche* dough *(see below)*
- 225 g (8 oz) apricot jam
- 100 g (4 oz) seedless raisins
- 1 egg for glazing (size 4)
- 1 tablespoon cold water

Cramique is a certain type of breakfast cake/*brioche* eaten in Belgium but Madame Legout's particular French genius produced a version that is far superior to the original. A 25-cm (10-in) baking tin, about 5 cm (2 in) deep, will be needed. (Or use a cheesecake tin with a removeable rim.)

Butter the tin. Preheat the oven to 200°C, 400°F, Gas Mark 6. Prepare the *brioche* dough and when it has risen to its full volume, pinch it into 7 pieces. Roll out each piece very lightly into a band 23 cm (9 in) long, 2 cm (¾ in) thick and 6 cm (2½ in) wide. Brush the pieces with apricot jam, scatter with the raisins and roll up lightly lengthways with the jam inside. Place the first one in the centre of the tin and the others around it. Leave in a warm place to rise again. Beat the egg with the water and brush over the *cramique*. Bake for 40–45 minutes.

Madame Legout's brioche sans tête

TO SERVE SIX

INGREDIENTS
- 4 tablespoons tepid water
- 10 g (⅓ oz) fresh yeast, obtainable at health food shops (or 2 teaspoons dried yeast plus ½ teaspoon sugar)
- 100 g (4 oz) granulated sugar
- ½ teaspoon salt
- 225 g (8 oz) flour
- 3 eggs
- 100 g (4 oz) unsalted butter
- 1 egg for glazing (size 4)
- 1 tablespoon water
- a ring mould approximately 25 cm (10 in) in diameter

In a large warm mixing bowl put the tepid water and disperse the fresh yeast into it. Mix lightly to dissolve. If dried yeast is used, dissolve the sugar in 2 tablespoons of water, sprinkle in the yeast, whisk well, and stand in a warm place for 15 minutes.

Then add the sugar, salt, and half the flour sifted in. Mix to obtain a very soft dough. Cover with a cloth and leave in a warm place to rise for 20 minutes.

Drop the eggs into this dough, one at a time, beating vigorously between each one – this is best done by beating the mixture with your hand. When all three eggs are worked in, add the softened butter by the same method, and finally the rest of the flour. Beat with the hand to obtain a very elastic dough. Pull it up in the air frequently so that it eventually detaches itself from the bowl. Keep on beating until it forms a ball.

Butter the ring mould and place the dough in it so that it three-quarter fills the mould. Cover with a clean cloth and leave in a warm place to rise for 1½–2 hours until the dough practically fills the mould.

Preheat the oven to 200°C, 400°F, Gas Mark 6 and place the shelf ready about 10 cm (4 in) from the bottom of the oven. Beat the egg for glazing with the water and brush the top of the *brioche*. Put it into the oven and quickly close the door. After 10 minutes reduce to 180°C, 350°F, Gas Mark 5; bake for a further 35 minutes.

This *brioche* is traditionally served warm on a wicker tray and is not cut but pulled apart. The tray allows the *brioche* to cool with air circulating around it and so keeps light. Butter and/or jam can be served with it. Stale *brioche* is good sliced thickly, toasted, buttered and served hot.

This recipe can be made as individual *brioches* in 6-cm (2½-in) diameter moulds.

Croissants

TO MAKE EIGHT

INGREDIENTS
8 tablespoons milk
20 g ($\frac{2}{3}$ oz) fresh baker's yeast (or $4\frac{1}{2}$ teaspoons dried yeast plus $\frac{3}{4}$ teaspoon sugar)
450 g (1 lb) flour
pinch of salt
225 g (8 oz) softened butter
150 g (5 oz) castor sugar
1 egg for glazing (size 4)
1 tablespoon water

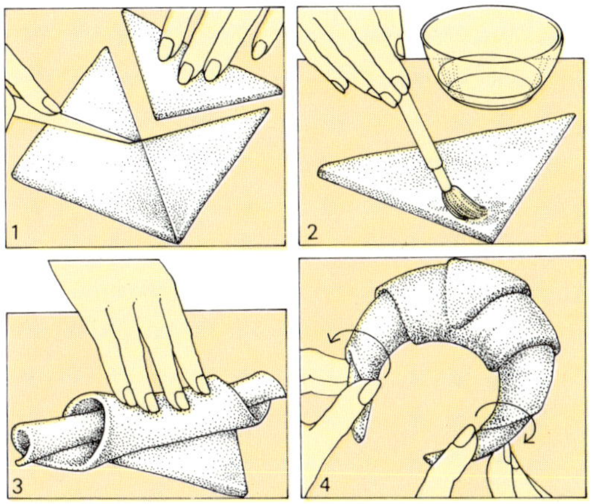

Left to right: Cramique, brioche, hazelnut and plain croissants

Warm the milk to blood heat and disperse the fresh yeast into it. Leave to dissolve. If dried yeast is used dissolve the sugar in 4 tablespoons of the milk, sprinkle in the yeast, whisk well, and stand in a warm place for 15 minutes before use.

Sift the flour and salt into a large bowl, work in the softened butter a little at a time, then add the sugar and mix it in thoroughly. Whisk the yeast mixture. Make a well in the centre of the flour mixture, and pour in the yeast. Beat the flour into the liquid with the hand and continue beating to obtain a very elastic dough. Pull it up in the air frequently so that it eventually detaches itself from the bowl, leaving it clean, and continue beating until the dough forms a ball. Cover with a clean cloth and leave in a warm place for 2 hours to rise.

Preheat the oven to 200°C, 400°F, Gas Mark 6. Beat the egg with 1 tablespoon of water. Divide the dough into halves and roll each half separately on a lightly floured board into a square. Cut each square into 4 triangles approximately 8 cm ($3\frac{1}{2}$ in) a side when cut across from corner to corner (1). Dab the point of each triangle in turn with beaten egg (2) and lightly roll up the long side towards it (3), then turn the ends inwards to form a tight crescent shape (4). Brush the surface with egg and place on a buttered and floured baking sheet. Leave in a warm place for 10 minutes to rise again. Bake for 15 minutes. Serve warm.

Croissants are best eaten the same day but they reheat very successfully the next day if placed in a hot oven for 5 minutes.

Croissants aux noisettes

Croissants with hazelnuts

TO MAKE EIGHT

INGREDIENTS
8 tablespoons milk
20 g ($\frac{2}{3}$ oz) fresh yeast (or $4\frac{1}{2}$ teaspoons dried yeast plus $\frac{3}{4}$ teaspoon sugar)
450 g (1 lb) flour
pinch of salt
225 g (8 oz) softened butter
150 g (5 oz) castor sugar

Filling
100 g (4 oz) castor sugar
100 g (4 oz) ground hazelnuts
75 g (3 oz) softened butter
1 egg, beaten
2 tablespoons apricot liqueur
1 egg for glazing (size 4)

Warm the milk to blood heat and disperse the fresh yeast into it. Leave to dissolve. If dried yeast is used, dissolve the sugar in 4 tablespoons of milk, sprinkle in the yeast, whisk well and stand it in a warm place for 15 minutes before using.

Sift the flour and salt into a large bowl, work in the softened butter a little at a time, then add the sugar and mix it in thoroughly. Whisk the yeast mixture. Make a well in the centre of the flour mixture and pour in the yeast. Beat the flour into the liquid with the hand and continue beating to obtain a very elastic dough. Pull it up in the air frequently so that it eventually detaches itself from the bowl, leaving it clean, and continue beating, until the dough forms a ball. Leave it in the mixing bowl in a warm place to rise for 2 hours.

To make the filling, mix the sugar and ground hazelnuts together in a small mixing bowl. Work in the beaten egg, then the softened butter and the liqueur last.

When the dough has risen, divide it into half and roll each piece separately on a lightly floured board into a square. Cut each square into 4 triangles approximately 9 cm ($3\frac{1}{2}$ in) a side when cut across from corner to corner (1). Dab the point of each triangle in turn with beaten egg (2) and place a portion of the filling on the long side. Lightly roll the long side of each piece towards the point (3), then turn the ends inwards to form a tight crescent shape (4). Beat the egg for glazing with 1 dessertspoon of cold water and brush this over the surface of the *croissants*. Place them on a lightly buttered and floured baking sheet. Leave in a warm place for 5–10 minutes to rise again. Preheat the oven to 200°C, 400°F, Gas Mark 6. Bake the *croissants* for 15 minutes and serve either warm or cold.

Soups

Good soup is an essential part of every French family's evening meal. They regard it as a meal in itself and not a prelude to it. Soup followed by a vegetable or egg dish makes a well-balanced meal at comparatively little cost. Thickening is usually provided by the ingredients themselves being passed through a mouli-légumes. Otherwise soup is thickened with semolina, rice, rice or potato flour, or potatoes themselves are included. Soup can also be thickened with breadcrumbs or an egg yolk and/or cream binding. Butter is sometimes used as an alternative to cream for smoothness, and in southern France, Provençal soups are bound with a delicious *pommade* made by pounding together fresh basil, *gruyère* cheese and olive oil. Serve clear soup in cups which prevent it cooling rapidly and serve thick soup in soup-plates or wide bowls, but serve them all as hot as possible.

Crème d'asperges

Cream of asparagus soup

TO SERVE SIX

INGREDIENTS
450 g (1 lb) green asparagus
salt
1 medium-sized onion
1 clove
1 litre ($1\frac{3}{4}$ pints) milk
6 peppercorns
bouquet garni (*page* 216)
50 g (2 oz) rice or potato flour
50 g (2 oz) butter
100 g (4 oz) double cream

Scrape and trim the asparagus and place in salted water to remove grit. Peel the onion, stick with a clove and simmer it in milk with the peppercorns and bouquet garni over low heat. Mix the rice flour to a smooth paste with cold water and mix into the milk stirring constantly. Reduce the heat and simmer slowly for 20 minutes, stirring occasionally. Cook the asparagus lying flat in a large roasting tin with just sufficient salted water to cover. Remove when still a little firm, and reserve the water. Cut off the asparagus tips about 3 cm (1 in) long and set aside. Cut the rest into short lengths and cook until softened in melted butter. Add them to the cream of rice with a large cupful of the cooking water and simmer until very soft. Pass the soup through a sieve, pressing the asparagus with a wooden spoon to force through as much pulp as possible.

Add sufficient cooking water to bring the quantity to 1.3 litres ($2\frac{1}{4}$ pints), reheat to boiling point, then draw the pan away from the heat and add the cream gradually, stirring constantly. Garnish with the reheated asparagus tips. Serve immediately. Do not reboil after adding cream.

Potage bonne femme

TO SERVE SIX

INGREDIENTS
225 g (8 oz) leeks
225 g (8 oz) carrots
450 g (1 lb) potatoes
25 g (1 oz) butter
1.4 litres ($2\frac{1}{2}$ pints) warm water
salt and black pepper
2 bayleaves
50 g (2 oz) double cream

Trim the leeks, remove faded parts but retain all the edible green. Chop small and place in a colander under running water to remove grit. Peel carrots and potatoes and chop into small pieces. Melt the butter and when it foams add leeks and carrots, and cook, covered, over a low heat until soft without colouring, stirring occasionally. Then add water, salt, pepper, bayleaves and potatoes, and simmer uncovered for 45 minutes.

To serve, remove the bayleaves, correct seasoning and crush the potatoes against the side of the pan with a fork. Remove the pan from the heat and stir in the cream gradually. Reheat without boiling.

Top: Crème d'asperges, potage bonne femme; *bottom:* potage au céleri

Potage au céleri

Celery soup

TO SERVE SIX

INGREDIENTS
675 g ($1\frac{1}{2}$ lb) celery
225 g (8 oz) potatoes
100 g (4 oz) onion
50 g (2 oz) butter
1 litre ($1\frac{3}{4}$ pints) warm water
275 ml ($\frac{1}{2}$ pint) milk
50 g (2 oz) double cream

Trim the celery, remove faded parts and retain all green leaves. Chop small and place in a colander under running water to remove grit. Chop potatoes into small pieces and place in a bowl of water. Chop the onion. Melt the butter and when it foams, add celery and onion, and cook covered over a low heat until soft without colouring, stirring occasionally. Then add water, milk, salt and pepper and potatoes. Bring to boiling point and simmer uncovered for 45 minutes. Blend in a mouli-légumes and return to pan, heat to boiling point. Remove from heat and add cream gradually. Serve scattered with chopped celery leaves.

This soup is also delicious when made with celeriac. Serve it sprinkled with parsley.

Potage Crécy

Carrot soup

TO SERVE SIX

INGREDIENTS
450 g (1 lb) carrots
350 g (12 oz) potatoes
100 g (4 oz) turnips
50 g (2 oz) butter
1.4 litres ($2\frac{1}{2}$ pints) warm water
salt and black pepper
175 g (6 oz) onion
Croûtons
3 slices bread (1 cm, $\frac{1}{2}$ in thick)
25 g (1 oz) butter

Peel and chop the vegetables into small pieces keeping the potatoes separate. Melt 25 g (1 oz) butter in a large pan and cook carrots and turnips in it over low heat, covered, until they soften without colouring. Stir occasionally and after 20 minutes add salt, pepper, water and potatoes. Simmer, uncovered, for 1 full hour after boiling point is reached.

Meanwhile peel and chop the onion medium fine and cook in the rest of the butter until soft but not coloured, and set aside. Blend the soup in a mouli-légumes, and if it is too thick dilute with a little milk, mix in the cooked onion, correct the seasoning and simmer for a further 10 minutes. Serve with croûtons.

In any soup containing potatoes do not cook them in butter with the other vegetables; they should be included after the water is added.

Croûtons
Remove crusts from the bread, cut each slice into small cubes and sauté in foaming butter until crisp and golden. Drain on kitchen paper and keep hot in a moderate oven. Croûtons can be made in advance and kept tightly covered in a plastic box in the refrigerator. To reheat, place in a hot oven.

Croûtons à l'ail (Garlic croûtons)
Cut a clove of garlic into halves and rub them over the bread before cutting it into cubes. Fry in hot olive oil instead of butter. Allow 2 tablespoons of oil for three slices of bread.

Potage aux fèves fraîches

Fresh broad bean soup

TO SERVE SIX

INGREDIENTS
675 g ($1\frac{1}{2}$ lb) broad beans
1.4 litres ($2\frac{1}{2}$ pints) water
salt and black pepper
15 g ($\frac{1}{2}$ oz) sugar
50 g (2 oz) butter
3 egg yolks

Make this soup when the beans are small, otherwise they have to be skinned.

Put the shelled beans, cold water and 1 teaspoon of salt into a large pan and cook, uncovered, until tender. Drain, reserve the water and blend the beans in a mouli-légumes.

Melt the butter in the same pan and when foaming add the bean purée. Stirring constantly, cook slowly for 2–3 minutes, add the cooking water and beat thoroughly with a whisk. Correct the seasoning, add pepper and sugar and simmer briskly, uncovered, for 10 minutes. Add a little milk if too thick.

To serve, put the egg yolks into a bowl and mix well. Remove the pan from the heat and beat a ladleful of soup into the eggs very gradually with a whisk. Stir well before adding another, then return this mixture slowly to the soup stirring constantly. Do not boil again. Serve immediately.

Potage aux fines herbes

TO SERVE SIX

INGREDIENTS
225 g (8 oz) lettuce
100 g (4 oz) sorrel
50 g (2 oz) chives
50 g (2 oz) butter
25 g (1 oz) flour
salt and black pepper
1.3 litres ($2\frac{1}{4}$ pints)
50 g (2 oz) semolina

Outside lettuce leaves can be used for this soup, leaving the hearts for salad.

Wash and pick over both lettuce and sorrel retaining the centre rib of the latter if tender. Drain well, then chop them finely with the chives and cook over gentle heat to a soft mass in 25 g (1 oz) foaming butter, stirring frequently with a wooden spoon. Work in the flour, season well and add warm water. Increase the heat slightly and simmer briskly for 45 minutes. Pour in the semolina and leave to cook another 10 minutes. To serve, place the remaining butter in the tureen and pour the boiling soup over it. Serve with croûtons if so desired (*see page* 33).

Potage aux fèves fraiches; potage aux fines herbes

Potage à la liégeoise

Vegetable and tomato soup

TO SERVE SIX

INGREDIENTS
225 g (8 oz) leeks
100 g (4 oz) sorrel
2 stalks celery
4 large sprigs chervil or parsley
75 g (3 oz) butter
450 g (1 lb) potatoes
salt and black pepper
2 bayleaves
1.4 litres ($2\frac{1}{2}$ pints) water
225 g (8 oz) tomatoes, skinned and roughly chopped

Trim the leeks and cut off any faded parts but reserve all edible green leaves, cut into short lengths and place in a colander under running water to clear the grit. Leave to drain. Wash the sorrel, celery and chervil but do not remove either the centre rib of the sorrel or the stalks of the chervil. Chop them finely together with the leeks and cook until soft, but not coloured, in half the butter melted to foaming stage in a large pan. Cover and leave over gentle heat for 10 minutes stirring occasionally. Peel the potatoes and cut into small chunks. Pour warm water over the vegetables, add potatoes and seasoning and one bayleaf. Bring to boiling point, cover and simmer briskly for 35 minutes. Remove the lid and cook for a further 10 minutes. Cook the tomatoes in a covered pan in the rest of the butter, with the other bayleaf and seasoning, until reduced to a thick purée. Cook them slowly at first and then when the soup is ready, remove the lid and simmer briskly for a further 5 minutes. Mix this purée into the soup. Boil for another 5 minutes, remove the bayleaves and blend in a mouli-légumes. Reheat and serve immediately.

Soupe à l'oignon

Onion soup

TO SERVE SIX

INGREDIENTS
450 g (1 lb) onions
50 g (2 oz) butter
25 g (1 oz) flour
1.2 litres (2 pints) beef *bouillon* (*page* 12)
salt and black pepper
6 slices of a French loaf
75 g (3 oz) grated *gruyère* cheese

Peel and slice the onions thickly. Melt the butter over a medium heat in a large pan, add the onions and stirring constantly cook to the blonde stage. Sprinkle with flour and cook until golden brown. Remove from the heat and add the beef *bouillon* all at once, beat well with a birch whisk until the flour is incorporated, season, and return to boiling point. Reduce the heat and simmer steadily, uncovered, for 20 minutes. Meanwhile grill the bread slowly until hard and lightly browned. Leave the grill on at a high temperature.

To serve, pour the soup into thick earthenware bowls (which must be heatproof), float the bread on top and sprinkle liberally with *gruyère*. Grill until the cheese is bubbling and brown.

Anti-clockwise from the top: Soupe au potiron; potage aux écosses de petits pois; soupe aux poireaux, pommes de terre

Soupe au potiron
Pumpkin soup

TO SERVE SIX

INGREDIENTS
50 g (2 oz) butter
675 g (1½ lb) pumpkin, peeled and seeded
150 ml (¼ pint) warm water
salt and grated nutmeg
1.3 litres (2¼ pints) milk
50 g (2 oz) rice

Melt the butter in a large pan and when foaming add the pumpkin cut into large pieces. Stir well to coat with butter and cook for 10 minutes over low heat. Add warm water, salt and nutmeg, cover, and cook rapidly until soft. Reduce to purée in a blender with a little milk and add to the rice and remaining milk in the pan. Bring to boiling point and cook, uncovered, over gentle heat for 30 minutes.

Serve with croûtons, garlic flavoured or plain (*see page* 33).

Potage aux écosses de petits pois
Pea-pod soup

TO SERVE SIX

INGREDIENTS
50 g (2 oz) onion
6 large outside lettuce leaves
1.4 litres (2½ pints) hot chicken *bouillon* (*page* 12), or water and 15 g (½ oz) of butter
1 kg (2 lb) fresh pea-pods
salt and black pepper
sugar
150 ml (¼ pint) milk
50 g (2 oz) double cream
a few cooked peas for garnishing

Choose the pods for their freshness and small size – preferably home-grown.

Peel and roughly chop the onion, wash and pick over the lettuce leaves and tear them into pieces. If water is used and not *bouillon*, melt the butter in a large pan over gentle heat and when it froths sauté the vegetables until they are soft without letting them colour. Add the pods, seasoning, and just enough water to cover. Bring to boiling point. Reduce the heat, cover, and simmer until the pods are soft. If *bouillon* is used do not sauté the vegetables in butter, just cook in stock to cover. Strain off the liquid and reserve it, purée the pods in a mouli-légumes, add the cooking liquid, sugar to taste (and additional seasoning if necessary), the milk and the rest of the stock or water. Simmer uncovered to reduce to about 1.2 litres (2 pints). Draw the pan from the heat when the contents are boiling steadily, slowly add a ladleful of soup to the cream, blend well and stir this mixture into the pan a little at a time. Add the cooked peas and serve immediately.

Soupe aux poireaux, pommes de terre
Leek and potato soup

TO SERVE SIX

INGREDIENTS
450 g (1 lb) potatoes
450 g (1 lb) leeks
75 g (3 oz) butter
1 litre (1¾ pints) warm water
salt and black pepper
275 ml (½ pint) milk

Peel the potatoes and cut into small chunks. Trim the leeks but retain all the edible green parts, and chop into 1-cm (½-in) lengths. Place in a colander under running water to remove grit. Leave to drain.

Melt the butter in a large pan and when foaming cook the leeks, covered, over low heat until soft but not coloured. Add water, potatoes, salt and pepper, cover, increase the heat slightly and when boiling, simmer steadily for 30 minutes. This soup can be blended in a mouli-légumes or electric blender, or pressed lightly with a potato masher. Then add the milk and reheat slowly to boiling point, and adding extra milk if necessary, simmer for a few minutes.

Serve with croûtons (*see page* 33).

Pistou

Provençal vegetable soup

TO SERVE SIX

INGREDIENTS
450 g (1 lb) courgettes
350 g (12 oz) leeks
675 g ($1\frac{1}{2}$ lb) large tomatoes (Mediterranean variety if possible)
175 g (6 oz) carrots
350 g (12 oz) onions
450 g (1 lb) young runner beans
450 g (1 lb) young broad beans (when shelled)
225 g (8 oz) French beans *(haricots verts)*
225 g (8 oz) tin of *flageolet* beans
2 litres ($3\frac{1}{2}$ pints) cold water
salt
100 g (4 oz) broken macaroni

Pommade
25 g (1 oz) fresh basil
4 cloves garlic
125 g (5 oz) freshly grated *gruyère* cheese
4 tablespoons olive oil

This soup is a meal in itself and needs only fruit to follow. Four kinds of green bean are necessary for this soup. To make up this number in England, a tin of *flageolet* beans has been substituted. They can be obtained from most Italian delicatessen shops.

Wash, top and tail the courgettes, do not peel. Clean and peel or trim leeks, tomatoes, carrots and onions and chop all into small chunky pieces. Top and tail the beans and cut into 1-cm ($\frac{1}{2}$-in) lengths. Drain the *flageolet* beans. Put all together in a large soup pan, add cold water, 2 teaspoons salt and place over a medium heat. Bring slowly to boiling point and skim off froth that rises until the surface is clear. Reduce the heat and simmer slowly, uncovered, until vegetables are soft. Meanwhile cook the macaroni in salted water until half cooked, drain and add to the *pistou* 10 minutes before serving.

Pommade
Wash the basil, shake dry and pick the leaves from the stalks. Peel the garlic and pound in a mortar, adding the basil leaves a few at a time. When reduced to a paste add 125 g (5 oz) of cheese gradually, and continue pounding until the mixture is thick and soft. Now beat in the oil drop by drop as for mayonnaise, until the pommade resembles a thick cream.

To serve, bring the soup to boiling point and remove the pan from the heat. Take a ladleful of soup and add it gradually to the *pommade* stirring continually with a wire whisk, add a little more and when incorporated return this mixture gradually to the pan. This must be done carefully or it will curdle. Mix well and ladle immediately into very hot soup plates. Sprinkle each one with grated *gruyère* and serve with French bread crisped for 5 minutes in a very hot oven.

Potage aux tomates

Fresh tomato soup

TO SERVE SIX

INGREDIENTS
575 ml (1 pint) fresh unthickened tomato purée (*page* 18)
1.3 litres ($2\frac{1}{4}$ pints) beef *bouillon* (*page* 12)
salt and black pepper
25 g (1 oz) semolina

Bring the tomato purée and beef *bouillon* to boiling point and simmer together for 30 minutes over a low heat. Season to taste and scatter the semolina over the surface, stir well and continue simmering for 10 minutes. Serve with garlic croûtons (*see page* 33).

Potage aux moules

Mussel soup

TO SERVE SIX

INGREDIENTS

- $1\frac{3}{4}$ litres (3 pints) mussels
- 50 g (2 oz) butter
- 40 g ($1\frac{1}{2}$ oz) flour
- 1 litre ($1\frac{3}{4}$ pints) hot milk
- salt
- cayenne pepper
- 1 large egg yolk
- 50 g (2 oz) double cream
- shredded saffron
- chopped parsley for garnishing

Scrub the mussels with a wire brush in several changes of cold water and discard any that are open. Place in a large dry pan over high heat, cover, and shake the pan occasionally. In about 5 minutes the mussels will open. Take them from the pan and remove the shells, discarding any that fail to open. Reserve all liquid.

Melt the butter over a medium heat, work in the flour, cook until foaming, add the hot milk, season with the salt and cayenne pepper and bring to boiling point. Reduce the heat and simmer steadily for 5 minutes, stirring constantly. Strain the mussel liquid through filter paper placed in a fine sieve and beat it into the sauce. Test for seasoning.

Whisk the egg yolk, cream and a pinch of cayenne together in a bowl, draw the pan from the heat when boiling, stir in the shelled mussels, then beat a ladleful of soup into the egg mixture. Return it slowly to the pan and mix well.

To serve, put a pinch of saffron into each heated soup plate, and pour the soup over it dividing the mussels equally. Then sprinkle with parsley and serve immediately.

Soupe de poisson

Fish soup

TO SERVE SIX

INGREDIENTS

- 1 kg (2 lb) mixed salt water fish (i.e. 1 small mackerel, 1 herring, fresh haddock, huss etc.)
- 450 g (1 lb) tomatoes (large Mediterranean variety if possible)
- 225 g (8 oz) onion
- $\frac{1}{2}$ head of fennel
- 3 cloves garlic
- 3 tablespoons olive oil
- salt and black pepper
- 1 sprig thyme
- 1 bayleaf
- 1.2 litres (2 pints) water
- $\frac{1}{2}$ litre ($\frac{3}{4}$ pint) dry white wine
- saffron shreds
- 100 g (4 oz) uncooked spaghetti
- 75 g (3 oz) grated Parmesan cheese

As it is not possible to obtain the kind of fish necessary for *bouillabaisse* other than in Mediterranean waters, the following fish soup is suggested instead.

Remove head and fins from the fish, scale, wash and cut into 5-cm (2-in) pieces.

Skin and quarter the tomatoes, peel the onion and slice it, with the fennel, into medium fine rings. Peel and crush the garlic. Heat the oil in a large pan and add these ingredients with salt, pepper and thyme and bayleaf tied together. Stir with a wooden spoon and cook over a medium heat for 5 minutes. Add water, wine and a large pinch of saffron. When boiling, skim off the froth that rises, reduce the heat and simmer steadily, uncovered, for 20 minutes.

Remove the herbs and pass the soup through a coarse sieve pressing the ingredients through with a wooden spoon to obtain as much pulp as possible. Reheat and when boiling add the broken spaghetti and leave to simmer steadily for 20 minutes. Serve immediately and sprinkle Parmesan cheese over each plate of soup according to taste.

Top to bottom: Potage aux moules; soupe de poissons

Garbure béarnaise

Pork and bean soup

TO SERVE EIGHT

INGREDIENTS

175 g (6 oz) dried haricot beans
450 g (1 lb) lean pickled belly pork (in one piece)
450 g (1 lb) potatoes
225 g (8 oz) leeks
100 g (4 oz) turnips
350 g (12 oz) onion
450 g (1 lb) firm cabbage heart
1 chili pepper
3 litres ($5\frac{1}{4}$ pints) cold water
1 teaspoon salt
1 sprig marjoram
bouquet garni
1 clove garlic
white pepper
6 thin slices light brown rye bread

Soak the haricot beans and pickled pork separately in cold water overnight. Drain and wash well in cold water.

Trim and peel potatoes, leeks, turnips and onion and chop roughly into small pieces. Remove the coarse ribs of the cabbage and shred the leaves. Set aside. Put the other vegetables with the chili, water and salt into a very large pan, add the beans and bring slowly to boiling point over low heat. Skim off the froth as it rises and when clear add the herbs, garlic and some pepper. Cover, and simmer slowly for $1\frac{1}{2}$ hours. Then add the shredded cabbage and the pork. Check that the ingredients are covered with water. Replace the lid and simmer again for $1\frac{1}{2}$ hours or until both pork and beans are tender. This soup should have the consistency of a stew.

To serve, remove the chili, cut the pork into slices, place them with the slices of bread in a heated tureen and pour the boiling soup over them. The native *béarnois* adds one or two tablespoons of red wine to his *garbure*. It is served as a complete meal with only fresh fruit to follow. Light rye bread is suggested as an alternative to the slightly sour-tasting *pain de campagne* used in France.

Pot-au-feu; poule au pot

Pot-au-feu

TO SERVE EIGHT

INGREDIENTS
2 kg (4½ lb) meat
3.7 litres (6½ pints) water
2–3 cracked beef bones
40 g (1½ oz) coarse salt crystals
12 peppercorns
450 g (1 lb) carrots
350 g (12 oz) leeks
1 head of celery
100 g (4 oz) small turnips
100 g (4 oz) small onions
2 cloves
1 sprig parsley
1 bayleaf
1 clove garlic or small piece of root ginger

This recipe economically provides two dishes in one, tender meat and vegetables to be eaten the day it is cooked and the best of all beef *bouillons* to serve the following day. Choose two cuts of beef from the following: leg of beef, lean boned brisket, blade bone, leg-of-mutton cut, oxtail. Allow 1 kg (2¼ lb) of each meat chosen but one of the two cuts should be on the bone.

Wipe the meat with a damp cloth and tie each cut into a neat parcel. Put into a very large pan over a low heat, add the water, beef bones, salt and pepper, and bring *slowly* to boiling point. At all times this recipe must cook slowly. As the scum rises skim it off with a slotted spoon, making sure the liquid always covers the meat. Add nothing further to the pan until the soup is quite clear. Peel and cut the carrots and leeks into 5-cm (2-in) lengths and tie into small bundles. Trim the celery, remove the coarse outer leaves. Quarter the celery through the length from the root end and chop into 8 cm (3 in) length pieces. Tie into small bundles. Quarter the turnips and leave the onions whole with the cloves stuck into one of them. Add these vegetables to the pan with the herbs and when the liquid returns to simmering, cover, reduce the heat to low and cook for 4–5 hours, lifting the lid only twice to add a cup of hot water if necessary. Remove the meat and drain well, cut into thick slices and surround it with the vegetables. Serve coarse crystal salt and French mustard with the *pot-au-feu.*

To serve *pot-au-feu bouillon* at a later date, leave in the pan until cold, and remove the solidified fat. If required when still hot remove the fat, first with a metal spoon, then by trailing bands of kitchen paper over the surface. Reheat to boiling point and pour into hot soup cups. Serve with thin dry toast.

Poule au pot

Chicken in the pot

TO SERVE EIGHT–TEN

INGREDIENTS
2–2.5 kg (4–5 lb) boiling fowl (with giblets)
3 small onions, peeled
5 cloves
450 g (1 lb) carrots
350 g (12 oz) white part of leeks
225 g (8 oz) button onions
a head of celery
225 g (8 oz) firm heart of young cabbage
40 g ($1\frac{1}{2}$ oz) coarse salt crystals
2.6 litres ($4\frac{1}{2}$ pints) water
12 peppercorns
1 sprig parsley
1 bayleaf
$\frac{1}{2}$ teaspoon nutmeg

This delicious chicken version of *pot-au-feu* made history and became the symbol of prosperity when Henri IV of France declared that his ambition was to see each of his subjects with a chicken in the pot on Sunday.

Wash and trim the giblets.

Wipe the chicken inside and out with a cloth wrung out in boiling water and fill with three small onions peeled and each stuck with a clove. Truss firmly and tie with string.

Prepare the carrots, leeks, onions and celery as for *Pot-au-feu* and divide the cabbage into 8 sections, trim and remove the toughest part of the core leaving enough to hold the leaves together.

Put the chicken, giblets, salt and water into a large braising pan, place over low heat and bring *very slowly* to boiling point. The pan should be just large enough to hold all the ingredients and allow the water to reach half-way up the breast.

As the liquid reaches boiling point remove the foam as it rises and continue until the surface is quite clear. Then add the bundles of prepared vegetables (except the cabbage), pepper corns, herbs, the remaining 2 cloves and the nutmeg.

When the liquid returns to simmering point lower the heat, half-cover the pan and simmer for approximately 3 hours. Add the cabbage 20 minutes before serving. This recipe must cook as slowly as possible throughout.

To serve, drain the chicken, peel off the skin, carve and arrange on a large heated serving plate. Drain the vegetables and place them in small groups around the meat. Cover with foil and keep hot.

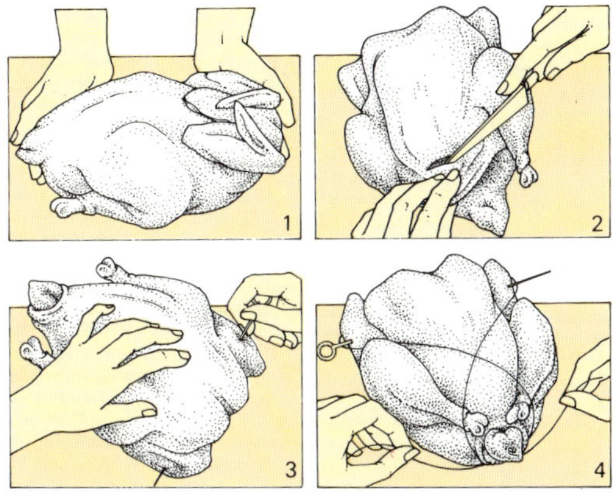

(1) Fold wing tips inward over back of chicken to hold neck skin in place. (2) Turn bird on to its back to slit the skin above the vent and, after stuffing, push the parson's nose through the slit. (3) Push skewer through body pinning wings to the side of the bird. (4) Loop string round the bird and knot securely around the drumsticks and parson's nose.

The classic sauce to serve with *poule au pot* is *sauce ivoire* (*see page* 16). Take the required amount of chicken *bouillon* from the pan before the cabbage is added and pour into a wide shallow bowl. Remove the fat first with a metal cooking spoon and then with strips of kitchen paper drawn over the surface. Pour a little of the *sauce ivoire* over the meat and serve the rest in a heated sauceboat.

The rest of the *bouillon* not used in the sauce may be served separately as soup or used to make the following delicately flavoured soup, *potage à la reine*.

Potage à la reine

TO SERVE EIGHT

INGREDIENTS
1.3 litres ($2\frac{1}{4}$ pints) chicken *bouillon* (*page* 12)
salt and ground allspice
75 g (3 oz) rice
100 g (4 oz) white meat of chicken
3 egg yolks

The chicken *bouillon* from *poule-au-pot* can be made into a delectable soup for a dinner party, especially to precede cold salmon or any other plainly cooked fish.

Remove the fat from the *bouillon* first with a metal cooking spoon and then by drawing strips of kitchen paper over the surface until clear. Season well with salt and ground allspice, add the rice and cook until tender. Stir in the finely chopped chicken meat and when simmering rapidly draw the pan from the heat. Whisk the egg yolks with a little salt in a bowl, add a ladleful of hot soup and stir it into the eggs. Add this into the soup a little at a time. Stir well until the soup thickens. Serve immediately in heated soup plates.

MARCHÉS DE FRANCE
MDF

Hors d'oeuvre, entrées and pâtés

The main event of the day in a French household is lunch. This substantial meal consists of an *hors d'oeuvre, entrée* or pâté, a main course of meat or fish served with noodles, rice or sometimes potatoes – vegetables are served separately after the meat – a green salad provides breathing space, and cheese and fresh fruit end the meal. It is evident that such a menu demands a first course calculated to stimulate the appetite, not satisfy it.

Hors d'oeuvre consists of raw vegetable salads, rice salads (both served with a *vinaigrette* or mayonnaise dressing), cooked or pickled vegetables and delicatessen foods such as sardines, olives, tuna, smoked ham and sausage, pickled and smoked fish.

Entrées, usually hot, are served on more formal occasions and consist of *choux* or other pastry with a savoury filling, egg or shellfish dishes and savoury pancakes. Most *entrées* fit into the English menu as a light lunch or supper dish.

Pâtés are the national stand-by, occasionally served with radishes but always with the midday baking of fresh bread.

Hors d'oeuvre

The quantities given in the following salad recipes are all to serve six people.

Salade de carottes rapées

Grated carrot salad

INGREDIENTS
450 g (1 lb) carrots
salt and black pepper
vinaigrette aux fines herbes (*page* 23)

Peel and grate the carrots, season well and mix with dressing. If the herbs suggested for the *vinaigrette* are not available use chopped parsley instead.

Salade de céleri rémoulade

Celeriac salad with rémoulade sauce

INGREDIENTS
450 g (1 lb) celeriac
salt and black pepper
sauce rémoulade (*page* 23)

Peel and trim both ends of the celeriac, cut into thin slices, then into fine strips, and throw them immediately into boiling salted water. Boil for 1 minute only, drain and dry, season lightly and mix thoroughly with the *sauce rémoulade*, omitting the gherkins if desired.

Salade de chou rouge

Red cabbage salad

INGREDIENTS
350 g (12 oz) red cabbage
salt
1 tablespoon chopped chives or onion and/or 3 tablespoons sliced radishes
vinaigrette à la moutarde (*page* 22)

Remove outer leaves from cabbage and cut into quarters. Cut away the core (1) and slice paper-thin (2), sprinkle liberally with salt and leave to soften for 1 hour. Drain and press dry in a cloth. Beat herbs and dressing together, pour over the cabbage, mix thoroughly and leave for at least 1 hour.

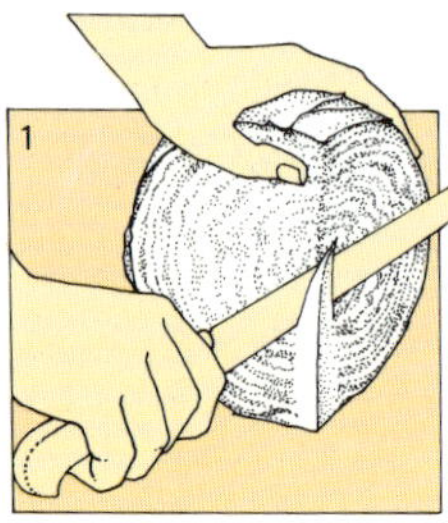

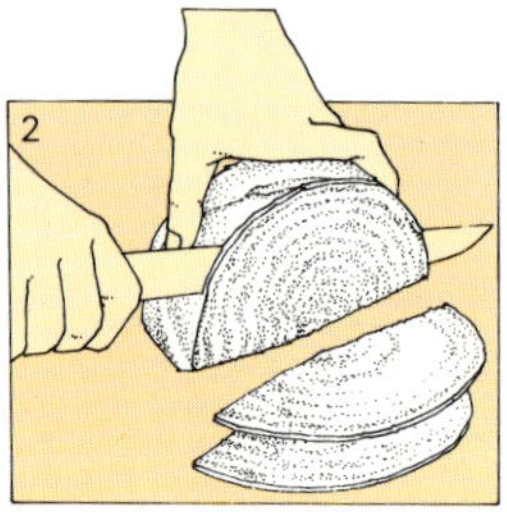

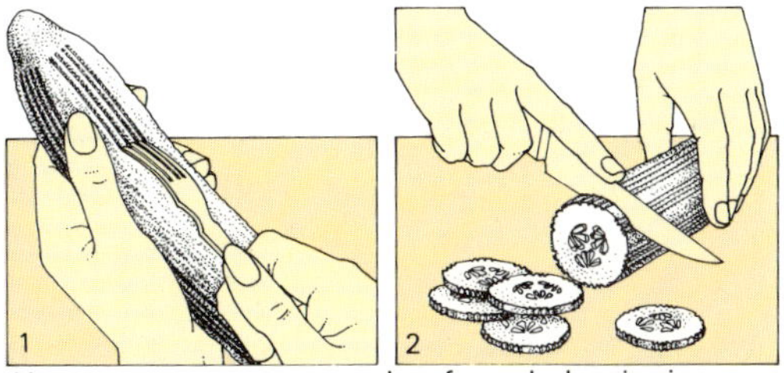

How to prepare a cucumber for salade niçoise

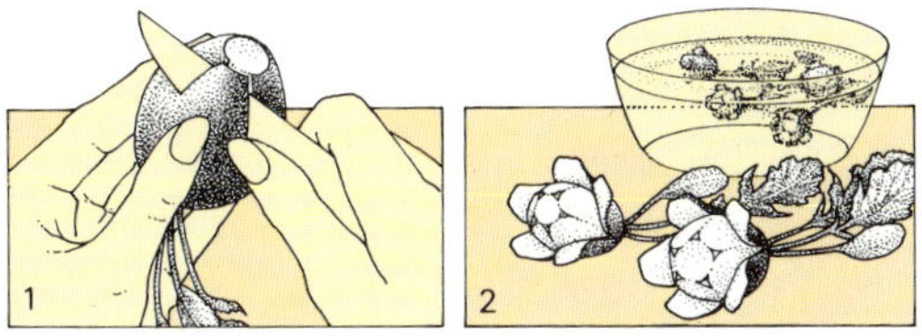

Radish roses: trim off root and any faded leaves. Peel back thin slices of red skin all round the radish (1). Leave in iced water for 1 hour (2).

Hors d'oeuvre salads; salade niçoise; crudités

Salade de chou-fleur

Cauliflower salad

INGREDIENTS
450 g (1 lb) cauliflower
salt and black pepper
mayonnaise (*page* 21)
1 tablespoon chopped tarragon or mint
juice of $\frac{1}{4}$ a lemon

Break the cauliflower into very small sprigs, season well, stir the chopped herbs into the mayonnaise, add a few drops of lemon juice, mix into the cauliflower and leave for 1 hour before serving.

Salade de concombres

Cucumber salad

INGREDIENTS
1 medium-sized cucumber
salt
1 tablespoon parsley, freshly chopped
vinaigrette (*page* 22)

Slice the unpeeled cucumber as finely as possible and spread out on a large plate. Sprinkle liberally with salt, cover with another plate, put weight on top and leave for at least 1 hour. Drain off the liquid, wash the cucumber in a sieve under cold water, and dry it. Cover with parsley and the *vinaigrette*. This treatment eliminates bitterness and aids digestion.

Salade de tomates

Tomato salad

INGREDIENTS
450 g (1 lb) tomatoes
vinaigrette (*page* 22)
2 sliced spring onions
chopped parsley

Peel and slice the tomatoes and dress with the *vinaigrette,* sliced spring onions, and chopped parsley. This is usually served with cucumber salad.

Salade niçoise

Mixed vegetable and anchovy salad

INGREDIENTS
350 g (12 oz) tomatoes
$\frac{1}{2}$ a large cucumber
1 green pepper
1 small onion
1 clove garlic
1 bunch radishes
1 tablespoon parsley
vinaigrette (*page* 22)
50 g (2 oz) anchovies and/or tuna fish
25 g (1 oz) small black olives

Skin the tomatoes, remove core and cut into wedges. Score the skin of the cucumber down the length using a fork (1), cut into $\frac{1}{2}$-cm ($\frac{1}{4}$-in) thick slices (2). Remove seeds and intersections from the pepper and slice coarsely. Peel and slice onion and crush the garlic, top, tail and slice radishes, mix vegetables, chopped parsley and dressing thoroughly. Drain and split the anchovies, mix half into the salad and use the rest with the olives as a garnish.

Crudités

Raw spring vegetables

Choose small vegetables young enough not to need peeling, carrots, courgettes, cauliflower sprigs, radishes, spring onions, little turnips, celery hearts, red and green peppers, and cucumber.

Wash, dry and trim the vegetables, cut the peppers into quarters and the cucumber into slices 3 cm (1 in) thick and arrange decoratively on a large dish.

Serve with mayonnaise, aïoli, *sauce verte* or *vinaigrette* (*see pages* 21–22).

Fenouil à la grecque
Pickled fennel

TO SERVE SIX

INGREDIENTS
450 g (1 lb) fennel
425 ml ($\frac{3}{4}$ pint) water
100 ml (4 fl oz) olive oil
juice of 1 large lemon
1 tablespoon each fennel seeds and coriander
4 large sprigs parsley and 1 sprig thyme tied together
salt

Trim the fennel and slice paper-thin. Put the rest of the ingredients into a wide-based pan and boil for 30 minutes. Add the fennel to this marinade so that the slices are covered by liquid and simmer gently for 8–10 minutes, no more. Remove the herbs and leave the fennel in the marinade for 24 hours before draining and serving.

Concombres à la grecque (Pickled cucumber)
Substitute 1 large cucumber for the fennel. Peel and cut into 1-cm ($\frac{1}{2}$-in) slices and remove the seeds. Cut the slices into halves. Proceed as in the above recipe.

Fenouil, concombres and courgettes à la grecque

Courgettes à la grecque
Pickled courgettes

TO SERVE SIX

INGREDIENTS
450 g (1 lb) courgettes,
425 ml ($\frac{3}{4}$ pint) water
100 ml (4 fl oz) olive oil
juice of 1 large lemon
2 cloves
1 small onion, sliced
2 peeled and quartered tomatoes
4 large sprigs parsley and 1 sprig of thyme tied together
salt

Cut the courgettes into thick slices but do not peel. Put the rest of the ingredients into a wide-based pan and boil for 30 minutes. Add the courgettes so that the slices are covered by liquid and cook for 5 minutes. Remove the herbs and leave the courgettes for 24 hours in the liquid before draining and serving.

Salade de riz
Rice salad

TO SERVE SIX

INGREDIENTS
1 green or red pepper
12 tablespoons cold cooked rice (*page* 163)
1 tablespoon finely chopped onion
1 tablespoon chopped chives
100 g (4 oz) cooked peas
1 tablespoon chopped parsley
vinaigrette (*page* 22)
salt and black pepper

Quarter the pepper and hold under running water to flush out the seeds, remove rib and chop the pepper into small pieces. Mix thoroughly with remaining ingredients, season well and leave for 1 hour before serving.

Salade de riz au poisson (Fish salad)
To serve as a lunch or supper dish add 225 g (8 oz) cooked, skinned and flaked fish, or peeled shrimps, or prawns.

Salade de riz; salade de riz au poisson

Aubergines en gigot

Baked aubergines, hot or cold

TO SERVE ONE

INGREDIENTS
1 small aubergine
1 rasher bacon
1 teaspoon fresh basil or marjoram ($\frac{1}{2}$ teaspoon dried)
1 clove garlic
salt and black pepper
1 teaspoon olive oil

Heat the oven to 180°C, 350°F, Gas Mark 4. Make four incisions across the length of each aubergine and stuff alternately with pieces of bacon rolled in herbs and slivers of garlic rolled in salt and pepper. Sprinkle oil over and bake for 1 hour or until soft.

If eaten cold, split open and sprinkle with olive oil and lemon juice.

Tomates farcies

Hot or cold stuffed tomatoes

TO SERVE SIX

INGREDIENTS

6 extra large tomatoes

Tuna fish

Serve cold

100 g (4 oz) tin of tuna fish
2 tablespoons fine breadcrumbs
3 tablespoons *vinaigrette* (*page* 22)
1½ tablespoons chopped parsley
salt and black pepper
juice of ¼ a lemon

Garlic and parsley

Serve either hot or cold

1 clove garlic, finely chopped
50 g (2 oz) finely chopped onion
4 tablespoons finely chopped parsley
salt and black pepper
juice of ½ a lemon
1 tablespoon olive oil

Eggs

Serve either hot or cold

6 eggs (sizes 3–4)
1 tablespoon cold water
1 tablespoon chopped chives or tarragon
salt and black pepper
25 g (1 oz) butter

For this recipe buy very large tomatoes, the Mediterranean variety if possible. To serve cold, skin the tomato and remove a thick top slice, hollow out with a teaspoon, salt lightly and leave upside down to drain. To serve hot do not skin. Fill with one of the following mixtures.

Tuna fish

Prepare the tomatoes. Drain the fish and flake finely, mix into the other ingredients, reserving some parsley for garnishing, season well, add lemon juice to taste, bind with *vinaigrette*, fill the tomatoes and garnish.

Garlic and parsley

Prepare tomatoes. Chop pulp finely, mix with garlic, onion and parsley, season well, add lemon juice and bind with oil. Fill the tomatoes and serve them chilled. To serve hot, brush the unpeeled tomatoes with oil and place upside down in a shallow oiled dish under a medium grill for 5 minutes. Fill and cook for 10 minutes turning over the filling twice.

Eggs

Beat the eggs, cold water, chives and seasoning together, and scramble very lightly in foaming butter. When still creamy fill the drained tomatoes and leave to cool completely before serving.

To serve hot, rub the prepared, unskinned tomatoes with oil and place upside down in a shallow oiled dish. Cook for 10 minutes under a medium grill until soft, and then fill. Serve immediately while the eggs are hot and creamy.

Tomates farcies: eggs, spinach and tuna fish; *foreground:* petit soufflé aux tomates

Petits soufflés aux tomates

Soufflés in tomato cases

TO SERVE SIX

INGREDIENTS

6 extra large tomatoes
salt
225 ml (8 fl oz) *sauce béchamel* made from 15 g (½ oz) butter, 15 g (½ oz) flour, 150 ml (¼ pint) milk (*page* 14)
2 eggs, separated
salt and black pepper

Heat oven to 200°C, 400°F, Gas Mark 6. Remove the tops of the unskinned tomatoes and scoop out with a teaspoon, reserving juice and pulp. Salt lightly and turn upside down to drain. Chop the pulp and, with the juice, cook to a thick purée. When cool mix into the *sauce béchamel* with the beaten egg yolks. Season well and fold in the stiffly beaten whites. Fill the tomatoes three-quarters full, and bake for 20–25 minutes according to their size and serve straight away.

Choux au fromage

Chou pastry filled with cheese

TO SERVE SIX

INGREDIENTS

Pâte à choux

(Chou pastry)
150 g (5 oz) flour
225 ml (8 fl oz) cold water
pinch of salt
75 g (3 oz) butter
4–5 eggs (size 3–4)

Filling

275 ml ($\frac{1}{2}$ pint) *sauce mornay* (*page* 16)
1 egg yolk
25 g (1 oz) grated *gruyère* cheese

To make the pastry, sieve the flour. Put the water, salt and butter into a heavy pan over a medium heat. Bring to boiling point. When the butter has melted, draw the pan from the heat, pour in the flour all at once and stir vigorously with a wooden spatula. Work the mixture thoroughly until smooth, return the pan to the heat and continue stirring until all moisture has evaporated and the mixture leaves the sides and bottom of the pan clean. The drier the mixture the more eggs are required, the more eggs used the lighter the choux.

Add the eggs one at a time working the mixture well between each one. Beat the last egg and add it gradually to avoid making the mixture too liquid. When finished, it should be supple and glossy. Leave to rest for 20 minutes.

Heat the oven to 220°C, 425°F, Gas Mark 7. Butter and flour a baking sheet and drop on to it heaped tablespoons of *pâte à choux* well spaced out.

Cook for 20 minutes until well risen and firm to the touch. Prepare the *sauce mornay* and reduce until fairly thick, then beat in the egg yolk and the *gruyère* cheese. Keep hot in a *bain-marie.* Cut the tops off the choux, fill them, and replace their tops and keep hot until all are filled. Serve immediately.

To make *choux Pignatelli,* substitute 100 g (4 oz) chopped boiled ham for the *gruyère* cheese.

Crêpes

TO MAKE SIX

INGREDIENTS
50 g (2 oz) flour
1 egg (size 4) plus 1 extra yolk
pinch of salt
1 tablespoon melted butter
2 tablespoons milk
1–2 tablespoons cold water

Mushroom filling
100 g (4 oz) mushrooms
50 g (2 oz) butter
salt, black pepper and grated nutmeg
25 g (1 oz) flour
275 ml ($\frac{1}{2}$ pint) hot milk
100 g (4 oz) grated *gruyère* cheese

Spinach filling
225 g (8 oz) cooked spinach, fresh or frozen
50 g (2 oz) butter
salt, black pepper, grated nutmeg
25 g (1 oz) flour
275 ml ($\frac{1}{2}$ pint) hot milk
100 g (4 oz) grated *gruyère* cheese

Ham and walnut filling
100 g (4 oz) lean boiled ham, thickly cut
50 g (2 oz) shelled walnuts
50 g (2 oz) butter
25 g (1 oz) flour
275 ml ($\frac{1}{2}$ pint) hot milk
100 g (4 oz) grated *gruyère* cheese
salt, black pepper, grated nutmeg

Sieve the flour into a mound in a mixing bowl, making a well in the centre. Break the egg into it and the extra yolk, add a pinch of salt and mix with a wire whisk. Add the milk and 1 tablespoon of cold water to form a very fluid paste. Melt the butter and when liquid mix into the paste. Leave the mixture in a cool place for at least 1 hour or preferably overnight.

Stir the batter well before use, and if it has thickened while standing, add a further 2–3 tablespoons of cold water. The pancakes must be very thin, therefore the batter must be almost as liquid as water.

Heat a small frying pan over a medium temperature, wipe it round with buttered paper and pour a large tablespoon of batter into it, rotating the pan so that the mixture runs evenly over the bottom. Cook for 1 minute shaking the pan, to loosen the pancake, turn it over and cook the other side for 1 minute. Keep hot between two soup plates placed over a pan of simmering water whilst cooking the rest of the batter.

Crêpes aux champignons (Pancakes filled with mushrooms)
Wash and trim mushrooms, but do not peel. Chop the stalks and slice the caps. Cook the stalks slowly for 10 minutes, in a covered pan, in 25 g (1 oz) of butter, add the caps, add seasoning and a pinch of nutmeg. Cook for 5 minutes uncovered. Melt the remaining 25 g (1 oz) of butter, work in the flour, add milk, and cook until thick, stirring briskly. Add the mushrooms and simmer for 5 minutes. Remove from the heat, and beat in two-thirds of the cheese. Correct the seasoning, put a tablespoon of filling centrally on each pancake, roll up and place in a buttered ovenproof dish. Cover with remaining sauce, sprinkle with remaining cheese, reheat and brown under a hot grill. To make this into an extra special dish, mix the cooked mushrooms and their juice with *sauce velouté* (*see page* 17) instead of *béchamel*.

Crêpes aux épinards (Pancakes filled with spinach)
Press the cooked spinach, chop finely and toss over a medium heat for 2–3 minutes until dry in 25 g (1 oz) butter. Add the seasoning and a pinch of nutmeg. In a second pan, melt the remaining butter, work in the flour, add milk, and cook until thick, stirring briskly. Add the spinach and simmer for 5 minutes. Remove from the heat and beat in two-thirds of the cheese and proceed as in above recipe.

Crêpes à la dauphinoise (Pancakes filled with ham and walnuts)
Cut the ham into very small dice and chop the nuts coarsely. Melt the butter, work in the flour, add milk and cook until thick, stirring briskly. Add the ham and nuts and remove the pan immediately from the heat. Beat in two-thirds of the cheese, add the seasoning and a pinch of nutmeg and proceed as in above recipe.

Top: Crêpes à la dauphinoise, aux épinards, aux champignons; *bottom:* Croque-monsieur

Croque-monsieur

TO SERVE SIX

INGREDIENTS
450 g (1 lb) milk loaf
100 g (4 oz) butter
175 g (6 oz) lean boiled ham
175 g (6 oz) *gruyère* cheese

Cut 12 slices of bread $\frac{1}{2}$ cm ($\frac{1}{4}$ in) thick and butter them lightly, remove all fat from ham and cut the cheese into thin slices. Cover 6 slices of bread first with ham and then with cheese and cover with another slice of bread. Tie each parcel crosswise with cotton.

Melt the butter in a large frying pan until foaming and sauté the parcels on both sides until golden. Remove cotton and serve immediately.

Tarte à l'oignon alsacienne

Onion tart

TO SERVE SIX–EIGHT

INGREDIENTS

175 g (6 oz) *pâte brisée* (*page* 204)
40 g (1½ oz) butter
350 g (12 oz) chopped spring onions, green included
2 slices lean bacon
3 eggs
225 ml (8 fl oz) single cream
salt and black pepper
1 20-cm (8½-in) loose-based flan tin

Heat oven to 200°C, 400°F, Gas Mark 6, with baking sheet inside. Line flan tin with the *pâte brisée* and chill until required. Melt butter until foaming and cook the onions until soft. Cut the bacon into small squares.

Beat eggs, cream and seasoning together. Season the onions and arrange in pastry case. Pour in the eggs, scatter with the bacon squares and place on the hot baking sheet. Bake for 30 minutes or until set and serve warm.

Flamiche aux poireaux (Leek tart)
Substitute 350 g (12 oz) white part of leeks for the spring onions in the above recipe and omit the bacon. Slice the leeks and cook in the same way as the onions. Proceed as above.

Tarte à l'oignon alsacienne; tourte ardennaise

Tourte ardennaise

Pork, apple and chestnut pie

TO SERVE SIX–EIGHT

INGREDIENTS

225 g (8 oz) chestnuts
225 g (8 oz) Cox apples
200 g (7 oz) lean pork, finely minced
100 ml (4 fl oz) Madeira
salt and black pepper
2 eggs
15 g (½ oz) butter
225 g (8 oz) *pâte brisée* (*page* 204)
1 20-cm (8½-in) loose-based flan tin

Heat the oven to 190°C, 375°F, Gas Mark 5 with a baking sheet inside.

Butter the flan tin. Slash chestnuts on one side and place under a slow grill until the skin bursts and they are cooked. Remove skins and break the nuts into pieces. Peel, core and finely slice apples and mix them with the chestnuts, pork, Madeira, salt, pepper and one beaten egg.

Roll out two-thirds of the pastry ½ cm (¼ in) thick and line flan tin, prick with a fork and spread with filling. Cover with remaining pastry, seal edges, brush with the other beaten egg and stick a small roll of cardboard (the diameter of a cigarette) into a little hole made in the centre to allow steam to escape. Bake for 45 minutes and cool for 10 minutes. Remove cardboard. Brush the surface with melted butter and serve warm.

Tartelettes au fromage

Cold cheese tartlets

TO SERVE SIX

INGREDIENTS
75 g (3 oz) butter
225 g (8 oz) flour
3 egg yolks (size 4)
100 ml (4 fl oz) milk
dried beans for baking

Filling
40 g ($1\frac{1}{2}$ oz) butter
225 ml (8 fl oz) milk
salt, pepper and grated nutmeg
4 egg yolks (size 4)
100 g (4 oz) grated Emmenthal cheese

Heat oven to 190°C, 375°F, Gas Mark 5. Rub butter into flour, beat in the egg yolks and sufficient milk to form a smooth dough. Chill for 2 hours. Roll out, cut to fit buttered tartlet tins, fill with dried beans and bake blind for 10-15 minutes. To make the filling soften the butter and beat to a mousse. Season the milk with salt, pepper and a pinch of nutmeg and heat to near boiling point. Beat the egg yolks in a bowl and pour the hot milk over them beating with a birch whisk. Strain the mixture through a fine sieve into a clean pan. Cook in a *bain-marie,* stirring constantly, until thick. Remove pan from the heat, beat in the cheese, and then the butter mousse. When the mixture is cold fill the tartlets.

Coquilles de moules au cari

Mussels in curry sauce

TO SERVE SIX

INGREDIENTS
2 litres ($3\frac{1}{2}$ pints) mussels
150 ml ($\frac{1}{4}$ pint) white wine
black pepper
2 shallots, peeled and chopped
25 g (1 oz) butter
25 g (1 oz) flour
1 dessertspoon curry powder
2 tablespoons double cream
6 scallop shells, or small dishes

Clean mussels thoroughly (*see page* 89). Put wine and a little pepper into a large pan, bring to boiling point. Add the mussels, cover and cook over a brisk heat for 5–10 minutes until open. Remove the mussels from the pan one at a time and shell, discarding any that do not open. Reserve the liquid and strain through filter paper placed in a very fine sieve. Cook the shallots in foaming butter in a small pan, work in the flour and curry powder and add the mussel liquid. Whisk until thick and simmer for 10 minutes. Add mussels to the sauce, stir in the cream gradually. Heat very gently for 1 minute, divide and serve.

This dish can also be prepared with *sauce mornay* (*see page* 16) and sprinkled with paprika.

Gratinée de poisson mornay

Fish in mushroom and cheese sauce

TO SERVE SIX

INGREDIENTS
175 g (6 oz) mushrooms
50 g (2 oz) butter
salt and black pepper
juice of $\frac{1}{2}$ a lemon
sauce mornay made from
40 g ($1\frac{1}{2}$ oz) butter
25 g (1 oz) flour
and 275 ml ($\frac{1}{2}$ pint) milk (*page* 16)
450 g (1 lb) cooked white fish (sole, plaice, cod, etc)
4 tablespoons *chapelure*
25 g (1 oz) grated *gruyère* cheese
6 scallop shells

Trim and chop the mushrooms coarsely. Melt 25 g (1 oz) of butter and when foaming add the mushrooms and cook them until tender. Season and add lemon juice to taste, mix in the *sauce mornay,* reheat gently. Divide the fish equally among 6 shells and pour the sauce over. Cover with *chapelure,* dot with butter, sprinkle with *gruyère* cheese and place under grill for 10 minutes or until crusted and browned.

This recipe is very suitable for use with frozen fish.

Chapelure (Browned breadcrumbs)
For the above and other *gratin* dishes, prepare the *chapelure* by baking pieces of bread and crusts in the bottom of the oven until hard and golden. Crush finely and store in screw-topped jars.

Coquilles de moules au cari; gratinée de poisson mornay

Tartelettes au fromage; tricornes du diable

Tricornes du diable

Devil's tricornes with cheese soufflé filling

TO SERVE SIX

INGREDIENTS

1 235 g ($7\frac{1}{2}$ oz) pack frozen flaky pastry
2 eggs (size 2), separated
100 g (4 oz) *petits Suisse* cheese or cream cheese
75 g (3 oz) grated *gruyère* cheese
large pinch cayenne pepper
large pinch black pepper
1 egg yolk (size 2)
1 tablespoon cold water

Heat oven to 220°C, 425°F, Gas Mark 7. Thaw pastry to room temperature.

Beat the egg yolks into the cream cheese until fluffy, and incorporate the *gruyère* cheese. Season with both cayenne and black pepper and beat until smooth. Fold in the stiffly beaten egg whites, adding a third at a time, using a wooden spatula. Roll out the pastry not too thickly and cut into 6 cm ($2\frac{1}{2}$ in) diameter circles. Put a heaped teaspoon of cheese mixture on one side and fold over the other, pressing the edges together to form a triangle. Glaze with egg yolk beaten with the cold water and bake for 15 minutes until puffed and golden. Serve immediately.

Pâté de campagne

Pork pâté

TO SERVE TEN

INGREDIENTS
- 375 g (¾ lb) pickled belly pork
- 750 g (1¾ lb) lean hand or spring of pork (when boned)
- 450 g (1 lb) pork fat
- 450 g (1 lb) pig's liver
- 2 shallots
- 100 g (4 oz) onions
- 2 tablespoons brandy or dry vermouth
- 1 tablespoon each of chopped parsley and chives
- 1 tablespoon mixed spices
- salt and black pepper
- 2 bayleaves
- 6 rashers green fat bacon

Heat the oven to 180°C, 350°F, Gas Mark 4. Soak the pickled pork in cold water overnight if very salty. Remove rind from pork and chop all meat and fat roughly. Peel and chop shallots and onions and mix all these ingredients together. Mince once or twice through mincing machine according to the texture preferred, and mix in brandy, parsley, chives, spices and seasoning. Blend this mixture thoroughly with the hands and pack into a heavy earthenware dish with the bayleaves on top and streaky bacon arranged over them in a criss-cross pattern. It must cover the surface completely.

Place in a *bain-marie* and cook in the oven for 30 minutes, then reduce the heat to 150°C, 300°F, Gas Mark 2, and cook for a further 1½–2 hours. When a metal skewer plunged into the centre comes out hot and the juice is clear remove the pâté from the oven and cover with a sheet of greaseproof paper. Put a small plate, and a weight of not more than 450 g (1 lb) on top. Leave until quite cold. Allow to mature for at least 24 hours before serving.

Do not remove the fat as this preserves the pâté. To serve, cut the required number of slices from out of the dish. Place a piece of cling film paper against the cut side to prevent drying out and cover. Remove all surrounding fat from the slices and arrange them overlapping on a long dish and garnish with sprigs of parsley.

Foie de volaille en pâté

Chicken liver pâté

TO SERVE SIX

INGREDIENTS
- 275 g (10 oz) onions
- 4 tablespoons chicken, duck or goose fat
- 600 g (1 lb 5 oz) chicken livers
- 1 teaspoon dried thyme
- salt and black pepper

Peel and slice the onions and cook over a low heat in 2 tablespoons chicken fat without letting them colour. Remove from the pan with a slotted spoon, add the remaining fat, trimmed chicken livers, thyme and seasoning. Cook gently until firm but still pink inside. Leave to cool and mix in onions, livers and fats in an electric blender until smooth. Correct the seasoning and smooth down in a 13 cm (5 in) diameter earthenware bowl. Serve with rye or brown bread, plain or toasted, and pickled gherkins.

For special occasions flambé the livers, when firm, in 2 tablespoons of brandy and add the thyme afterwards.

Top to bottom: Pâté de canard; pâté de campagne; foie de volaille en pâté

Pâté de canard

Duck pâté

TO SERVE TEN

INGREDIENTS
- 1 orange
- 225 g (8 oz) pork back fat
- 2 kg ($4\frac{1}{2}$ lb) duck
- 200 g (7 oz) pie veal
- 200 g (7 oz) lean pork
- 2 chicken livers
- 1 shallot
- 2 eggs, beaten
- salt, ground allspice, pinch of mixed spices and thyme
- 2 tablespoons or 1 miniature bottle orange Curaçao or Grand Marnier
- 1 bayleaf
- a 1.7 litre (3 pint) earthenware pâté or soufflé dish

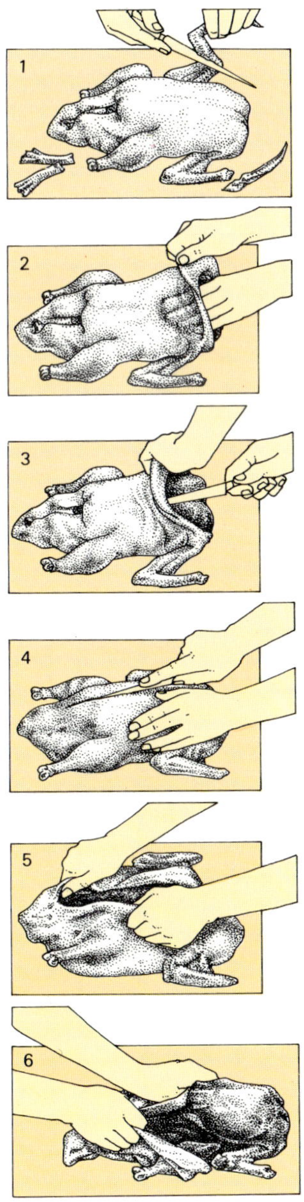

Remove rind from half the orange with a potato peeler, cut into fine strips and simmer in water until tender. Trim the meats and set the duck liver aside. Remove wing tips from the duck, and the feet at leg joint (1). Pull back the neck skin with one hand (2) and sever the adhering membranes with small sharp knife (3). Make a slit down the back (4) and work the skin off with the thumbs (5). When loose, pull off the skin inside out and cut away, keeping it as undamaged as possible (6). Pull off excess fat, and blanch the skin in boiling water for 5 minutes. Drain and dry. Joint the duck, remove the breast meat in thin slices cutting parallel to the breast bone, cut all meat away from the carcass and scrape the bones clean. Scrape away the flesh from sinews and membrane. Keep the carcass for making stock.

Render down the scraps of duck fat over a medium heat and in the liquid fat firm the duck liver and chicken livers. They must not cook but remain pink inside. Drain and chop them finely. The rendered fat can be used for cooking instead of butter.

Roughly chop all other meats (except the sliced breast meat), fat, shallot, and drained orange peel and pass the mixture twice through the mincing machine. In a large bowl mix the minced meats, chopped livers and beaten eggs before adding seasoning, spice and thyme to taste. Mix thoroughly with the hands until soft and smooth.

Line the bottom of the dish with half of the skin, fill with half of the minced meats, lay the strips of breast meat evenly over the surface and fill with the rest of the minced meats. Plunge in a skewer to make 10–15 holes and fill them with the liqueur. Lay the split bayleaf on top, cover with the remaining skin and a sheet of kitchen paper, tucking it well down the sides, and bake in the oven in a *bain-marie* at 180°C, 350°F, Gas Mark 4, for 2 hours. Test with a skewer by plunging it into the centre and if it comes out hot and the juice clear, remove the pâté from the oven. Allow to cool for 20 minutes, remove paper and top skin, and cover with a clean sheet of greaseproof paper. Put a plate and a weight of not more than 450 g (1 lb) on top. Allow to mature for at least 48 hours before use.

Do not remove the congealed fat as this preserves the pâté. To serve, cut the required number of slices from out of the dish. Place a piece of cling film paper against the cut side to prevent drying out and cover. Remove all surrounding fat from the slices and arrange them overlapping on a long dish and garnish with sprigs of parsley.

Soufflés, omelettes and egg dishes

Soufflés

The basis of all soufflés, savoury or sweet, is *sauce béchamel* to which different flavoured ingredients are added with egg yolks. The stiffly beaten egg whites are then folded in. In this folding, and in cooking at a rising temperature, lies the secret of success. Remember that a soufflé waits for no one, so serve from oven to plate without delay.

Savoury soufflés served with a green salad make a good lunch or supper dish.

Making soufflé au fromage

Soufflé au fromage

Cheese soufflé

TO SERVE SIX

INGREDIENTS

- *sauce béchamel* made from 50 g (2 oz) butter, 50 g (2 oz) flour, 275 ml (½ pint) milk
- salt, black pepper and grated nutmeg
- 6 eggs (size 2), separated
- 50 g (2 oz) grated *gruyère* cheese
- 50 g (2 oz) grated Parmesan cheese
- an 18-cm (7¼-in) diameter soufflé dish

Soufflé Furstenbourg

- 6 eggs (size 3–4)
- juice of ½ a lemon

Buy the cheeses in a whole piece and grate as required in order to obtain their full flavour. Use a large pan so that there will be room to incorporate the egg whites easily. Heat the oven to 200°C, 400°F, Gas Mark 6.

Make the *sauce béchamel* by melting the butter over a medium heat until foaming. Add the flour and work it in thoroughly with a wooden spoon. Remove the pan from the heat, add all the milk at once and beat with a whisk until smooth. Return the pan to the heat and cook until thick, stirring constantly, drawing in the mixture from the sides of the pan to avoid lumps. Season, add a generous pinch of nutmeg and taking the pan off the heat, beat in the egg yolks one at a time and the two cheeses and stir until dissolved. Leave to cool. This mixture can be made early in the day for serving later. In this case press a piece of buttered paper over the surface to prevent a skin forming.

Beat the whites to a stiff peak 35 minutes before serving, place a third on top of the *sauce béchamel*, and fold in using a wooden spatula. Add the rest of the egg whites in the same way. Do not stir or beat.

Pour into a buttered soufflé dish to three-quarters full, place in the oven immediately, cook for 20 minutes, then increase the heat to 230°C, 450°F, Gas Mark 8, for a further 10 minutes and serve without delay.

Soufflé Furstenbourg (cheese soufflé with poached eggs inside)
Heat the oven to 180°C, 350°F, Gas Mark 4. Poach the eggs in boiling water with the lemon juice added. Poach for 3 minutes only and then drain on a cloth. Pat dry with kitchen paper and trim the whites with scissors. Make the cheese soufflé as indicated in the above recipe, pour half into a buttered 18-cm (7¼-in) diameter soufflé dish, arrange the poached eggs on top, well spaced out and cover carefully with the remaining mixture. Cook for 10 minutes, then increase the heat to 200°C, 400°F, Gas Mark 6 and cook for a further 20 minutes. Serve immediately.

Soufflé au crabe

Crab soufflé

TO SERVE SIX

INGREDIENTS

- 20 g (⅔ oz) butter
- 1 teaspoon paprika
- 1 teaspoon curry powder
- 275 g (10 oz) crab meat, preferably all white
- *sauce béchamel* made from 50 g (2 oz) butter, 50 g (2 oz) flour, 275 ml (½ pint) milk
- salt, black pepper and grated nutmeg
- 25 g (1 oz) double cream
- 6 eggs (size 2), separated
- an 18-cm (7¼-in) diameter soufflé dish

Heat the oven to 200°C, 400°F, Gas Mark 6. Melt the butter in a large pan, add the paprika and curry powder, mix well and cook together for 1 minute. Mix in the crab meat and cook for 1 minute, stirring constantly. Draw the pan from the heat. In a second pan make the *sauce béchamel* by melting the butter over a medium heat until foaming. Add the flour working it in thoroughly with a wooden spoon. Remove the pan from the heat, add all the milk at once and beat with a whisk until smooth. Season, return the pan to the heat for 10 minutes, stirring frequently. Add the sauce to the crab mixture, add the cream, stir well, correct the seasoning, and beat in the egg yolks, one at a time. When the mixture has cooled fold in the stiffly beaten egg whites, three-quarters fill a buttered soufflé dish and cook for 25 minutes. Serve without delay.

Soufflé au crabe et fines herbes
For paprika and curry powder in the above recipe, substitute 1 heaped tablespoon of finely chopped fresh tarragon or parsley and chives mixed together.

Soufflé au jambon et épinards

Ham and spinach soufflé

TO SERVE SIX

INGREDIENTS
225 g (8 oz) fresh or frozen spinach, leaf not purée
25 g (1 oz) butter
sauce béchamel made from 50 g (2 oz) butter, 50 g (2 oz) flour, 275 ml (½ pint) milk
salt, black pepper and grated nutmeg
100 g (4 oz) lean boiled ham
50 g (2 oz) grated Parmesan cheese
6 eggs (size 2), separated
an 18-cm (7¼-in) diameter soufflé dish

Heat the oven to 200°C, 400°F, Gas Mark 6. If using fresh spinach, wash it and cook in just the water clinging to the leaves. If using frozen spinach, cook while still frozen with no water. When tender, drain well and press out all moisture between the palms. Chop finely. Melt the butter in a large pan and when it foams add the spinach and dry without it colouring, stirring constantly.

In a second pan make the *sauce béchamel* by melting the butter over a medium heat until foaming. Add the flour, working it in thoroughly with a wooden spoon. Remove the pan from the heat, add all the milk at once and beat with a whisk until smooth. Season, return the pan to the heat for 10 minutes, stirring frequently. Add the sauce to the spinach. Remove any fat from the ham and finely chop. Add to the spinach and stir together before adding the Parmesan cheese. Mix well. Correct the seasoning and beat in the egg yolks one at a time, fold in the stiffly beaten egg whites and pour into a buttered soufflé dish. Cook for 20 minutes then increase the heat to 230°C, 450°F, Gas Mark 8 and cook for a further 10 minutes. Serve immediately.

Soufflé au jambon et épinards

Soufflé aux oignons

Onion soufflé

TO SERVE SIX

INGREDIENTS
900 g (2 lb) onions
100 g (4 oz) butter
sauce béchamel made from 50 g (2 oz) butter, 50 g (2 oz) flour, 275 ml (½ pint) milk
pinch of grated nutmeg and paprika
salt and black pepper
50 g (2 oz) double cream
6 eggs (size 2), separated
an 18-cm (7¼-in) diameter soufflé dish

Heat the oven to 200°C, 400°F, Gas Mark 6. Peel and finely slice the onions and blanch them in boiling water for 5 minutes. Drain well. Melt 50 g (2 oz) of butter in a large pan and when it foams cook the onions until tender but not coloured. In a second pan make the *sauce béchamel* by melting the butter over a medium heat until foaming. Add the flour working it in thoroughly with a wooden spoon. Remove the pan from the heat, add all the milk at once and beat with a whisk until smooth. Season with salt and pepper, return the pan to the heat and cook for 5 minutes, stirring frequently. Add the sauce to the onions, season highly, adding a pinch of nutmeg and paprika to taste. Cook for 10 minutes, stirring constantly, until the sauce is very thick. Then reduce to a purée in a blender, beat in the double cream and the remaining butter cut into small pieces. Then beat in the egg yolks, one at a time. When cool, fold in the stiffly beaten egg whites and three-quarters fill the buttered soufflé dish. Cook for 20 minutes, then increase the heat to 230°C, 450°F, Gas Mark 8 and cook for a further 10 minutes. Serve immediately.

Soufflé de poisson

Fish soufflé

TO SERVE SIX

INGREDIENTS

- 100 g (4 oz) cold, cooked fish (not fried)
- *sauce béchamel* made from 50 g (2 oz) butter, 50 g (2 oz) flour, 275 ml ($\frac{1}{2}$ pint) milk
- salt, black pepper and grated nutmeg
- 5 eggs (size 2), separated
- 50 g (2 oz) grated *gruyère* cheese
- 50 g (2 oz) grated Parmesan cheese
- 50 g (2 oz) peeled shrimps or 1 tablespoon concentrated tomato purée
- an 18-cm ($7\frac{1}{4}$-in) diameter soufflé dish

If the fish is fresh, put in a saucepan with enough milk to cover and cook until tender. Drain thoroughly and chop finely. Heat the oven to 200°C, 400°F, Gas Mark 6. Prepare the *sauce béchamel* by melting the butter in a pan over a medium heat until foaming. Add the flour, working it in thoroughly with a wooden spoon. Remove the pan from the heat, add all the milk at once and beat with a whisk until smooth. Season well with salt, black pepper and grated nutmeg and return the pan to the heat to cook for 10 minutes, stirring frequently. Remove the pan from the heat, beat in the egg yolks, one at a time. Stir in the cheese until dissolved. Add the fish and peeled shrimps and leave to cool. This mixture can be made early in the day for serving later. In this case, press a piece of buttered paper over the surface to prevent a skin forming.

Beat the egg whites to a stiff peak 35 minutes before serving, place a third on top of the *sauce béchamel* and fold in using a wooden spatula. Add the rest of the egg whites in the same way. Do not stir or beat.

Pour into a buttered soufflé dish to three-quarters full, place in the oven immediately, cook for 20 minutes, then increase the heat to 230°C, 450°F, Gas Mark 8 for 10 minutes and serve without delay.

Soufflé de potiron

Pumpkin soufflé

TO SERVE SIX

INGREDIENTS

- 450 g (1 lb) pumpkin, peeled and seeded
- 1 teacup cold water
- salt
- juice of $\frac{1}{2}$ a lemon
- 1 dessertspoon cornflour
- 425 ml ($\frac{3}{4}$ pint) milk
- salt and black pepper
- 3 eggs (size 2), separated
- 75 g (3 oz) grated *gruyère* cheese
- an 18-cm ($7\frac{1}{4}$-in) diameter soufflé dish

Heat the oven to 190°C, 375°F, Gas Mark 5. Cut the pumpkin into pieces and cook in a large pan with the cold water, salt and the lemon juice. When just tender drain thoroughly, press out excess moisture and blend until smooth. Mix the cornflour with a little cold milk, heat the rest of the milk and when warm add the cornflour. Season and cook until thick. Cool a little and whisk in the pumpkin purée, the egg yolks, one at a time, and the grated cheese. When cold, fold in the stiffly beaten whites, pour into a buttered soufflé dish and cook for 30 minutes. Serve straight away.

Soufflé de purée de pommes de terre

Soufflé with potato, ham and cheese

TO SERVE SIX

INGREDIENTS

- 225 g (8 oz) mashed potatoes
- 25 g (1 oz) butter
- 3 eggs (size 2), separated
- 50 g (2 oz) lean boiled ham, finely chopped
- 25 g (1 oz) grated *gruyère* cheese
- salt, black pepper and grated nutmeg
- an 18-cm ($7\frac{1}{4}$-in) diameter soufflé dish

Heat the oven to 180°C, 350°F, Gas Mark 4. Pass the potatoes through a mouli-légumes to ensure smoothness. Beat in the softened butter, egg yolks, ham and grated cheese. Season and add a pinch of grated nutmeg to taste. Beat the mixture thoroughly. Fold in the stiffly beaten egg whites and pour into a thickly buttered soufflé dish. Bake for 30 minutes. Serve straight away.

Soufflé aux fraises

Soufflé au chocolat

Chocolate soufflé

TO SERVE SIX

INGREDIENTS
200 g (7 oz) cooking chocolate
1 dessertspoon water
6 eggs (size 2), separated
100 g (4 oz) sugar
40 g (1½ oz) flour
1 teaspoon vanilla sugar – castor sugar in which a vanilla pod has been stored
15 g (½ oz) butter
icing sugar for dusting
a 16-cm (6½-in) diameter soufflé dish

Heat the oven to 220°C, 425°F, Gas Mark 7. Break up the chocolate and melt it with the water in a large pan standing in a *bain-marie*. When liquid, remove the pan from the heat and beat in the egg yolks, two at a time. Sieve two-thirds of the sugar and the flour together with the vanilla sugar and beat this into the chocolate and egg mixture. Beat the egg whites to a soft peak and then add the rest of the sugar, beating constantly until very stiff. Butter and sugar the soufflé dish right up to the top. Fold in the egg whites carefully with a wooden spatula, a third at a time. Do not stir or beat. Fill the dish to the top and bake for 30–35 minutes. Dust with icing sugar and serve immediately.

Both the yolk mixture and the whites need to be very well beaten to counteract the density of the chocolate.

Soufflé aux fraises

Strawberry soufflé

TO SERVE SIX

INGREDIENTS
450 g (1 lb) strawberries, 350 g (¾ lb) if frozen
3 eggs (size 2), separated, plus 1 extra white
200 g (7 oz) castor sugar
25 g (1 oz) cornflour
50 g (2 oz) double cream
1 dessertspoon strawberry liqueur or kirsch
juice of ¼ a lemon
an 18-cm (7¼-in) diameter soufflé dish

Heat the oven to 190°C, 375°F, Gas Mark 5. Hull the strawberries and reduce to purée in an electric blender. If frozen, thaw and drain first. Butter the soufflé dish. Beat the yolks and sugar together until white and frothy. Add the cornflour, cream, liqueur and a few drops of lemon juice and beat until smooth. Add the strawberry purée and mix well. Beat the whites to a stiff peak and fold them into the strawberry and egg yolk mixture very carefully. Pour into the soufflé dish to three-quarters full and bake in the oven for 30 minutes. Serve straight away.

Soufflé au Cointreau/Grand Marnier/rhum

Liqueur or rum flavoured soufflé

TO SERVE SIX

INGREDIENTS
275 ml (½ pint) milk
100 g (4 oz) castor sugar
75 g (3 oz) unsalted butter
50 g (2 oz) flour
6 eggs (size 2), separated
4 tablespoons liqueur or rum
pinch of salt
an 18-cm (7¼-in) diameter soufflé dish

Heat the oven to 200°C, 400°F, Gas Mark 6. Heat the milk slowly and stir in 75 g (3 oz) of the sugar until dissolved. Melt the butter over a medium heat in a large pan and when foaming work in the flour with a wooden spoon, cook for 1 minute but do not colour. Remove the pan from the heat and add the sweetened milk all at once. Beat with a whisk until smooth. Cook over a slightly increased heat until thick, stirring constantly. Remove the pan from the heat and beat in the egg yolks, one at a time. Stir in the liqueur gradually.

Beat the whites with a pinch of salt and add the remaining sugar gradually until a very stiff peak is formed. When the *sauce béchamel* is cold fold in the egg whites. Pour into the buttered soufflé dish and cook for 40 minutes. Serve at once.

Omelette

TO SERVE SIX

INGREDIENTS
8 eggs (size 2)
salt and pepper
50 g (2 oz) butter

Entire chapters have been written on the way to make a classic French omelette, but practice and a few special tricks soon give good results. When served the omelette should be soft, plump, golden outside and creamy inside, in fact 'runny' say native experts.

Mix the eggs with a fork; they should not be beaten or whisked. Season them and set aside for a while. Some cooks add a tablespoon of cold water during the mixing, others a few small flecks of soft butter, to make the texture lighter. But milk or cream are never included as this would have the opposite effect.

The pan must be very large so that the finished omelette will be thin and pliable and it must also be of a heavy metal to cook the eggs more by the heat of the pan than by the heat under it.

Place the dry pan over a medium heat for a full minute so that when the butter is dropped in, it froths immediately and colours soon afterwards. Swirl it round the pan, give the eggs a final stir and pour them into the pan all at once. Reduce the heat immediately to low and with the back of the fork draw a figure 8 on the surface several times so as to distribute the eggs evenly. Lift up the edges as they begin to set, all round the pan, to allow the liquid

Omelette aux champignons; omelette aux croûtons

to run under and shake the pan often to loosen the omelette which must remain liquid on the surface. Lift up the edge with a fork and drop a few little pieces of butter underneath to make it slide out easily, fold over once on the handle side and tilt the pan over on to the serving dish so that the omelette folds over once more on to itself. Eggs in any form continue cooking by their own heat so do not overcook, and serve immediately.

Omelette aux fines herbes
Add 2 tablespoons finely chopped chives and parsley, or tarragon, chervil or basil to the eggs when mixing them.

Omelette aux croûtons

Omelette with croûtons, onions and bacon

TO SERVE SIX

INGREDIENTS
4 tablespoons croûtons (*page* 33)
100 g (4 oz) thickly cut lean streaky bacon, cut into strips
40 g (1½ oz) butter
175 g (6 oz) coarsely chopped onions
6 eggs (size 2)
salt and black pepper

Rub the pan over with a buttered paper and sauté the bacon, until crisp and golden. Keep the bacon and croûtons hot in the oven. In the same pan melt half the butter and over a low heat cook the onions in it to the golden stage, stirring occasionally. Season, drain and keep hot. Mix the eggs in a bowl with a fork and season. Wipe out the pan used for the onions and place over a medium heat for a full minute so that when the remaining butter is dropped in it froths immediately and colours soon afterwards. Swirl it round the pan, give the eggs a final stir and pour them into the pan. Reduce the heat immediately to low and with the back of the fork draw a figure 8 on the surface several times to distribute the eggs evenly, lifting up the edges as they begin to set to allow the liquid to run under. Shake the pan often to loosen the omelette which must remain liquid on the surface. When set underneath and still liquid on top loosen the edges, slide a few extra pieces of butter underneath, shake the pan, spread the onions, bacon and croûtons on one side, fold the other side over on top and slide the omelette on to a heated serving dish.

Omelette aux champignons

Mushroom omelette

TO SERVE SIX

INGREDIENTS
225 g (8 oz) mushrooms, peeled and coarsely chopped
40 g (1½ oz) butter
sauce béchamel made from 25 g (1 oz) butter, 25 g (1 oz) flour, 150 ml (¼ pint) milk
salt and black pepper
6 eggs (size 2)
50 g (2 oz) butter

Peel and chop the mushrooms coarsely. Melt the butter in a pan, add the mushrooms and cook, uncovered, until soft. Make the *sauce béchamel* by melting the butter in a second pan over a medium heat until foaming. Add the flour, working it in with a wooden spoon. Remove the pan from the heat, add the milk all at once and beat with a whisk until smooth. Season. Add the mushrooms and juices, stir well and simmer for 5 minutes, stirring frequently.

Prepare the omelette by mixing the eggs in a bowl and whisking with a fork. Season. Place the omelette pan over a medium heat for a full minute so that when the butter is dropped in, it froths immediately and colours soon afterwards. As this happens, swirl it round the pan, give the eggs a final stir and pour them into the pan all at once. Reduce the heat immediately to low and with the back of a fork draw a figure 8 on the surface several times to distribute the eggs evenly, lifting up the edges as they begin to set to allow the liquid to run under. Shake the pan often to loosen the omelette which must remain liquid on the surface. When set underneath, lift up the edges, slide a few small pieces of butter under and pour half of the sauce across the centre of the omelette. Fold over once on to the filling and slide out on to a heated serving dish before pouring the rest of the sauce on top.

Omelette du curé

Omelette with sorrel and cream

TO SERVE SIX

INGREDIENTS
100 g (4 oz) sorrel
6 large tender lettuce leaves
40 g ($1\frac{1}{2}$ oz) butter
salt and pepper
6 eggs (size 2)
50 g (2 oz) double cream

Wash the sorrel and lettuce, remove the centre ribs and shred the leaves. Melt half the butter in a small pan, add the leaves and cook until soft. Season well and keep hot.

Mix the eggs in a bowl with a fork and season. Place the pan over a medium heat for 1 minute so that when the remaining butter is dropped in it froths immediately and colours soon afterwards. Swirl it round the pan, give the eggs a final stir and pour them into the pan all at once. Reduce the heat immediately to low and with the back of the fork draw a figure 8 on the surface several times to distribute the eggs evenly, lifting up the edges all round the pan as they begin to set to allow the liquid to run under. Shake the pan often to loosen the omelette which must remain liquid on the surface. When the omelette is half cooked, stir the cream into the sorrel, mix well and pour across the centre of the omelette. When the omelette is set underneath and still liquid on top, stir the cream into the sorrel, mix well and pour across the centre of the omelette. Fold it once on to the filling and again on to itself before sliding it on to a heated serving dish.

Omelette aux foies de volaille

Chicken-liver omelette

TO SERVE SIX

INGREDIENTS
175 g (6 oz) chicken livers
25 g (1 oz) butter
25 g (1 oz) chopped onion
4 tablespoons white wine or dry sherry
salt and black pepper
6 eggs (size 2)
25 g (1 oz) butter

Trim the livers and cut each lobe into half. Melt the butter over a medium heat and when foaming add the onion and cook until transparent. Add the white wine and reduce by half. Reduce the heat and add the livers. Cook for no more than 2 minutes, stirring continually. Season well and draw the pan away from the heat.

Make the omelette by mixing the eggs in a bowl and whisking with a fork. Season. Place the omelette pan over a medium heat for a full minute so that when half the second amount of butter is dropped in, it froths immediately and colours soon afterwards. Swirl it round the pan, give the eggs a final stir and pour them into the pan all at once. Reduce the heat immediately to low and with the back of a fork, draw a figure 8 on the surface several times to distribute the eggs evenly, lifting up the edges all round the pan as they begin to set to allow the liquid to run under. Shake the pan often to loosen the omelette which must remain liquid on the surface. When set underneath and still liquid on top loosen the edges, slide a few little pieces of butter underneath to make the omelette slide out easily and fold over once on the handle side. Tilt the pan over on to the heated serving dish so that the omelette folds over once more on to itself. Make a slash down the centre and pour in the livers, onion and juice. Serve immediately.

Omelette aux tomates et poivron

Omelette with tomatoes, green pepper and garlic

TO SERVE SIX

INGREDIENTS
1 green pepper
2 dessertspoons olive oil
1 clove garlic
450 g (1 lb) tomatoes
175 g (6 oz) onion
1 tablespoon chopped basil or parsley
salt and pepper
6 eggs (size 2)
40 g ($1\frac{1}{2}$ oz) butter

Split open the pepper, remove ribs and seeds and brush the outside with some of the oil. Place under a hot grill until blistered and peel off the skin. Peel and crush the garlic. Skin tomatoes and onions and chop together, add the chopped pepper and garlic, season highly and cook in the remaining olive oil until soft and thick. Add the fresh herbs, stir well and keep hot while making the omelette.

Mix the eggs in a bowl with a fork and season. Place the pan over a medium heat for 1 minute so that when the butter is dropped in it froths immediately and colours soon afterwards. Swirl it round the pan, give the eggs a final stir and pour them into the pan all at once. Reduce the heat immediately to low and with the back of the fork draw a figure 8 on the surface several times to distribute the eggs evenly, lifting up the edges all round the pan as they begin to set to allow the liquid to run under. Shake the pan often to loosen the omelette which must remain liquid on the surface. Lift up the edges with a fork and drop a few small pieces of butter underneath to make it slide out easily. Pour the sauce into the centre, fold over once and slide on to the serving dish.

This omelette is also extremely good when eaten cold, in fact lightly chilled, and served with a green salad.

Omelette soufflée à la vanille

Vanilla soufflé omelette

TO SERVE SIX

INGREDIENTS
100 g (4 oz) castor sugar
5 eggs (size 2), separated
1 teaspoon vanilla sugar (*page* 217)

Heat the oven to 190°C, 375°F, Gas Mark 5. Butter a shallow oval ovenproof dish and sprinkle with a little of the castor sugar. Beat the yolks in a large bowl with both the castor and vanilla sugar until thick and smooth. Whisk the whites until stiff, place a third on top of the yolk mixture and fold it in with a wooden spatula. Do not stir or beat. Add the rest of the whites all at once, and fold in.

Pour into the prepared dish, smooth over and up with a knife blade to form a dome and make shallow slits along the top and sides to help the heat penetrate. Bake for 20–22 minutes. Serve immediately.

This omelette can also be flambéd, with 3 tablespoons of rum gently warmed with a teaspoon of sugar. Pour this over the omelette at table and ignite. Baste and serve as the flames die down.

Omelette soufflée à la vanille

Omelette soufflée au Grand Marnier

Soufflé omelette flavoured with liqueur

TO SERVE SIX

INGREDIENTS
6 boudoir biscuits or sponge fingers
4 tablespoons liqueur
100 g (4 oz) castor sugar
5 eggs (size 2), separated
1 teaspoon vanilla sugar (*page* 217)

Dip the biscuits lightly on both sides into the liqueur, making sure they are not soaked. Butter a shallow oval metal gratin dish and sprinkle with a little of the castor sugar. Place the biscuits in the bottom.

Beat the egg yolks in a large bowl with both the castor and vanilla sugar until thick and smooth. Whisk the whites until stiff, place a third on top of the yolk mixture and fold it in with a wooden spatula. Do not stir or beat. Add the rest of the whites all at once and fold in.

Pour over the biscuits, smooth over and up with a knife blade to form a dome and make shallow slits along the top and sides to help the heat penetrate. Bake for 20–22 minutes. Serve immediately.

Slices of *brioche* (*see page* 28) can be used instead of biscuits or sponge fingers.

Oeufs Auckland

Eggs poached in cream and sherry

TO SERVE SIX

INGREDIENTS
- 25 g (1 oz) butter, cut into small pieces
- 275 ml (½ pint) single cream
- 3 tablespoons medium dry sherry
- 6 eggs (size 2)
- 40 g (1½ oz) grated *gruyère* cheese
- salt and black pepper
- 6 rounds hot buttered toast

Place a sauté pan or large frying pan over low heat, add the butter and when half melted, beat in the cream and the sherry. Do not boil or the cream will curdle.

Break the eggs into a wet saucer one at a time and slide them into the pan. Poach gently and as soon as the white starts to set sprinkle with grated cheese, add seasoning and finish cooking. Lift out on to the toast with a slotted spoon and pour the sauce over them.

Oeufs aux crevettes

Eggs with shrimps and cream sauce

TO SERVE SIX

INGREDIENTS
- 450 g (1 lb) milk loaf
- 6 eggs (size 2)
- salt and black pepper
- 100 g (4 oz) butter
- 1 tablespoon olive oil
- 150 g (5 oz) peeled shrimps
- 75 ml (3 fl oz) dry white wine
- 25 g (1 oz) rice or potato flour
- 1 tablespoon milk
- 425 ml (¾ pint) single cream
- 25 g (1 oz) concentrated tomato purée

Heat the oven to 190°C, 375°F, Gas Mark 5. Thinly slice the crust off the side of the loaf and cut 3 slices 2 cm (¾ in) thick. Cut each slice into halves and stamp out each one with a round cutter making 6 circles in all. Thickly butter 6 dariol moulds or ramekin dishes. Break the eggs into a saucer and slide one into each mould, season and place in a *bain-marie*, cover, and bake for 8–10 minutes until the eggs are sufficiently set to turn out.

Meanwhile heat the butter and oil together in a large frying pan and when hot sauté the bread until golden. Put these *canapés* in the bottom of the oven on kitchen paper to drain and keep hot.

Put the shrimps and wine into a small pan over a low heat and simmer until the liquid is reduced by half. Dilute the rice flour in the milk and add to the cream. Stir gradually into the pan and cook slowly for 3 minutes before adding the tomato purée. Bring slowly to boiling point and season highly. Keep hot by standing the pan in a *bain-marie*.

Pass a sharp knife blade around the inside of the dariol moulds and turn out the eggs on to the hot *canapés*, cover with the sauce and serve immediately.

Oeufs frits jardinière

Eggs deep-fried with aubergine, rice, and ham

TO SERVE SIX

INGREDIENTS
- 350 g (12 oz) aubergine
- salt and black pepper
- 200 g (7 oz) onions
- 50 g (2 oz) butter
- 200 g (7 oz) rice
- 575 ml (1 pint) warm water
- 2 tablespoons olive oil
- 225 g (8 oz) frozen peas
- 200 g (7 oz) boiled ham, cut thick
- 6 eggs (size 2)
- pinch of paprika
- 4 tablespoons cooking oil

Wipe the aubergine with a damp cloth, remove the stem but do not peel. Cut the flesh into thick slices. Sprinkle with salt on both sides and press between two plates to extract the liquid. Leave on one side.

Peel and chop the onions. Melt the butter in a deep frying pan over a low heat. When foaming, add the onions and cook until transparent. Add the rice to the onions, season well and, stirring all the time, cook together for 3 minutes. Add the warm water. Stir well, cover and leave over a medium heat for 15 minutes until the liquid is absorbed and the surface of the rice pitted with little holes.

Meanwhile drain, wash and dry the aubergine, cut into dice and cook for 10 minutes until golden in the hot olive oil.

Blanch the peas in salted water for 5 minutes. Cut the ham into cubes, add to the aubergines to colour, then mix them and the drained peas into the rice. Correct the seasoning, pour into a heated serving dish and keep hot. Pour the cooking oil into a small pan and when it is hot poach the eggs one at a time. Flip the white over the yolk with a spoon and when lightly coloured, drain and place on top of the rice.

Serve immediately with *sauce tomate* (*see page* 18).

Anti-clockwise: Oeufs aux crevettes; oeufs frits jardinière; oeufs mollets aux épinards

Oeufs mollets aux épinards

Eggs soft-boiled with spinach

TO SERVE SIX

INGREDIENTS

900 g (2 lb) fresh or frozen spinach, leaf not purée
100 g (4 oz) butter
salt, black pepper
pinch of sugar
grated nutmeg
sauce béchamel made either from 15 g ($\frac{1}{2}$ oz) butter, 15 g ($\frac{1}{2}$ oz) flour, 150 ml ($\frac{1}{4}$ pint) milk
or 150 ml ($\frac{1}{4}$ pint) double cream
4 slices bread
6 eggs (size 2)

Heat the oven to 180°C, 350°F, Gas Mark 4. If using fresh spinach, wash it and cook in just the water clinging to the leaves. If using frozen spinach, cook while still frozen with no water. When tender, drain well and press out all moisture between the palms. Chop finely. Melt the butter in a large pan and when it foams add the spinach and dry for 2–3 minutes, stirring constantly. Add a pinch of salt, black pepper and sugar. Either make the *sauce béchamel* and stir a generous pinch of nutmeg into it and stir into the spinach. Or, if cream is used instead, season with salt, pepper, and nutmeg before stirring it into the spinach. Heat gently until the first bubble rises. Beat in 25 g (1 oz) of butter in small pieces, pour into a heated serving dish and keep hot in the oven.

Butter the bread on both sides and place in the middle of the oven to colour.

Lower the eggs into boiling water, boil for 4 minutes, plunge into very cold water for 2 minutes, crack the shells and peel off under a running tap. Dry on kitchen paper and set deeply into the spinach. Cut the bread into triangles and stand them upright around the eggs. Serve immediately.

If sorrel is available it can be included with the spinach. Substitute 175 g (6 oz) of sorrel for 175 g (6 oz) of spinach in the quantity given and cook in 50 g (2 oz) butter. Mix into the dried spinach before the *sauce béchamel* or cream is added. Sprinkle Parmesan cheese on top before serving.

Oeufs normande

Eggs with onions, mussels and cream

TO SERVE SIX

INGREDIENTS
6 hard-boiled eggs
1 litre ($1\frac{3}{4}$ pints) mussels
50 g (2 oz) butter
50 g (2 oz) chopped onion
25 g (1 oz) flour
200 ml (7 fl oz) single cream
salt and black pepper
2 tablespoons chopped parsley and chives

Peel the eggs and cut them in halves lengthways. Scrape and wash the mussels thoroughly (*see page* 89). Melt half the butter in a large pan and when foaming add the onions and cook over a medium heat until soft. Throw in the mussels, increase the heat and shake briskly until the mussels open. Throw away any that do not open. Reserve all the liquid, shell the mussels and place them in an ovenproof dish. Set aside.

Strain the liquid through filter paper placed in a very fine sieve and set aside. Heat the oven to 230°C, 450°F, Gas Mark 8. Melt the remaining 25 g (1 oz) butter in a small pan, work in the flour, add sufficient mussel liquid to obtain a thick sauce, season lightly, and cook, stirring constantly, for 5 minutes. Stir in the cream gradually, adding more liquid if too thick. Place the eggs on top of the mussels and cover with the hot sauce. Cover with foil and place in a very hot oven for 5 minutes, just long enough to heat through. Sprinkle with the herbs and serve immediately.

Oeufs soubise

Eggs with onion cream sauce

TO SERVE SIX

INGREDIENTS
sauce soubise (*page* 17)
6 eggs (size 2)
salt and paprika

Pour the sauce into a shallow serving dish and reheat by standing it, covered, in a *bain-marie* in a moderate oven. Meanwhile place the eggs in boiling water and cook for 4 minutes. Then plunge them into very cold water for 2 minutes, crack all over and peel under a running tap. Dry on kitchen paper and set deeply into the hot sauce. Sprinkle with salt and paprika and serve immediately.

Piperade basquaise

Eggs with green pepper, tomatoes and onions

TO SERVE SIX

INGREDIENTS
100 g (4 oz) onions
1 clove garlic
1 green pepper
225 g (8 oz) tomatoes
1 tablespoon olive oil
1 chili pepper
salt and black pepper
175 g (6 oz) slice of gammon, cut into narrow strips
25 g (1 oz) butter
6 large eggs (size 2)

Peel and coarsely chop the onions and peel and crush the garlic. Remove seeds and ribs of the green pepper and chop coarsely with the skinned tomatoes. Heat the olive oil in a large frying pan and when hot add onion and garlic and cook for 5 minutes, add tomatoes, green pepper and chili, season well and cook, uncovered, over a low heat for 10 minutes, stirring occasionally. Add the gammon and cook for a further 10 minutes. Remove the chili pepper. Add the butter cut in small pieces. Beat the eggs and add to the pan, cook for 6–8 minutes, stirring once round the pan at 2-minute intervals. When set underneath, cut into 6 portions. Serve immediately with French bread.

Suprêmes au fromage

Egg custards with cheese

TO SERVE SIX

INGREDIENTS
575 ml (1 pint) milk
salt and black pepper
4 eggs (size 2), plus 1 extra yolk
50 g (2 oz) grated *gruyère* cheese
sauce tomate (*page* 18)

Heat the oven to 180°C, 350°F, Gas Mark 4. Season the milk with salt and pepper and heat to boiling point. Meanwhile beat the eggs with a pinch of salt in a large bowl. Pour the boiling milk over them, little by little, beating constantly. Beat in the grated cheese gradually and continue beating until it melts.

Butter 6 dariol moulds (or ramekin dishes), and fill with the mixture. Stand them in a *bain-marie* and cook for 20 minutes or until set in the centre. Meanwhile make the *sauce tomate*.

When the *suprêmes* are set in the centre, pass a sharp knife round the inside of the moulds and turn out the contents on to a heated serving dish. Pour the sauce around them and serve immediately.

This recipe can also be cooked in a 1-litre (2-pint) mould. Allow 1 hour's cooking time.

Top : Oeufs normande; piperade basquaise; *bottom :* oeufs soubise; suprêmes au fromage

HUITRES
HUITRES
A EMPORTER

Fish and shellfish

A notable difference between the French ways of cooking fish and the English is that the French rarely fry it. Whatever the variety, from sea or river, they mainly bake, sauté in butter, or cook fish in *court-bouillon*. This mixture of wine, or wine vinegar and water flavoured with vegetables and herbs in its turn flavours the fish which is then served with a delicious sauce. Sometimes the fish is cooked in the sauce itself to the same effect.

How to clean a round fish: Make a slit along the length of the belly (1). Scrape out the insides. Trim off the gills with scissors (2).
How to clean a flat fish: Cut off the head and remove, together with the insides (3). Trim the tail and remove the fins (4).

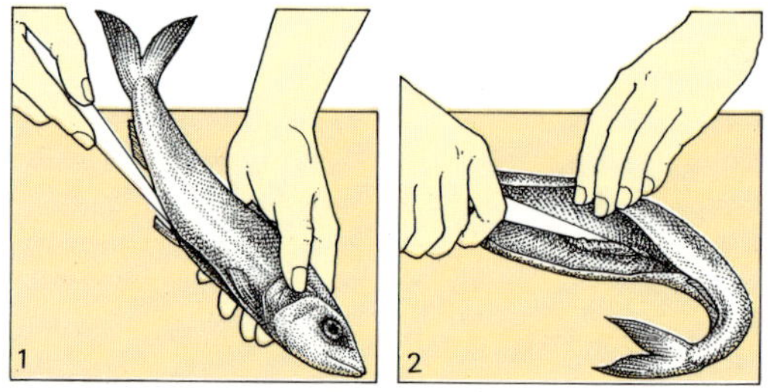

How to clean a round fish

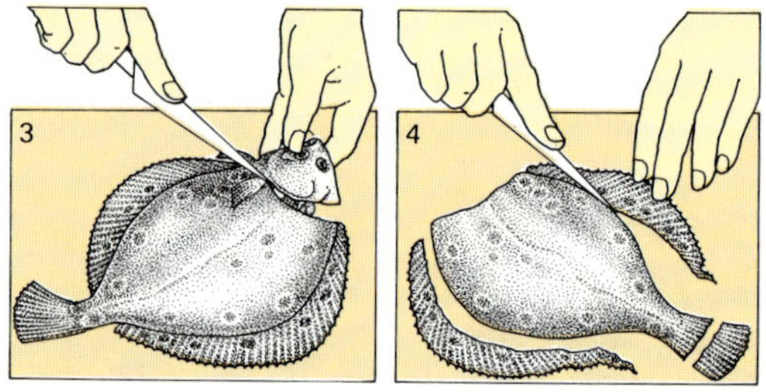

How to clean a flat fish

Court-bouillon

INGREDIENTS
- 1 litre ($1\frac{3}{4}$ pints) water
- 75 ml (3 fl oz) wine vinegar or 150 ml ($\frac{1}{4}$ pint) dry white wine
- 50 g (2 oz) sliced carrots
- 50 g (2 oz) sliced onion
- 1 tablespoon coarse crystal salt
- 1 teaspoon black peppercorns
- 2 cloves
- bouquet garni or 1 large sprig parsley
- 1 small sprig thyme
- 1 bayleaf

The technique of cooking in *court-bouillon* consists of concentrating the liquid ingredients in a covered pan by simmering, and plunging in the whole fish to seal in the flavours while cooking. This method is suitable for any firm-fleshed white fish, which retains its full savour much more this way than if bought and cooked in small pieces. The whole fish may also be cheaper.

Put all the ingredients together in a pan just large enough to contain them, bring to boiling point, reduce the heat, cover and simmer for 30 minutes to concentrate.

Whiting cooked in court-bouillon with white sauce piquante

Fish cooked in court-bouillon

TO SERVE SIX

INGREDIENTS

Codling, haddock or whiting

1 whole fish, or 1 piece weighing 1 kg (2 lb) or more
court-bouillon (*see facing page*)
parsley for garnishing

Turbot or halibut

1 piece of fish weighing 1 kg (2 lb)
court-bouillon made from 1 litre ($1\frac{3}{4}$ pints) water, 275 ml ($\frac{1}{2}$ pint) milk, 1 dessertspoon coarse crystal salt, 1 teaspoon black peppercorns, juice of 2 small lemons

Codling, haddock or whiting

When cooking whiting or any loosely flaked fish in *court-bouillon* it is advisable to wrap it in a piece of cheesecloth so that it may be easily removed from the pan without breaking.

Clean the fish and scale by scraping with a knife blade from tail to head. Wash under running water and place in a pan. Add just enough *court-bouillon* to cover the fish. Return to boiling point and simmer slowly, without a lid, for about 25 minutes or until the fish is tender when pierced with a pointed knife. Drain, reserving the liquid, and place on a table napkin folded on a heated serving dish.

Remove the top skin of the fish, garnish with sprigs of parsley and serve with *sauce piquante* (white), made with the reserved *court-bouillon* (*see page* 16). Other sauces to serve with fish cooked in *court-bouillon* are *sauce poivrade* (*see page* 17) or *béarnaise* (*see page* 20).

Fish cooked in this way can be served either hot or cold. To serve cold, drain the fish on kitchen paper and remove the top skin. When cold, chill for 1 hour and transfer to a folded table napkin placed on a serving dish, garnish and serve with mayonnaise (*see page* 21) or *sauce verte* (*see page* 22).

Hake cooked in *court-bouillon* and served with *sauce gribiche* (*see page* 23) makes a delicious summer dinner-party dish.

Pike, or *brochet au beurre blanc*, is the speciality of Anjou and the Nantes area. The fish is cooked in *court-bouillon* with a teaspoon of fennel seeds added, and served with white butter sauce, *beurre blanc* (*see page* 20).

Turbot or halibut

To make the *court-bouillon*, mix together the ingredients and pour them into a large pan, bring slowly to simmering point, put in the fish immediately and cook for about 25 minutes, until tender when pierced with a pointed knife. Drain and place on a table napkin folded on a heated serving dish.

Remove the top skin of the fish and garnish with a few sprigs of parsley and serve with *sauce hollandaise* (*see page* 20).

With any fish cooked in *court-bouillon* serve a Barsac or Anjou for those who do not relish a dry white wine, a Pouilly-Fuissé for those who do.

Alose à la méridionale

Shad, mackerel or herring with tomatoes, peppers, herbs and white wine

TO SERVE SIX

INGREDIENTS
450 g (1 lb) large tomatoes
350 g (12 oz) onions
2 green peppers
100 g (4 oz) mushrooms
1 kg (2 lb) fish, whole if possible
2 tablespoons olive or corn oil
2 tablespoons chopped parsley and chives
salt and black pepper
25 g (1 oz) butter
1 finely chopped clove garlic
75 ml (3 fl oz) white wine

This recipe for cooking shad, a popular fish in Brittany, is also a delicious way of cooking large mackerel, herrings, sea perch or codling.

Heat the oven to 180°C, 350°F, Gas Mark 4. Peel and slice tomatoes and onions thinly. Split open the peppers, remove ribs and seeds and brush the outside with oil. Place under a hot grill until blistered and peel off the skin. Cut into strips. Wash, dry and slice the mushrooms. Clean and scale the fish, remove the fins, leave the head and tail on. Dry well and brush with half the oil. Pour the rest into a large shallow dish, cover with half the tomatoes, onions and pepper, sprinkle with half the herbs, lay the fish on top, season and cover with the remaining vegetables.

Melt half the butter in a pan, add the mushrooms and cook for 5 minutes over a medium heat. Spread them over the vegetables and cover with the garlic mixed into the rest of the herbs. Salt lightly and

pour the wine over the surface. Dot with the remaining butter, cover and cook for approximately 45 minutes. Serve with cider.

Anguilles à la bière

Eels cooked in beer, also suitable for cooking huss (rock salmon)

TO SERVE SIX

INGREDIENTS
1 kg (2 lb) eels, skinned and cleaned
75 g (3 oz) butter
1 litre ($1\frac{3}{4}$ pints) light ale
bouquet garni
salt and pepper
$\frac{1}{2}$ teaspoon of grated nutmeg
6 rounds bread, cut 1 cm ($\frac{1}{2}$ in) thick
40 g ($1\frac{1}{2}$ oz) butter
1 egg yolk (size 2)
20 g ($\frac{2}{3}$ oz) flour
1 tablespoon chopped parsley

This recipe comes from Amiens in the hop-growing north of France.

Wash and dry the eels and cut into short lengths. Melt half the butter in a large pan and when foaming, add the eels and colour to the blonde stage on both sides. Pour in the ale, add bouquet garni, salt, pepper and the nutmeg. Bring slowly to boiling point, cover and simmer very gently for approximately 45 minutes until tender. Huss will cook in 20 minutes.

Heat the oven to 180°C, 350°F, Gas Mark 4. Remove crusts and corners from the bread and sauté quickly in foaming butter until golden. Place these *canapés* in a deep serving dish and keep hot. Soften the remaining butter and mix with the egg yolk and flour to form a smooth paste. Remove the eels from the pan with a slotted spoon, drain, place on the *canapés* and keep hot. Pass a few bands of kitchen paper over the surface of the liquid in the pan to remove the fat, add the flour and egg mixture, beat briskly and allow to thicken very slowly over a low heat. Pour the sauce over the eels and sprinkle with parsley. Serve with beer.

Eperlans en escabêche

Sprats or smelts in marinade

TO SERVE SIX

INGREDIENTS
1 kg (2 lb) sprats
seasoned flour
4 tablespoons frying oil
100 g (4 oz) chopped onions
6 chopped cloves garlic
1 sliced carrot
75 ml (3 fl oz) olive oil
225 ml (8 fl oz) white wine vinegar
½ litre (18 fl oz) water
2 bayleaves
1 sprig thyme
1 chili pepper
salt and black pepper
saffron
slices of lemon

Open and clean the sprats but do not remove either head or tail. Wipe with a damp cloth, dry and dip into seasoned flour. Heat half the oil in a large frying pan and fry one layer of fish very lightly to the blonde stage. Heat the rest of the oil and cook the remaining fish. Drain on kitchen paper and arrange in one layer, head to tail, in a large shallow dish.

Put onions, garlic and carrot into a saucepan, add the olive oil, vinegar and water, herbs, chili, and a generous pinch of saffron. Bring to boiling point and simmer for 20 minutes. Leave until cold and then strain over the fish. Garnish with the bayleaves, sliced carrot and slices of lemon and chill for 24 hours.

Serve with rye bread and a bottle of dry or medium Vouvray, or Sancerre.

Top left : filets de sole Nelly; *top right :* filets de sole au gratin; *bottom :* filets de sole à l'estragon

Filets de sole Nelly

TO SERVE SIX

INGREDIENTS
100 g (4 oz) button mushrooms
1 hard-boiled egg
6 fillets of sole
flour for coating
100 g (4 oz) butter
25 g (1 oz) fine breadcrumbs
25 g (1 oz) finely chopped parsley
salt and black pepper
juice of 1 lemon
Sauce
$1\frac{1}{2}$ tablespoons lemon juice
$\frac{1}{2}$ teaspoon salt
100 g (4 oz) softened butter
black pepper

In the following recipe for cooking fillets of sole, brill, plaice or other fillets can be used just as well.

Trim, wash and dry the mushrooms. Pass the hard-boiled egg through a coarse sieve.

Wash and dry the fish thoroughly and dip lightly into seasoned flour. Melt 50 g (2 oz) of butter in a large shallow pan over a medium heat and when foaming sauté the fillets, shaking the pan occasionally. Increase the heat for the final few minutes to colour the fish. Drain, place on a serving dish and keep hot.

Melt the remaining butter until foaming, add the mushrooms and cook for 5 minutes. Increase the heat and add the sieved egg, breadcrumbs, parsley, salt and pepper and stir vigorously for 2 minutes. Sprinkle this over the fish and flavour generously with lemon juice. Serve immediately.

Sauce is not usually served with this recipe, but if one is required heat the lemon juice with the salt in a small saucepan over a *low heat* and whisk in the softened butter, cut into small pieces. Season with freshly ground black pepper. By beating constantly with a birch whisk, this sauce will thicken slightly and become creamy. Serve immediately.

Filets de sole au gratin

Fillets of sole with white wine sauce

TO SERVE SIX

INGREDIENTS
knob of butter
6 large fillets of sole
1 shallot
salt and pepper
150 ml ($\frac{1}{4}$ pint) white wine
4 tablespoons cold water
50 g (2 oz) butter
1 dessertspoon flour
150 ml ($\frac{1}{4}$ pint) milk
4 tablespoons *chapelure* (*page* 54)

Filets de sole mornay
100 g (4 oz) *gruyère* cheese

In the following recipe for cooking fillets of sole, brill, plaice or other fillets can be used just as well.

Heat the oven to 190°C, 375°F, Gas Mark 5. Butter a large gratin dish with the knob of butter and lay the fish in it, brushing in between the fillets with melted butter to prevent them sticking together.

Peel and finely chop the shallot, sprinkle over the fish and season well. Mix the wine and water, pour down the sides of the dish, cover with buttered greaseproof paper and bake for 15 minutes.

Drain off and reserve the liquid without removing the fish from the dish and keep it hot. Melt 25 g (1 oz) butter in a small pan until foaming, work in the flour, add the cooking liquid and whisk until smooth, add the milk and cook over a medium heat until thick. Simmer for 5 minutes, add the seasoning and pour over the fish, scatter the *chapelure* thickly on top and dot with the remaining 25 g (1 oz) butter. Place under a hot grill until bubbling and the top crusted.

If no wine is available for cooking it can be replaced by a mixture of 150 ml ($\frac{1}{4}$ pint) water and 1 dessertspoon of tarragon vinegar.

Filets de sole mornay
When the sauce is made, add half the cheese with the seasoning and pour over the fish. Mix the rest of the cheese with the *chapelure*, scatter the dish and dot with the remaining pieces of butter before placing under the grill.

Filets de sole à l'estragon

Fillets of sole with tarragon

TO SERVE SIX

INGREDIENTS
100 g (4 oz) butter
6 large sprigs of tarragon, about 10 cm (4 in) long
flour for coating
6 thick fillets of sole
salt
150 ml ($\frac{1}{4}$ pint) white wine
black pepper

In the following recipe for cooking fillets of sole, brill, plaice or other fillets can be used just as well. Henri de Toulouse-Lautrec was a great cook as well as a great painter. Love of food and cooking bound him closely to his friend Maurice Joyant, director of the Joyant Gallery in Paris. Together they collected and perfected recipes. The following recipe, supreme in its simplicity, was created by Toulouse-Lautrec.

Heat the oven to 200°C, 400°F, Gas Mark 6. Melt the butter in a large metal gratin dish and place 3 sprigs of tarragon in the bottom. Lightly flour the fish and place on top. Salt lightly and cook over a brisk heat for 3 minutes. Then add the wine, and cover with the rest of the herbs. Turn down the heat and reduce the liquid for 10 minutes. Turn the fish over and put the dish into the oven for 10 minutes to reduce the sauce still further. Remove the herbs, sprinkle with pepper at the last minute and serve in the same dish.

Filets de sole au vermouth

Fillets of sole in vermouth

TO SERVE EIGHT

INGREDIENTS
knob of butter
2 large soles, filleted
150 ml ($\frac{1}{4}$ pint) dry vermouth
225 g (8 oz) mushrooms
6 tablespoons water
$1\frac{1}{2}$ tablespoons lemon juice
25 g (1 oz) butter, cut into pieces
275 ml ($\frac{1}{2}$ pint) double cream
4 egg yolks (size 2)

Fish stock
fish bones and trimmings of filleted soles
275 ml ($\frac{1}{2}$ pint) white wine
275 ml ($\frac{1}{2}$ pint) water
100 g (4 oz) chopped onion
1 sprig thyme
4 sprigs parsley
1 bayleaf
salt and black pepper

Top: filets de sole au vermouth, *bottom:* flétan au Muscadet

Put the stock ingredients, with plenty of seasoning, into a large saucepan and boil until reduced by half. Strain and set aside.

Butter a *sauteuse* or heavy pan well and place the fillets in it without overlapping them. Pour on the vermouth and reduced stock and poach gently for 10 minutes. Drain, reserve the liquid, and keep warm in a covered serving dish.

Meanwhile, wipe the mushrooms with a damp cloth, trim the ends, slice thickly and cook in the water, lemon juice and butter. Season well and stir with a wooden spoon over a brisk heat for 5 minutes. Strain the juice into a small saucepan and garnish the fish with the mushrooms. Put the reserved liquid into a pan and reduce by half. Reduce the mushroom liquid to 3 tablespoons, mix the two liquids together, add the cream and heat slowly until *almost* boiling. Remove the pan from the heat and whisk in the egg yolks. Place over a very low heat, season and add lemon juice to taste, beating constantly and heat until the sauce is thick.

Pour the hot sauce over the fish and serve immediately. This delectable sauce must be made with great care. To prevent it from boiling it can be finished off in a *bain-marie* (*see page* 14). Serve with a dry white burgundy, or *champagne nature*, the non-vintage wine of Champagne made into a still wine.

Flétan au Muscadet

Halibut in white wine sauce

TO SERVE SIX

INGREDIENTS
75 g (3 oz) butter
6 chopped shallots
1 kg (2 lb) halibut
salt and pepper
1 bottle Muscadet
bouquet garni
1 tablespoon potato or plain flour
275 ml ($\frac{1}{2}$ pint) single cream
juice of $\frac{1}{2}$ a lemon
2 tablespoons chopped parsley and chives

Heat the oven to 200°C, 400°F, Gas Mark 6. Line a large flat dish with cooking foil in order to lift out the fish without breaking it.

Melt the butter in a small pan and when foaming, add the shallots and cook until soft. Pour this over the foil and place the fish on top. Season well, pour the wine over, add the bouquet garni and place the dish in the oven. As soon as the contents start to simmer, after about 15 minutes, reduce the heat to 180°C, 350°F, Gas Mark 4, baste the fish and cook for approximately 25 minutes or until tender when pierced with a pointed knife. The liquid must simmer very slowly and the fish must not colour. Cover if necessary.

When cooked, transfer the fish to the serving dish, remove the skin and keep hot wrapped in fresh foil. Pour the cooking liquid into a saucepan placed over brisk heat. Reduce by half, strain and return to the pan. Stir the flour into the cream until smooth and add to the fish liquid. Simmer and stir continually until the sauce is thick. Unless a sauce containing cream has a starch binding it must not boil or it will curdle. Cook for 5 minutes, correct the seasoning and add lemon juice to taste, pour over the fish and garnish with herbs. Serve very hot with steamed new potatoes and a pot of strong French mustard. Serve with the same wine as that used in the cooking.

Harengs farcis en papillotes

Stuffed herrings baked in parcels

TO SERVE EIGHT

INGREDIENTS
50 g (2 oz) fine breadcrumbs
4 finely chopped shallots
6 herrings with roes
5 tablespoons chopped parsley and chives or green onion tops
4 tablespoons cream
100 g (4 oz) butter
salt, black pepper, and cayenne pepper

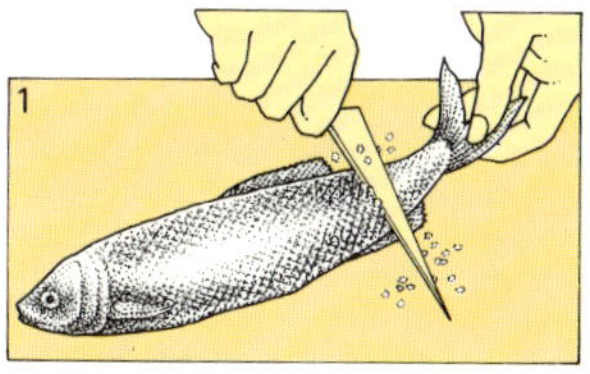

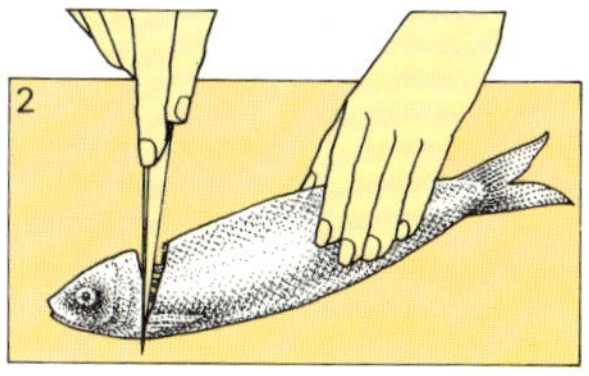

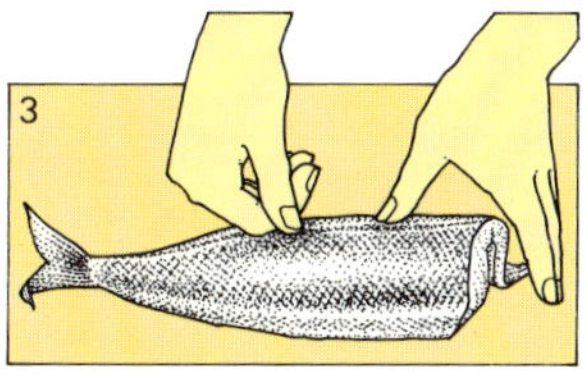

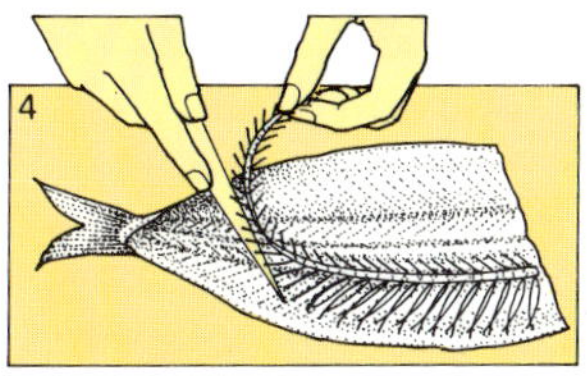

Soak the breadcrumbs in cream and set aside. Scale the herrings by scraping from tail to head with a knife blade (1). Slit open the belly and remove entrails, roes, head, and fins (2). Set the roes aside. Turn skin-side up, spread flat and press firmly along the backbone (3). Turn the fish over and, starting at the head end, ease out the backbone with the knife (4). Wash and dry thoroughly.

Work 3 tablespoons of herbs into the butter and add the rest of the herbs and the shallots to the breadcrumbs and cream. Season and add a generous pinch of cayenne pepper. Spread the mixture inside the herrings, lay the roes on top, season lightly and wrap them separately in buttered foil, crimping the ends to seal them.

Heat the oven to 200°C, 400°F, Gas Mark 6, and cook the parcels on the middle shelf, for about 10–12 minutes, until the paper is well coloured on top, turn and bake until the other side is coloured. Serve in the papers with the herb butter and plain boiled potatoes. Cider or beer can be served with this dish or a Muscadet if white wine is preferred.

Harengs en matelote

Herrings in red wine sauce

TO SERVE SIX

INGREDIENTS
6 medium-sized herrings
seasoned flour
25 g (1 oz) butter
1 tablespoon corn oil
sauce matelote (*page* 18)

Remove head, tail and fins from the fish, clean, scale and wash, dry well and cut each one into 3 pieces. Dust lightly with seasoned flour. Put butter and oil into a large frying pan and heat until the butter foams. Sauté the fish in this until golden brown but not fully cooked. Cover and keep hot.

Meanwhile make the *sauce matelote* and when it is thick, add the fish and cook for 10–15 minutes over a low heat until the sauce has reduced, and the fish is cooked.

Pour into a deep serving dish, garnish with fingers of hot toast and serve with boiled potatoes. Serve with Beaujolais-villages.

Kofta

Algerian fish cakes

TO SERVE SIX

INGREDIENTS
175 g (6 oz) sliced onions
salt
100 g (4 oz) fine fresh breadcrumbs
150 ml ($\frac{1}{4}$ pint) milk
3 eggs (size 2)
675 g ($1\frac{1}{2}$ lb) skinned and boned white fish, cod or whiting
black pepper
pinch of ground cinnamon
pinch of ground cloves
flour for dusting
100 g (4 oz) butter
1 teaspoon oil

Sprinkle the sliced onions with salt, cover and set aside. Soak the breadcrumbs in milk for 10 minutes, then squeeze out the excess moisture and mix into the well beaten eggs.

Chop the fish and onions as finely as possible, or pound in a mortar until smooth and add to the egg and bread mixture. Season well with pepper, cinnamon and cloves and mix thoroughly. Form into small round cakes and dust with flour.

Heat the butter in a sauté pan or large frying pan until foaming, add a teaspoon of oil to prevent it burning and sauté the fish cakes over a medium heat until crisp and golden brown on both sides. Serve with *sauce tomate* (*see page* 18).

Maqueraux à l'oléronnaise

Grilled mackerel with mustard and spices

TO SERVE SIX

INGREDIENTS
6 medium-sized mackerel
oil
salt and black pepper
paprika and cayenne pepper
3 bayleaves
juice of 1 large lemon
75 g (3 oz) butter, cut into small pieces
4–5 tablespoons strong French mustard

Heat the grill to a medium temperature. Clean, scale and wash the mackerel and dry inside and out. Brush the inside with oil, sprinkle lightly with salt, and generously with black pepper, paprika and cayenne. Add half a bayleaf to each fish and brush the outside with oil. Turn up the grill heat to high and cook the fish about 12 cm (5 in) below the element until the skin is brown and crisp. Turn and cook on the other side.

Meanwhile strain the lemon juice into a small pan, add salt and pepper, heat for a moment, then beat in the butter and the mustard alternately, a little at a time and continue beating until thick. If the sauce thickens too much, thin down with lemon juice. Pour over the fish and serve very hot with red-skinned potatoes boiled in the skin. Serve with strong cider.

Truites grillées, sauce piquante

Grilled trout with *sauce piquante*

TO SERVE ONE

INGREDIENTS
sauce piquante (*page* 17)
1 200-g (7-oz) trout
1 teaspoon oil
Beurre maître d'hôtel
15 g (½ oz) butter
½ teaspoon chopped fresh or dried tarragon
salt and black pepper
1 teaspoon lemon juice

Prepare the *sauce piquante* (*see page* 17) and keep hot in a *bain-marie*. Heat the grill to a medium temperature.

Clean, scale and wash the fish and dry thoroughly. Make the *beurre maitre d'hôtel* by mixing the butter, chopped herbs and seasoning together, working in the lemon juice until incorporated. Stuff the belly with this mixture and sew up with cotton. Brush with oil and place under the grill, but not too close to the element. Increase the heat to high and cook for 7–8 minutes on each side, until the skin is brown and crisp and the flesh tender when pierced with a sharp knife. Serve at once accompanied by the sauce. Serve with a Riesling or Chablis.

Truites à la Bresle

Trout cooked in vine leaves

TO SERVE ONE

INGREDIENTS
2 large vine leaves
cider
1 200-g (7-oz) trout
25 g (1 oz) butter
25 g (1 oz) shelled shrimps
salt and black pepper
1 teaspoon fresh chopped tarragon or ¼ teaspoon dried thyme
melted butter for coating

Heat the oven to 150°C, 290°F, Gas Mark 2. Put the vine leaves to soak in sufficient cider to cover. Clean, scale and wash the trout, dry thoroughly. Mix together the butter, shrimps, seasoning and herbs and work into a paste. Stuff the inside of the trout with this mixture and sew up the belly with cotton. Remove the vine leaves from the cider but do not dry them. Salt and pepper them and brush with softened butter. Wrap them around the trout to cover it completely, and secure with cotton. Place on an oiled grill rack, cover and bake for 35–40 minutes, until tender when pierced with a pointed knife.

To serve, place the fish on to a heated serving dish, cut away the cotton, and serve it with a good dry white wine, Graves, Pouilly-sur-Loire, or Chablis.

Top left: harengs en matelote; *top right:* maquereaux à l'oléronnaise; *centre:* truites grillées, sauce piquante; *bottom:* truites à la Bresle

Pain de poisson

Hot fish mousse with tomato cream sauce

TO SERVE SIX

INGREDIENTS

550 g ($1\frac{1}{4}$ lb) skinned whiting fillets
100 g (4 oz) peeled shrimps
2 eggs, plus 5 extra yolks
40 g ($1\frac{1}{2}$ oz) butter
3 tablespoons flour
425 ml ($\frac{3}{4}$ pint) milk
salt, black pepper, nutmeg
200 ml (7 fl oz) double cream
2 tablespoons concentrated tomato purée
a few drops of lemon juice
deep soufflé dish 18-cm ($7\frac{1}{4}$-in) diameter

Heat the oven to 200°C, 400°F, Gas Mark 6, for 30 minutes. Blend the fish in a liquidizer until smooth.

In a large bowl mix fish, shrimps, the eggs, plus 3 extra yolks. Mix thoroughly and set aside. Make a *sauce béchamel* by melting the butter in a small pan until foaming, work in the flour, remove the pan from the heat to add the milk, beat well and cook over a medium heat until thick. Season well and when cooked remove the pan from the heat and beat in the 2 remaining yolks until well incorporated. Add half the sauce to the fish mixture. Correct the seasoning and add grated nutmeg to taste. Pour it into a buttered charlotte mould or deep soufflé dish, place in a *bain-marie* with water 5 cm (2 in) deep in it, and put in the oven. Reduce the heat to 180°C, 350°F, Gas Mark 4, and cook for 1 hour, covering the mould with a sheet of foil if the fish begins to colour on the surface. Test with a knife blade which should come out clean when the dish is cooked. Meanwhile reheat the rest of the *sauce béchamel* in a *bain-marie,* correct the seasoning, and add nutmeg to taste. Beat in the cream and tomato purée and sharpen with a few drops of lemon juice. To serve, turn out the *pain de poisson* on to a hot dish and pour the sauce around it. Serve with a Riesling or Vouvray.

Poisson à la moutarde

Fillets of lemon sole, whiting, plaice or other white fish with mustard sauce

TO SERVE SIX

INGREDIENTS

6 fillets of fresh fish (frozen fish also gives good results)
15 g ($\frac{1}{2}$ oz) butter
2 tablespoons strong French mustard
2 tablespoons double cream
1 tablespoon chopped gherkins
salt and black pepper

Heat the oven to 220°C, 425°F, Gas Mark 7. Butter a gratin dish thickly and place the fillets in it without overlapping them. Put into the oven for 15 minutes. By this time the fish will have rendered its liquid. Pour this away.

In a small bowl mix the mustard, cream, chopped gherkins, salt and pepper. Coat the fish with this mixture and put back into the oven for a further 10 minutes.

Serve immediately with plain boiled potatoes and either beer or cider. The mustard in the sauce would overshadow the flavour of wine.

From left to right: poissons à la moutarde, ragoût de poisson and raie a la crème

Ragoût de poisson

Fish casserole

TO SERVE SIX

INGREDIENTS
900 g (2 lb) fillets of fish
175 g (6 oz) onions
675 g (1½ lb) small potatoes
225 g (8 oz) large tomatoes
75 g (3 oz) butter
salt and black pepper
1 sprig each thyme, rosemary, fennel and/or mint
1 bayleaf

This is an excellent recipe for cooking the less expensive kinds of fish, such as whiting, haddock or huss (rock salmon).

Wipe the fillets of fish with a damp cloth and cut into 3-cm (1-in) wide strips. Finely slice the onions, potatoes and tomatoes.

Melt 40 g (1½ oz) butter in a large iron cocotte and cook the onions to the blonde stage. Fill up the cocotte with slices of potato, tomato and fish. Salt each layer lightly and pepper well. Finish with overlapping slices of potato. Dot with the remaining butter and lay the herbs on top. Cover and cook for 1 hour over a low heat until the ingredients are tender when pierced with a pointed knife.

If using an earthenware dish cook the onions in a frying pan and then transfer them to the dish from the bottom layer. Cook in the oven at 180°C, 350°F, Gas Mark 4, for 1½ hours and test in the same way.

When cooked remove the herbs and brown under a very hot grill. Serve with cider or beer.

Raie à la crème

Skate with cream sauce

TO SERVE SIX

INGREDIENTS
1.2 kg (2½ lb) skate
100 g (4 oz) butter
150 ml (¼ pint) milk
2 tablespoons flour
salt and pepper
1 tablespoon French mustard
275 ml (½ pint) double cream
juice of ½ a lemon

English habits and fashions in food have changed with the times. Oysters, like skate, were, in Dickens' time, considered a poor man's dish. Not so in France where skate has always been regarded as one of the delicacies of the marine world.

Poach the pieces of fish in salted water in a *sauteuse* or large frying pan for 10 minutes. Drain, remove the skin and set the fish aside.

Wash and dry the pan and melt the butter in it over a medium heat. Dip each piece of fish first in milk and then in seasoned flour, then cook in the foaming butter until golden on both sides. Arrange on a heated serving dish and keep hot. In the same pan work the mustard into the butter with a wooden spoon over a low heat. Stir in the cream, correct the seasoning, add lemon juice to taste and, when hot, pour over the fish.

Serve with small new potatoes and a chilled Chablis or Muscadet.

Crabes toulonnais

Fresh baked crab with mussels

TO SERVE SIX

INGREDIENTS

1 sprig fresh fennel, 8 cm (3 in) long
2 hard-boiled eggs
1 clove garlic
1 litre ($1\frac{3}{4}$ pints) mussels
salt and black pepper
1 tablespoon olive or corn oil
1 dessertspoon flour
150 ml ($\frac{1}{4}$ pint) milk
4 small dressed crabs
25 g (1 oz) butter
chapelure (*page* 54)
6 shells

Chop the fennel and hard-boiled eggs together. Peel and crush the garlic in a mortar and pound all 3 ingredients together until smooth.

Scrub the mussels with a wire brush and wash in several changes of water. Throw them into a dry pan placed over a brisk heat, shake the pan vigorously and take out the mussels as they open. Throw away any that do not open. Remove the mussels from their shells, season and chop coarsely. Remove the liquid and strain through a fine sieve lined with filter paper.

Heat the grill to a medium temperature. In a large pan heat the oil, add the flour and colour it lightly. Remove the pan from the heat and add the milk. Stir with a wooden spoon until smooth. Now add enough of the reserved mussel liquid to make the sauce up to 425 ml ($\frac{3}{4}$ pint) and simmer over a medium heat for 10 minutes until thick.

Mix in the egg and herb mixture, the dark flesh of the crab, chopped mussels and the white crab meat. Correct the seasoning, and heat slowly for a few minutes, stirring constantly. Turn up the grill to high. Pour the prepared crab meat into the buttered shells, sprinkle generously with *chapelure*, dot with flecks of butter and place under the grill until brown and crusted. Serve with a Maçon or Chablis.

Homard grillé maître d'hôtel

Grilled lobster with lemon and herb butter

TO SERVE TWO

INGREDIENTS
1 cooked lobster
50 g (2 oz) butter
salt and black pepper
2 tablespoons fresh or 1 teaspoon dried chopped fennel or tarragon
juice of 1 lemon

Heat the oven to 190°C, 375°F, Gas Mark 5. If the lobster is whole straighten it out by pushing the palm firmly down the underside (1) and cut into halves beginning at the head end (2). Remove the stomach sac (3) and discard. Remove the flesh from the body in one piece and the coral. Crack the claws carefully (4) and remove the flesh. Season the butter, work in the herbs and the lemon juice. Spread half in the bottom of the shell, replace the lobster meat, the coral and the claw meat, and dot with the remaining herb butter. Cover and place in the oven for 10 minutes if it is a small lobster, 20 minutes if large. Serve with *Blanc de blancs*, a sparkling wine made by the champagne method from young non-vintage wine.

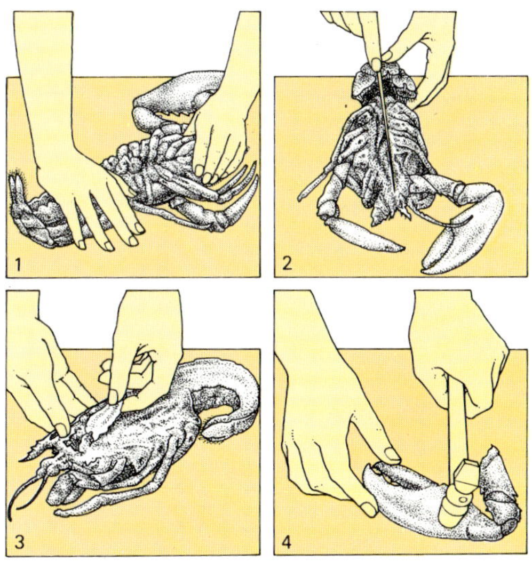

Langouste au Xérès

Crayfish tails in sherry

TO SERVE SIX

INGREDIENTS
- 6 large fresh or packet of frozen crayfish tails
- 100 g (4 oz) butter
- 75 g (3 oz) finely chopped onions
- salt and black pepper
- 425 ml ($\frac{3}{4}$ pint) double cream
- 1 dessertspoon flour
- 150 ml ($\frac{1}{4}$ pint) medium dry sherry

If the crayfish are frozen, thaw for 24 hours in the refrigerator, and then at room temperature until completely thawed.

Melt 50 g (2 oz) butter in a *sauteuse* or a shallow wide-based pan and when foaming, cook the onions over a low heat for 5 minutes until soft. If large crayfish tails are used, cut into thick pieces and add to the pan. Season lightly, lower the heat and cook very gently until the onion is pale gold but the fish uncoloured. Turn over the slices, season the second side, add the cream and heat through over a low heat. Remove the crayfish with a slotted spoon, arrange on a heated serving dish, cover and keep hot.

Work the remaining butter into the flour, drop it into the cream, stir until smooth, add the sherry and correct the seasoning. Put into a pan and cook very slowly until thickened, then simmer for 3 minutes. Pour over the crayfish and serve with *Riz créole* (*see page* 163). Serve with a white burgundy, such as Meusault-Charmes or Montrachet.

Moules à la marinière

TO SERVE SIX

INGREDIENTS
3 litres (4¼ pints) cleaned mussels
50 g (2 oz) chopped onions
2 chopped shallots
100 g (4 oz) chopped parsley
275 ml (½ pint) white wine
black pepper
100 g (4 oz) butter, cut into small pieces
juice of ½ a lemon

To clean mussels
Scrub with a wire brush and wash in several changes of cold water. Scrape them and remove the beard. To make them extra plump they should be bought 2 days beforehand. Place them in the bottom of a large bowl and cover well with cold water. Add a large handful of oatmeal and keep in a cool dark place for 2 days, changing the water and oatmeal every 24 hours.

Scrape the mussels well and wash them in several changes of water. Throw them into a very large pan with the onion, shallot, parsley, wine and plenty of freshly ground pepper. Add half the butter, place the pan over a brisk heat, shaking it to ensure even cooking. When the shells open, remove the mussels and keep hot in a large covered dish. Discard any that do not open. Strain the juice through a fine sieve lined with filter paper, return it to the pan, and reduce by half. Remove the pan from the heat, beat in the remaining butter and the lemon juice. Pour over the mussels and serve very hot. The same wine as that used for the cooking can be served, Graves or Pouilly-Fuissé.

Moules aux épinards

Mussels with garlic and spinach

TO SERVE SIX

INGREDIENTS
2 litres (3½ pints) cleaned mussels (*see above*)
1.3 kg (3 lb) fresh or frozen spinach, leaf not purée
25 g (1 oz) butter
1 tablespoon olive oil
100 g (4 oz) chopped onions
1 dessertspoon flour
275 ml (½ pint) milk
salt and black pepper
1 chopped clove garlic
1 bayleaf
1 carrot, unpeeled
75 ml (3 fl oz) white wine or the same amount of water plus 1 teaspoon wine vinegar
2 stalks parsley
chapelure (*page* 54)

Heat the oven to 150°C, 290°F, Gas Mark 2. Wash the fresh spinach in several changes of water, tear out the centre rib and cook in just the water clinging to the leaves. If frozen, cook without thawing in 3 cm (1 in) boiling, salted water. When tender, drain, squeeze out all moisture, then chop coarsely. In the same pan melt the butter until foaming, add the spinach and stir occasionally until it is dry.

In a second pan heat the oil, add the onions, cook together for 5 minutes and work in the flour. Add the milk, season well, and then add the garlic and bayleaf. Cook for 15 minutes, stirring occasionally, remove the bayleaf, then mix into the spinach, place in a deep dish and keep hot.

Meanwhile cut the carrot into slices, put it into a large pan with the wine or flavoured water, parsley and seasoning. Place over a brisk heat and throw in the mussels. As they open, remove the mussels from the shell and keep hot between two plates. Discard any that do not open. Strain the liquid through a fine sieve lined with filter paper and add a little to the spinach to flavour it. Increase the oven heat to 230°C, 450°F, Gas Mark 8. Bury the mussels in the spinach, sprinkle with *chapelure*, dot with butter and place in the oven for 5 minutes. Serve straight away. Any dry white wine is good with this dish. Muscadet, Pouilly-Fuissè or Champagne Nature.

Top: moules à la marinière; *bottom:* moules aux épinards

Coquilles St Jacques à la provençale
Scallops with garlic

TO SERVE SIX

INGREDIENTS
12 scallops
2 cloves garlic
100 g (4 oz) butter
3 tablespoons chopped parsley
salt and black pepper
6 scallop shells

Wash and dry the scallops and separate the coral from the white flesh. Peel and finely chop the garlic.

Melt 50 g (2 oz) butter in a saucepan and cook the white flesh very gently for 10 minutes, until tender. Season, place on kitchen paper and keep hot between two plates over a pan of hot water.

Pour out the butter from the pan, wipe it out with paper and add the remaining butter and the coral, cook for 1 minute only on each side, add the white flesh and the herbs and garlic, leave over the heat just long enough to mix thoroughly and divide between the heated shells. Serve immediately with a dry rosé wine.

Coquilles St Jacques au gratin
Scallops with white wine

TO SERVE SIX

INGREDIENTS
2 shallots
100 g (4 oz) mushrooms
275 ml ($\frac{1}{2}$ pint) water
1 teaspoon wine vinegar
salt
9 large scallops
100 g (4 oz) butter
1 tablespoon chopped parsley
black pepper
25 g (1 oz) flour
75 ml (3 fl oz) white wine
1 egg yolk
chapelure (*page* 54)
6 scallop shells

Peel and chop the shallots finely and the mushrooms coarsely. Mix the water and vinegar, add salt and bring to boiling point over a medium heat. Poach the scallops for 3 minutes, drain and keep hot between two plates over a pan of hot water. Reserve the cooking liquid.

Melt 25 g (1 oz) butter until foaming and cook shallots, mushrooms and parsley for 5 minutes, stirring occasionally, and season well. Set aside.

Heat the grill to a medium temperature and put the scallop shells under to warm. In a saucepan melt 25 g (1 oz) butter, work in the flour, season and cook to the blonde stage. Remove the pan from the heat, add the wine and beat until smooth, return to the heat, add sufficient cooking liquid to form a thick smooth sauce and simmer for 5 minutes.

Cut the scallops into pieces, divide between the heated shells and cover with the mushroom mixture. Beat the egg yolk into the sauce, pour it equally over the fish, sprinkle thickly with *chapelure* and dot with the remaining butter, cut into little pieces. Brown under the grill and serve immediately.

Serve with a medium dry wine such as Vouvray, or a dry Côtes du Rhône.

Coquilles St Jacques mornay
Scallops in cheese sauce

TO SERVE SIX

INGREDIENTS
9 scallops cooked as in previous recipe
sauce mornay (*page* 16)
chapelure (*page* 54)
25 g (1 oz) butter
6 scallop shells

Cut the scallops into pieces and divide between the heated shells, cover with *sauce mornay*, sprinkle liberally with *chapelure*, dot with butter and place under a hot grill to brown and crust over.

Serve with Anjou rosé, Cabernet or Pinot Gris.

From top to bottom:
coquilles St Jacques à la provençale, au gratin and mornay

VOLAILLE

Meat

The ancient French method of cooking a joint of meat in a heavy cast-iron pot with a lid, on top of the cooker, dates back to the sixteenth century when these *cocottes* were first made. The vessels themselves have hardly changed since, the technique of using them not at all.

The technique consists of first sealing the meat, then cooking it in a confined space which preserves maximum flavour and reduces shrinkage to a minimum. The French eat all their roast or grilled meat underdone, which is the best way of preserving vitamins. This question of well-done or underdone meat is, however, a matter of very personal reaction. In England, the tendency is to serve it well-done. In consequence the periods of cooking time given for joints and grills, though already slightly extended from the French original, can be extended further according to taste.

Beef

Rosbif cocotte

TO SERVE SIX

INGREDIENTS
- 1.5 kg (3 lb) fillet or rump of beef
- 3 strips barding fat or fat green bacon, 8 cm (3 in) wide and long enough to cover length of meat
- 3 shallots, peeled
- bouquet garni or 1 sprig parsley
- 1 small sprig thyme
- 1 bayleaf

While the cuts of meat in France are very different from those in England, the favourite cut of beef for roasting is sirloin – either sirloin proper, boned and rolled, fillet or rump. In all cases it is barded, that is covered top and sides with a thin sheet of fat, and well secured with string.

Wipe the meat with a damp cloth, cover top and sides with the barding fat and tie securely into place to make a compact joint.

Heat the dry *cocotte*, or heavy cast-iron pot, over a medium heat for a few moments and put in the meat, bard-side down. Colour well before turning to seal and colour other sides. Add the shallots, herbs and 2 tablespoons of water, cover and reduce the heat to very low. Cook for 15 minutes. Turn the meat, cover again and cook for a further 15 minutes. Press the top of the meat and if still soft cook for another 10 minutes. When tested with a long-pronged kitchen fork the juice should run pink and the prongs be hot to the touch. French cooks allow 10 minutes per 450 g (1 lb) cooking time after sealing.

To serve, remove the *cocotte* from the heat, tilt the lid so that it only half covers the contents and leave for 5 minutes to swell the meat. This makes carving easier. Transfer the meat to a heated serving dish and deglaze the pan with 2 tablespoons of boiling water (not stock), working in the meat residue on the bottom by scraping it up with the back of a fork. Season, and having carved sufficient meat for the first serving add its juice to that in the *cocotte*, mix well, allow to bubble once, and strain into a heated *gras-maigre* sauceboat.

There should not be a great amount of this delicious *jus*, otherwise it will lose its concentrated flavour.

Aloyau au cèpes

Marinaded beef fillet with marron mushrooms

TO SERVE SIX

INGREDIENTS
- 1.5 kg (3 lb) fillet or sirloin steak, rolled and tied
- 225 g (8 oz) button mushrooms, preferably marron variety
- 150 g (5 oz) gammon, cut 2 cm (½ in) thick
- 50 g (2 oz) butter
- 2 tablespoons brandy
- salt, black pepper, nutmeg
- 15 g (½ oz) flour
- 100 g (4 oz) beef marrow (optional)

Marinade
- ½ bottle full-bodied red wine
- 1 tablespoon olive oil
- 175 g (6 oz) carrots, peeled and sliced
- 4 shallots, peeled and sliced
- 1 clove garlic, crushed
- 1 bouquet garni
- buttered paper

To make the marinade

Twenty-four hours before cooking make a marinade of the wine, oil, carrots and shallots, the crushed garlic and bouquet garni. Place the meat in an earthenware or other non-metallic container just large enough to hold it, and pour the marinade over. Cover and leave for 24 hours, turning the meat once.

Wipe the mushrooms with a damp cloth and trim the stalks. Cut the gammon into narrow strips. Melt 25 g (1 oz) butter in a *cocotte* over a low heat and bring to foaming stage. Add the gammon strips and colour them. Remove them with a skimmer, leaving the fat in the pan. Slice the mushrooms into medium thick slices and add them to the fat, allowing their juices to render. As they start to colour remove them from the pan and set aside.

Pour the marinade, including the vegetables, into the pan, bring to boiling point, then reduce the heat to very low and simmer steadily for 20 minutes. Strain through a sieve, pressing the solids against the side with a wooden spoon. There should be about 275 ml (½ pint) of sauce. While the marinade is cooking, rub a pan over with a buttered paper and colour the meat in it on all sides. Place the meat in the *cocotte* with the mushrooms and strips of gammon. Pour in the marinade, add the brandy and seasoning and a generous pinch of nutmeg. Cover and bring slowly to boiling point over a medium to low heat, reduce the heat to very low and leave to simmer as slowly as possible for 45 minutes, turning the meat once. Allow 15 minutes cooking time to each 450 g (1 lb).

If the beef marrow is included, cut it into small dice and blanch in boiling, salted water for 3 minutes. Drain and set aside.

After 35 minutes cooking time, make a *beurre manié* with the flour and remaining 25 g (1 oz) butter, working them together to form a smooth paste. Draw the *cocotte* from the heat and add the *beurre manié* to the sauce, stir well to melt and incorporate. Then add the blanched marrow if used, and replace over the heat for the remaining 10 minutes.

To serve, carve the meat into ½ cm (⅛ in) thick slices, place on a heated serving dish and pour the sauce over.

Daube des gardiens

TO SERVE SIX

INGREDIENTS
1.5–1.8 kg (3–3½ lb) lean, unsalted silverside or braising beef
175 g (6 oz) pork rind
450 g (1 lb) sliced onions
450 g (1 lb) large tomatoes, preferably the Mediterranean variety

Marinade
1½ bottles Côtes du Rhône
1 sprig thyme
1 sprig rosemary
1 bayleaf
3 cloves garlic
salt, black peppercorns

A *daube* is a dish as old as any in France and in consequence has its variations of ingredients and methods according to the region in which it originated. These recipes cover a wide range from the simple to involved, some of them require the meat to be larded, others not; but in all cases the meat is marinated. This first recipe does not require larding. An economical cut of beef used for making a *daube* is lean, unsalted silverside.

To make the marinade
Twenty-four hours before cooking make a marinade of the wine, herbs, garlic, salt and 8 or 10 peppercorns. The above quantity of wine allows one bottle of the preparation for the sauce to serve with the *daube* and the extra half bottle to make *sauce poivrade* (*see page* 17) for another dish. Cut the meat into cubes of an average serving size and place them in an earthenware dish or other non-metallic container just large enough to hold them. Pour the marinade over, cover and leave overnight.

To prepare the *daube*, drain the meat from the marinade, reserve the liquid and the herbs. Cut the pork rind into 3 large pieces, place one in the bottom of a *cocotte* and cover with pieces of beef and sliced onions. Cover with a second piece of rind, layer with meat and onions and fill the dish in this way, finishing with a layer of meat. Peel, remove the seeds and roughly chop the tomatoes and arrange them in one layer over the meat. Peel and chop the garlic finely, sprinkle over the tomatoes and lay the herbs on top.

Strain the marinade and pour over the meat, cover and place over gentle heat. When boiling point is reached reduce heat to very low and cook, tightly covered, and as slowly as possible, for 4 hours.

To serve, remove the pork rind and remove the excess fat from the surface of the sauce first with a slotted spoon and then by trailing bands of absorbent kitchen paper across the surface.

Serve with plain boiled potatoes and another bottle of Côtes du Rhône.

Daube à l'aigre doux

TO SERVE SIX

INGREDIENTS
1.5 kg (3 lb) point or rump beef
100 g (4 oz) back fat of pork or fat streaky bacon, cut into long narrow strips
100 g (4 oz) sultanas
1 teaspoon potato flour
100 g (4 oz) double cream

Marinade
450 g (1 lb) carrots
450 g (1 lb) onions
275 ml ($\frac{1}{2}$ pint) dry white wine
75 ml (3 fl oz) white wine vinegar
1 stalk parsley
1 sprig thyme
1 bayleaf
salt, 6 black peppercorns

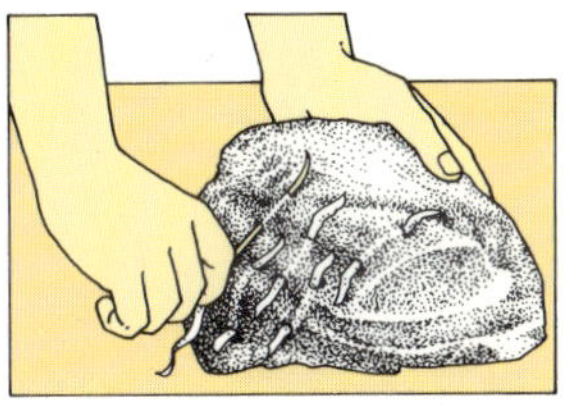

This second recipe for a *daube* is very delectable and suitable for entertaining.

Larding

The cut of meat used makes larding necessary. This consists of threading long strips of pork fat through the meat with the aid of a larding needle (*see diagram*). Cut the fat into long narrow strips, thread them into the needle and draw it through the meat at regular intervals, trimming off the ends of the fat not too closely in order to tuft the surface. Larding can also be done with a metal skewer, plunging it into the meat, first to make a hole and then pushing in the strips of fat afterwards. In warm weather this is made easier if the fat is chilled first.

To make the marinade

Peel the carrots and cut into thick slices, peel the onions but leave whole. Mix together wine, wine vinegar, herbs, seasoning and vegetables. Place the larded meat in an earthenware casserole or other non-metallic container just large enough to hold it and add the marinade. Cover and leave for at least 48 hours, turning the meat 3–4 times and making sure that it is always covered with liquid. Add a little more wine if necessary to raise the level.

Remove the meat from the marinade and dry on kitchen paper. Place a *cocotte* over a medium heat and add the meat to seal and colour it on all sides. The fat protruding from the larded meat will be sufficient to do this as it melts.

Cover, reduce the heat to very low and simmer as slowly as possible for 3–3$\frac{1}{2}$ hours. Meanwhile put the sultanas to soak in enough warm water to cover. Test the meat with a long-pronged kitchen fork and when tender, remove it from the *cocotte*, carve into fairly thick slices and keep hot between two plates.

Strain the marinade, put the vegetables in little groups around the serving dish and keep hot. Pour the marinade back into the *cocotte* and place over a medium heat. Mix the potato flour to a paste with a tablespoon of cold water. Add to the marinade and stir until thick and smooth. Add the sultanas, allow to bubble for a minute or two, remove from the heat and beat in the cream, little by little. Place the carved meat in the sauce and simmer very gently together for 5 minutes. Do not boil. Arrange the meat in the serving dish and pour the sauce over both meat and vegetables.

Serve with either rice or buttered noodles (*see page* 162–3) and a bottle of the same wine as that used in the cooking.

This *daube* improves on reheating so it is advisable to prepare a large one. It must, however, be reheated with care and over a very low heat. It is also delicious when served cold, cut into thin slices and accompanied by a green salad.

Carbonade flamande

Beef cooked in beer

TO SERVE SIX

INGREDIENTS

1.3 kg ($2\frac{1}{2}$ lb) chuck steak or thick skirt – fillet end

3 tablespoons pork dripping or pure lard

225 g (8 oz) onions, peeled and chopped coarsely

275 ml ($\frac{1}{2}$ pint) beer

salt and black pepper

1 bouquet garni

75 g (3 oz) wholemeal or light rye bread (1 slice)

1 tablespoon French mustard

1 tablespoon sugar

1 tablespoon wine vinegar

Cut the beef into thick strips 5 cm (2 in) long. Melt 1 tablespoon of dripping or lard in a *cocotte* or heavy metal pan over a medium heat and seal the meat on both sides. If the lard becomes dark in colour remove the meat, throw away the fat, and wipe out the pan. Melt the remaining 2 tablespoons of fat in which to soften the onions without colouring them. Replace the meat, add the beer and sufficient warm water to cover. Season well with salt and pepper, add the bouquet garni, spread the bread with mustard and float it in the pan, cover and bring to boiling point. Reduce the heat immediately to very low and simmer for 2 hours. If a greater quantity of meat is used, allow 30 minutes for each extra 450 g (1 lb).

When tender, remove the meat and keep hot between two plates. Strain the sauce through a coarse sieve, pressing the bread against the sides to force it through. This binds the sauce. In a small heavy saucepan mix the sugar and vinegar and cook over a medium heat until it bubbles and a dark caramel forms. Take care it does not burn. Stir in 2 tablespoons of fast boiling water to dilute it, stir vigorously and add to the sauce. This will intensify its colour. Put the meat back into the sauce and heat slowly until boiling point is reached. Simmer again for a further 30 minutes. Serve with plain boiled potatoes and beer to drink.

If an even thicker sauce is preferred stir a *beurre manié* into the sauce before the caramel is made. This thickening is made by working 1 tablespoon of flour into 1 tablespoon softened butter to form a paste.

Entrecôte à la moutarde

Sirloin steak with mustard and cream dressing

175–200 G (6–7 OZ) SIRLOIN STEAK FOR EACH PERSON

INGREDIENTS
- 1 tablespoon olive or corn oil
- 2 tablespoons French mustard
- salt and black pepper
- 8 tablespoons double cream
- 2 tablespoons cognac

To serve steak in the French manner have the butcher cut the required weight in one large piece 5 cm (2 in) thick. When cooked it is served whole and cut across into thick slices at table. In this way the meat is savoured at its best.

An hour before cooking nick the outside rim of fat with a sharp knife in several places to prevent curling, brush both sides of the steak with oil and spread with half the mustard. Place a heavy iron frying pan, dry, over a brisk heat for a few moments, brush with oil, seal the meat and cook to taste – 5 minutes each side for rare, and 7–8 minutes for medium-rare. Season with salt and pepper and keep hot on the serving dish covered with a plate.

Put the remaining mustard and 4 tablespoons cream into the pan over a very low heat and scrape up the meat residue with the back of a fork, working it into the cream. Stir for a minute or two, add the cognac, stir well and add the rest of the cream gradually. Bring slowly to the first bubble, draw the pan from the heat, correct the seasoning and pour over the meat.

Serve immediately with either *sauté* or chipped potatoes. If the steaks are cut individually prepare in the same way and cook according to thickness. Serve with a good red burgundy, such as Nuits St Georges or Corton.

Estouffade de boeuf

Beef cooked in red wine with garlic

TO SERVE SIX

INGREDIENTS
- 450 g (1 lb) chuck steak
- 550–800 g ($1\frac{1}{4}$–$1\frac{3}{4}$ lb) lean shoulder of beef or top of rump
- 225 g (8 oz) pickled belly pork
- 2 tablespoons olive or corn oil
- 2 tablespoons flour
- 450 g (1 lb) medium-sized onions, peeled and quartered
- salt and pepper
- 1 bottle full-bodied red wine
- 1 small sprig rosemary
- 1 large sprig thyme
- 1 bayleaf
- 2 cloves garlic, peeled
- 225 g (8 oz) button mushrooms
- 2 tablespoons concentrated tomato purée
- 100 g (4 oz) small black olives

Heat the oven to 180°C, 350°F, Gas Mark 4. Wipe the meat with a damp cloth and cut into pieces weighing about 75 g (3 oz) each. Remove the rind from the pork and discard. Cut the pork into small thick strips or *lardons*, put them into a pan half full of boiling water and blanch over a medium heat for 5 minutes. Drain and dry thoroughly.

Heat 1 tablespoon of oil in a *cocotte* or large frying pan and colour the *lardons* to the blonde stage over a medium-low heat. Remove with a slotted spoon and set aside, reserving the oil and pork fat. Dust the pieces of meat with flour, colour them lightly in the fat, add the onions and colour both meat and onions fully. Add salt, pepper and wine, increase the heat slightly and simmering gently, reduce the liquid by half. Add sufficient boiling water to cover the ingredients sparingly, stir well and add the herbs and garlic cloves. Lay a sheet of cooking foil or double greaseproof paper over the rim and press down the lid firmly to seal as tightly as possible. Place the *cocotte* in the bottom half of the oven and cook for 3 hours without lifting the lid. The ingredients can also be prepared in a frying pan and then transferred to an earthenware casserole.

Wipe the mushrooms with a damp cloth, trim the stalks and cut into quarters, then sauté them in the remaining tablespoon of oil. Place a colander over a large bowl and strain the contents of the *cocotte*, return the meat and *lardons* to it. Add the mushrooms. Remove the fat from the sauce first with a large metal cooking spoon and then by passing bands of absorbent kitchen paper over the surface. Correct the seasoning, stir in the tomato purée and olives, pour over the meat, cover and simmer again for 30 minutes before serving.

Serve the *estouffade* with *purée de pommes de terre* (*see page* 168). A bottle of the same wine as that used in the cooking should accompany this dish.

Epaule d'agneau aux haricots blancs

Shoulder of lamb with haricot beans

TO SERVE SIX

INGREDIENTS
225 g (8 oz) haricot beans
black pepper
225 g (8 oz) very small onions (pickling size)
2 cloves garlic, peeled
salt
1.6 kg ($3\frac{1}{2}$ lb) shoulder of lamb, boned and rolled, or small leg
100 g (4 oz) butter

This classic dish of lamb with white haricot beans is perhaps the most popular Sunday lunch in France. For this recipe buy the haricot beans from an Italian or French grocery shop where they will be of the correct variety.

Soak the beans overnight in enough cold water to cover generously. About 2 hours before they are required for cooking drain them, place in a large heavy pan and cover with cold water. Season with freshly ground black pepper, and add the onions and one clove of garlic. Cover and cook over a very low heat for $1\frac{1}{2}$ hours. Season with salt and cook for a further 30 minutes. If the water level becomes too low add a little hot water. When the beans are cooked, the water should be nearly absorbed, leaving the beans soft and moist.

Whilst the beans are cooking prepare the meat by cutting the remaining clove of garlic into thin slivers; make several holes in the meat with a skewer and push the garlic into them. In a heavy metal *cocotte* melt 50 g (2 oz) butter, add the meat and brown on all sides over a gentle heat. Reduce this to very low, cover and cook for $1\frac{1}{2}$–2 hours. Turn the meat once and replace the lid quickly. The condensation produced inside bastes the meat and forms the juices. If a *doufeu* (*see page* 8) is used, the hot water placed in the indented lid will create even greater condensation. Replenish the water when necessary.

Test the meat after $1\frac{1}{2}$ hours and when tender remove from the pan and keep hot on a serving dish. Pour 2–3 tablespoons of hot water into the pan, scrape up the meat residue with the back of a fork, season and heat together until bubbling. Pour into a heated *gras-maigre* sauceboat.

Correct the seasoning of the beans, add more salt and pepper if required and stir in the remaining 50 g (2 oz) of butter in small pieces.

Serve the meat cut into thick slices with the beans, and meat juice. *Sauce soubise* (*see page* 17) makes an additional accompaniment to this dish. A full-flavoured red burgundy, such as Côtes-de-Beaune or Pommard is well suited to this dish, or if claret is preferred, St Estèphe or Pomerol.

Epaule d'agneau farcie

Stuffed shoulder of lamb

TO SERVE SIX

INGREDIENTS
1.5 kg ($3\frac{1}{2}$ lb) boned shoulder of lamb
50 g (2 oz) butter
1 dessertspoon oil
The stuffing
50 g (2 oz) wholemeal bread
150 ml ($\frac{1}{4}$ pint) white wine or *bouillon*
2 lamb's kidneys
50 g (2 oz) bacon rasher, cut thick
100 g (4 oz) coarse sausagemeat
2 hard-boiled egg yolks, crushed
25 g (1 oz) finely chopped onion
1 tablespoon chopped parsley
1 tablespoon concentrated tomato purée
1 large clove garlic, peeled
salt and black pepper

Heat the oven to 180°C, 350°F, Gas Mark 4. To make the stuffing soak the bread in wine or bouillon and reduce to a purée with a fork. Slice the kidneys into halves, and trim. Cut the bacon into small cubes and sauté in its own fat until lightly coloured. In the same fat cook the kidneys gently until just firm enough to chop. They must remain pink inside. Chop coarsely and add to the bread with the bacon cubes, sausagemeat, crushed egg yolks, onion, parsley, tomato purée and half the garlic clove, crushed. Season well and mix thoroughly.

Spread the meat out flat, cover with the stuffing, roll and tie securely with string. Cut the rest of the garlic clove into slivers, make several holes in the meat with a skewer and push the garlic into them. Put the butter into a small deep roasting tin just large enough to hold the joint, add the oil to prevent it burning during the cooking and colour the meat on all sides. Place in the oven and cook for $1\frac{1}{2}$ hours, basting frequently with the juices.

To serve, place the meat on a serving dish and put it back in the turned-off oven, leaving the door ajar. If left for 10 minutes the meat will swell and be easier to carve. Put the roasting tin over a low heat, add 3 tablespoons of hot water, scrape up the meat residue from the bottom with the back of a fork, season, allow to bubble for a moment and pour into a heated *gras-maigre* sauceboat.

Serve hot with brussels sprouts or *pommes sautées* (*see page* 168), and if cold, with a mixed green salad. Serve with a very full-bodied red burgundy.

Top : épaule d'agneau aux haricots blancs
bottom : épaule d'agneau farcie

Gigot à la Septaine

TO SERVE SIX

INGREDIENTS
- 100 g (4 oz) butter
- 1.5 kg (3 lb) leg of young lamb
- 12 small young carrots
- 12 very small onions (pickling size)
- 2 cloves
- 1 clove garlic, peeled
- salt and black pepper
- 75 ml (3 fl oz) veal or chicken stock (*pages* 12–13)
- 4 tablespoons Madeira
- 1 teaspoon potato flour

The Plateau de la Septaine in the Bourges area produces lamb judged, even in a country of connoisseurs, to be unrivalled. This traditional recipe presents it in full flavour.

Melt the butter in a *cocotte* or large braising pan and when foaming add the meat and brown over a low heat. Peel the carrots and onions but leave them whole. Then add them to the *cocotte* together with the cloves, the garlic, salt and freshly ground black pepper. When they are well coloured, add the stock and Madeira, cover, reduce the heat to very low and cook for 1 hour without lifting the lid.

When tested with a metal skewer the juice should run pink and the meat should be pink inside also.

Place the meat on a heated dish in a warm oven with the door ajar. Take out the vegetables with a slotted spoon and keep hot. Mix the potato flour to a smooth paste with 1 tablespoon of water. Strain the pan juices and bind with the potato flour, season, and allow to simmer for a few minutes. Carve the meat into thick slices and place on a heated serving dish with the vegetables around it. Pour the sauce into a heated sauceboat to be served separately. Serve with small new potatoes.

A fine wine, either white or red, should honour this delicious dish. A good claret, Château Margaux, or burgundy, Volnay or Beaune, or white burgundy, a Meursault for example, or a Loire wine such as Sancerre or Pouilly-sur-Loire – any of these would be suitable.

Filet de mouton à l'aneth

Grilled fillet of lamb with dill

TO SERVE SIX

INGREDIENTS
1 kg (2 lb) fillet of lamb steaks or 6 double lamb chops
350 g (12 oz) onions
350 g (12 oz) large tomatoes, Mediterranean variety preferably
75 g (3 oz) pure pork dripping or lard
$\frac{1}{2}$ teaspoon dill seed or more to taste
salt and black pepper

Fillet of lamb steak is a thick slice cut from the top of the leg. Double lamb chops are cut in two ways – straight across the loin to give two chops joined together or cut in double thickness. The latter gives the juiciest meat when grilled.

Remove the outer skin from the fillet or lamb chops and nick the surrounding fat with a sharp knife to prevent them curling. Peel and slice the onions. Peel and thickly slice the tomatoes. Melt 50 g (2 oz) fat in a *cocotte* and when hot add the onions and colour. Add the tomatoes, salt, pepper and dill. Melt the rest of the fat in a large frying pan and when hot brown the meat on both sides. Place in the *cocotte* with the vegetables, cover and cook over a low heat for 1 hour. Serve with *Riz créole* (*see page* 163) and a full-bodied red burgundy.

Filet d'agneau au romarin

Grilled fillet of lamb with rosemary

TO SERVE SIX

INGREDIENTS
1 kg (2 lb) of fillet of lamb steaks or 6 double lamb chops
1 clove garlic
2 tablespoons olive oil
2 teaspoons dried rosemary
salt and black pepper (freshly ground)
juice of ½ a large lemon
50 g (2 oz) butter

Prepare the fillets or lamb chops as indicated in the previous recipe. On both sides rub the meat with the cut clove of garlic, brush with oil and press the rosemary into the surface to cover evenly. If convenient prepare and leave for 1 hour before cooking. Turn the grill on full and preheat.

Grill the meat for 5 minutes on each side for fillets or single lamb chops, 7 minutes for double chops. To serve, sprinkle the meat with salt and black pepper, arrange on a heated serving dish and cover to keep hot. Pour off the excess fat from the grill pan. Deglaze the bottom with the strained lemon juice and over a low heat scrape up the meat residue with the back of a fork, beat in the butter, cut in small pieces, and when cloudy, pour over the lamb and serve immediately.

With this very simple but delicious dish serve a light white Muscadet wine – Sévres-et-Maine.

Sauté d'agneau au paprika

Lamb cooked with paprika

TO SERVE SIX

INGREDIENTS

1.3 kg ($2\frac{1}{2}$ lb) neck of lamb
350 g (12 oz) green and red peppers
oil for brushing
salt and black pepper
150 ml ($\frac{1}{4}$ pint) dry white wine
150 ml ($\frac{1}{4}$ pint) water
$1\frac{1}{2}$–2 level tablespoons paprika
1 bayleaf
1 teaspoon dried thyme
1 clove garlic
100 g (4 oz) onions
1 large Cox's apple
225 g (8 oz) tin peeled tomatoes

With the aid of a *sauteuse*, a pan resembling a large straight-sided frying pan with a lid, all the ingredients of a dish can be cooked together without further supervision once the meat has been browned. It is an invaluable time, labour and fuel saver. If a *sauteuse* is not available, prepare the ingredients in an ordinary frying pan and transfer to an earthenware casserole.

Cut the meat into serving pieces, trim, and put them into a *sauteuse* over a gentle heat, covered, to render the fat. Turn the pieces over after 15 minutes, drain off the fat, replace the lid and render for a further 15 minutes.

Meanwhile halve the peppers lengthways, cut out the stem and white intersections and hold under running water to flush out the seeds. Dry and brush with oil and place under a very hot grill, skin side uppermost, until blistered, then pick off the skin. Cut the peppers into long strips.

Remove the meat from the pan, season lightly and keep hot between two plates.

Pour away the excess fat and deglaze the bottom of the pan with the wine and water mixed together. Heat the liquids slowly, bring to boiling point and simmer for a few minutes to reduce a little before adding the meat. Then mix in the paprika until thoroughly incorporated, and add the herbs. Peel and crush the garlic, peel and coarsely chop the onion, peel and slice the apple into 8 pieces. Add them to the pan with the juice from the tin of tomatoes. Cover and simmer very slowly for $1\frac{1}{2}$ hours. Test for seasoning and correct if necessary. Cover the meat with the whole tomatoes and the peppers, replace the lid and simmer for a further 20 minutes.

To serve, carefully lift out the meat on to a heated serving dish, rearrange the vegetables on top, simmer the liquids quickly for a moment and pour into the dish. Serve either claret or burgundy with this dish, a St Emilion, St Estèphe or a Pommard.

Porc farci au pruneaux

Pork stuffed with prunes

TO SERVE SIX

INGREDIENTS
- 12 large prunes
- 1 tablespoon seedless raisins
- 1 large Cox's apple
- juice of 1 lemon
- salt and black pepper
- a generous pinch of mixed spice
- 2 kg (4 lb) fillet of pork (without rind)
- 2 tablespoons corn oil
- 275 ml ($\frac{1}{2}$ pint) dry white wine
- 150 ml ($\frac{1}{4}$ pint) double cream
- 2 tablespoons redcurrant jelly

Crackling on roast pork is unknown to the French. The rind is removed and used to make meat tender in dishes such as *Daube des gardiens* (*see page* 96).

Heat the oven to 190°C, 375°F, Gas Mark 5. Put the prunes and raisins into a small bowl, cover with boiling water, place a lid over them and leave for 30 minutes. Peel and core the apple and cut into thin slices, sprinkle with lemon juice to prevent them discolouring and set aside. Drain the prunes and remove the stones, and mix them with the apple and raisins. Season with salt, pepper and a generous pinch of spice. Mix thoroughly.

Lay the meat flat on the board, place the stuffing in the centre in a roll, leaving a margin at both ends, and fold the meat around it. Tie securely at frequent intervals with fine string, passing it round the end of the fillet to close the ends. Heat the oil in a *cocotte* and brown the fillet slowly on all sides over low heat. Drain off all oil and fat, clean out the *cocotte* and replace the meat.

Moisten with the wine, and three-quarters of the cream. Season, cover and place in the oven. Cook for 1$\frac{1}{2}$ hours making sure that the meat cooks slowly at simmering point and turning it over from time to time.

When the meat is cooked, remove to a heated serving dish and leave in the turned-off oven, with the door ajar, and cover with a piece of foil. Remove the excess fat from the pan juices, first with a large metal cooking spoon and then by drawing bands of absorbent kitchen paper over the surface. Place over a low heat and reduce the juices to 150 ml ($\frac{1}{4}$ pint). Add the redcurrant jelly, stir until dissolved and, removing the pan from the heat, gradually add the remaining cream. Do not allow to boil again. Correct the seasoning, add a few drops of lemon juice to taste and pour into a heated *gras-maigre* sauceboat.

Serve the meat cut into slices and surrounded by steamed new potatoes. A soft full white wine or medium dry rosé can be served with this dish, such as a Barsac, Cabernet de Saumur or Tavel. For those who prefer a dry wine serve a lightly chilled Pouilly-Fuissé.

Filet de porc à l'ail

TO SERVE SIX

INGREDIENTS
7 cloves garlic
1 thin-skinned lemon
3 tablespoons corn or olive oil
1–1.5 kg (2–3 lb) fillet of pork (without rind)
2 tablespoons flour
salt and black pepper

Peel the garlic, crush lightly and place in a small pan with 75 ml (3 fl oz) cold water, cover and simmer until quite soft. Wash the lemon and slice thinly and cook in a covered pan with 275 ml ($\frac{1}{2}$ pint) cold water until tender. Strain and reserve both liquids and the lemon slices. Discard the garlic cloves.

Tie the meat securely with string in several places.

Heat the oil in a cast-iron *cocotte* and brown the fillet, colouring it well on all sides. Remove from the pan and work the flour into the juices with a wooden spoon. Leave to colour golden brown. Add the reserved liquids and whisk until smooth. Season well and add 75 ml (3 fl oz) warm water. Replace the fillet in the pan, cover and leave to simmer over a very low heat for about 2 hours. During the last 30 minutes if the sauce has not reduced sufficiently, tilt the lid slightly to allow evaporation and reduction to about half.

Test the meat with a long-pronged kitchen fork. When tender, remove from the pan and carve into thick slices, arrange on a heated serving dish, pour the sauce over them and garnish with the reserved slices of lemon. Serve with *Purée de pommes de terre* (*see page* 168).

This dish requires a fairly robust red wine such as a Médoc, Côtes de Beaune or Beaujolais.

Left: porc en papillotes; *right:* l'oignée du midi

Porc en papillotes

TO SERVE SIX

INGREDIENTS
3 thin slices gammon
50 g (2 oz) pure pork lard
6 thick pork chops, boned
2 shallots
225 g (8 oz) button mushrooms
5 tablespoons dry vermouth
1 tablespoon chopped parsley
salt, white and black pepper
150 ml (¼ pint) double cream

Remove the rind from the gammon and chop the slices medium fine. Melt the lard in a *sauteuse* or large frying pan over a low heat and colour the chops well on both sides. Remove from the pan and set aside, leaving the juices behind.

Heat the oven to 200°C, 400°F, Gas Mark 5. Peel the shallots. Wipe the mushrooms with a damp cloth and trim them. Finely chop shallots and mushrooms together. Melt these vegetables in the meat juices until soft but without colouring further, deglazing the pan with the additional juices they create by scraping the bottom with the back of a fork. Add the vermouth, chopped gammon and parsley. Salt lightly and add a little of both peppers. Leave to simmer until the liquid starts to evaporate but the mixture remains very moist. If the cream is liquid beat until thick.

Arrange each chop on a large sheet of foil between two layers of this stuffing, place a heaped teaspoon of cream on each one and close the parcel, crimping the foil around the edges tightly without crowding the contents. Place on a baking sheet in the oven and cook for 25 minutes.

Serve the *papillotes* as they come from the oven without opening the parcels.

With this delicious preparation serve an Arbois if white wine is preferred, otherwise a Beaujolais, Juliénas or Brouilly.

L'oignée du midi

TO SERVE SIX

INGREDIENTS
450 g (1 lb) waxy potatoes
1.5 kg (3 lb) large onions
2 tablespoons olive oil
675 g ($1\frac{1}{2}$ lb) sausagemeat
salt, black and white pepper

Not all delicious and memorable dishes are complicated or extravagant as the practised gourmet well knows, and the following country recipes for pork proves that sophisticated food can find its match in simplicity.

Choose potatoes that remain firm when cooked; a waxy variety is essential. Peel and slice the potatoes thickly and leave them in a bowl covered with cold water. Peel and slice the onions medium fine.

Heat the oil in a *cocotte* or large heavy pan over a gentle heat and cook the onions for 10 minutes, stirring frequently until the blond stage is reached. Dry the potato slices thoroughly and mix into the onions. Season with salt only, cover and leave to simmer until the vegetables start to render their juice. Roll the sausagemeat into short thick shapes, bury them deeply in the onions and season generously with white and freshly ground black pepper. Cover, and continue cooking gently, mixing from time to time very carefully to avoid breaking the potatoes. Remove the lid so that the excess moisture evaporates and when the potatoes are tender, empty the *oignée* into a deep gratin dish and place under a hot grill. When brown and crusted, serve immediately with coarse wholemeal bread.

In the Midi a strong local wine is served with this Provençal dish but in England a Chianti could well be substituted. It would be wasteful to serve any fine wine with this dish as onions in quantity are detrimental to a good bottle.

Pieds de porc grillés

Grilled pigs' trotters

TO SERVE SIX

INGREDIENTS
8 large trotters
1 large onion
3 cloves
3 carrots
1 clove garlic
1 bouquet garni
salt, 8 black peppercorns
2 tablespoons olive oil
chapelure (*page* 54)

Not only do *Pieds de porc grillés* receive the approval of the Académie Gastronomique de France as a national speciality and quite delicious of its kind, but also that of the meat porters in *Les Halles de Paris*. It had been their favourite dawn snack for as long as they could remember. But what these mighty eaters regarded as a snack is greatly appreciated on the family table as a main course.

Have the trotters split cleanly down the length into halves by the butcher. Plunge them into boiling water for a few minutes and scrape off any discolouration. Wrap each half in cheesecloth wrung out in boiling water and secure the ends with string. Peel the onion, cut it into halves and stick the cloves into them. Peel and thickly slice the carrots, and peel the garlic. In a large pan, place onion, carrots, bouquet garni, garlic, 2 teaspoons of salt and 8 peppercorns. Place the trotters on top and hold them down with a small cutting board placed on top. Cover generously with cold water, bring to boiling point and simmer for 2–3 hours. When tender leave to cool in the pan. Drain, brush all the surfaces of the trotters with oil and roll in *chapelure*.

Heat the grill to a medium temperature. Place the trotters under the grill, but not too near the element, until browned and well crusted.

Serve with *sauce poulette* (*see page* 16) and chipped potatoes, or apple or chestnut purée. With potatoes, French mustard is served as well. Either white wine or rosé can be served with this dish, such as a Muscadet, Cabernet de Saumur, or Tavel.

La Potée lorraine

TO SERVE SIX

INGREDIENTS

- 225 g (8 oz) dried haricot beans
- 450 g (1 lb) firm white cabbage heart
- 1 clove garlic, peeled
- 225 g (8 oz) small turnips
- 675 g ($1\frac{1}{2}$ lb) lean pickled belly pork
- salt and black pepper
- 1 large sprig parsley
- 1 small sprig thyme
- 1 bayleaf
- 1 branch celery, cut into short lengths
- 450 g (1 lb) smoked sausage boiling ring
- 1 kg (2 lb) small potatoes – a firm variety
- 50 g (2 oz) butter

If a leaner meat than pickled belly pork is preferred substitute a piece of pickled blade-bone of pork and cover the bottom of the cooking pot with a piece of pork rind before putting in the cabbage.

Soak the beans overnight in enough cold water to cover generously. Cut the cabbage into 8 sections, remove the core and place in the bottom of a large soup pot. Add the garlic. Peel the turnips and cut into halves or quarters depending on their size. Drain the beans and spread them over the cabbage and cover in turn with the turnips. Place the pork on top, cover with about 3 litres ($4\frac{1}{2}$ pints) of cold water (enough to cover generously) bring slowly to boiling point over a low heat and skim the surface until clear. Add half a teacup of cold water once or twice to hasten the skimming process. When the water is quite clear add salt but only very little at this stage, plenty of freshly ground pepper, the celery, and the herbs tied together with a long string. Attach the other end to the pan handle. Cover and cook slowly at simmering point for $1\frac{1}{2}$–2 hours, until the beans are almost tender. Add the whole boiling ring and the potatoes. Cook for a further 30 minutes until beans, meat and sausage are tender.

Drain well, reserving the liquid to serve the following day as soup. Place the vegetables on a large heated dish, dot liberally with butter cut into pieces and place in a hot oven until melted.

Meanwhile carve the pork and sausage into thick slices, arrange them on top of the vegetables and serve very hot, with coarse crystal salt and strong mustard. With this rugged dish drink a Beaujolais-Villages, a Fleurie or a Bourgeuil.

Blanquette de veau

TO SERVE SIX

INGREDIENTS
1 kg (2 lb) breast of veal
12 button mushrooms
12 very small onions (pickling size)
1 large veal bone, chopped
1 teaspoon salt
25 g (1 oz) butter
25 g (1 oz) flour
575 ml (1 pint) boiling water
freshly ground white pepper
1 bouquet aromatique (*page* 216)
rind and juice of 1 lemon
2 egg yolks (size 2)
150 ml ($\frac{1}{4}$ pint) double cream

Veal is a very popular meat in France and there are therefore innumerable recipes for cooking it. Some of the simplest are regarded as a gastronomic treat, especially in this case when lemon juice is used to enhance the delicate flavour of the meat.

Cut the veal into thick strips 5 cm (2 in) long. Wipe the mushrooms with a damp cloth, and trim the stalks. Peel the onions.

Put the veal and chopped bone into a large braising pan or *cocotte,* cover with cold water, add 1 teaspoon of salt and bring very slowly to boiling point over a medium heat. This should take about 30 minutes. Skim off the froth as it rises, adding half a cup of cold water once or twice to help this process, until the surface is clear. Simmer for 5 minutes, remove the meat with a slotted spoon and keep hot between two plates. Empty the pan, discarding the liquid and reserving the bones.

Wash and dry the pan, put it back on the heat and melt the butter. Work in the flour with a wooden spoon and cook together for a minute without colouring. Add the boiling water gradually to this *roux*, whisking continually until smooth. Stir in the salt, half a teaspoon of the pepper, the bouquet aromatique, the thinly peeled lemon rind and the strained juice, reserving 1 teaspoon of lemon juice for later use. Test the seasoning and correct if necessary, add the meat, bones and onions. If the meat is not covered by liquid, add a little boiling water. Cover and simmer over a low heat for 1 hour, add the mushrooms and simmer for a further 30 minutes.

Remove the bones from the pan and discard. Drain the contents of the pan through a sieve placed over a large bowl. Arrange the meat, onions and mushrooms in a deep serving dish, cover and keep hot. Return the liquid to the pan and place over medium heat. Simmer briskly for a moment and draw the pan to the side of the cooker.

Beat the remaining teaspoon of lemon juice into the egg yolks, beat in the cream, add a ladleful of cooking liquid, stirring it in gradually, and add this binding to the pan, whisking it in a little at a time. Stir well until the sauce thickens slightly. Pour over the meat and serve with *Riz créole* (*see page* 163) or with small new potatoes.

A bottle of Vouvray can be served with this simple, yet delicious dish.

Côtes de veau Foyot à la sauce périgueux

TO SERVE SIX

INGREDIENTS
6 thick veal chops on the bone
175 g (6 oz) grated *gruyère* cheese
75 g (3 oz) white breadcrumbs
salt and a pinch ground allspice
40 g ($1\frac{1}{2}$ oz) unsalted butter

The marinade
40 g ($1\frac{1}{2}$ oz) salted butter
3 tablespoons finely chopped onion
either 150 ml ($\frac{1}{4}$ pint) white wine and 150 ml ($\frac{1}{4}$ pint) veal stock (*page* 13) or 275 ml ($\frac{1}{2}$ pint) wine
salt and pepper

Sauce périgueux
100 g (4 oz) large button mushrooms
$\frac{1}{2}$ clove garlic
1 large truffle or 1 tin (smallest size) truffle trimmings
1 tablespoon finely chopped parsley
1 tablespoon finely chopped chives
1 tablespoon olive oil
salt and black pepper
40 g ($1\frac{1}{2}$ oz) flour
150 ml ($\frac{1}{4}$ pint) hot water
275 ml ($\frac{1}{2}$ pint) dry white wine

Truffles and thick luscious veal chops are two of the delicacies for which France is famous. Like most delicacies both are expensive but when combined, in the following recipe, the result is a connoisseur's dish. It is essential to have very thick veal chops on the bone, 3 cm (1 in) thick.

To make the marinade
Melt the salted butter in a small pan and when foaming add the onion. Stir well and cook over a brisk heat until golden, add wine and/or stock and season. Place the chops closely together in a deep earthenware dish just large enough to hold them. Pour the marinade over the meat, cover and leave overnight. Turn once.

Heat the oven to 140°C, 290°F, Gas Mark 2. When ready to cook, mix the *gruyère* cheese and breadcrumbs, salt and a pinch of allspice. Remove the chops from the marinade and dip them into the cheese and breadcrumb mixture, coating them thickly on one side only. Make sure that the edges are coated also. Place them cheese-side uppermost in a gratin dish, just large enough to hold them, dot with small pieces of unsalted butter and carefully pour the marinade down the side of the dish so that the prepared surface is not disturbed. Bake in the oven for $1\frac{1}{2}$ hours, shaking the dish occasionally and adding a little wine if the liquids reduce too rapidly. When the meat is browned and crusted on top arrange the chops on a heated serving dish and pour the juices over them.

To prepare the sauce
Wipe the mushrooms with a damp cloth, trim the stalks. Peel the garlic. Chop garlic and mushrooms finely together with the truffle. Add the parsley and chives.

Heat the oil in a small saucepan, add the chopped vegetables with a saltspoonful of salt and 2 good pinches of freshly ground pepper. Melt together over a medium heat for 5 minutes, sprinkle with flour and work it in with a wooden spoon. Add the hot water, whisk until smooth and add the white wine. Bring slowly to simmering point and stir constantly until thickened. Continue simmering for 15 minutes until reduced. If the sauce thickens too much add a little more wine.

When ready to serve correct the seasoning, and should there be a film on the surface draw several bands of absorbent kitchen paper over it until clear. Pour into a heated sauceboat and serve very hot.

This sauce, and the *côtes de veau* it accompanies, both merit a very good white burgundy – a Meursault would be perfect.

Falette auvergnate

Stuffed breast of veal

TO SERVE SIX

INGREDIENTS
1.5 kg (3 lb) breast of veal
675 g (1½ lb) spinach
225 g (8 oz) raw gammon
200 g (7 oz) fat pickled pork
1 clove garlic, peeled
3 shallots, peeled
2 eggs (size 4)
salt, black pepper, mixed spices
1 tablespoon pork dripping or pure lard
225 g (8 oz) very small onions (pickling size)
1 bouquet garni

This old country dish is excellent served either hot or cold.

Remove the bones from the veal using a sharp-pointed knife and spread the meat out flat. Reserve the bones. Wash the spinach thoroughly and remove the centre rib. Place in a large saucepan over a medium-high heat with a cupful of water, cover and blanch for 5 minutes until wilted. If frozen, drop into a cupful of boiling salted water, simmer until melted and drain. Squeeze out all moisture between the palms and chop. Chop the ham, pickled pork, peeled garlic and shallots, and mix with the spinach. Beat the eggs and add to the mixture. Season with pepper and a generous pinch of spices but do not salt until the mixture has been tasted. The pickled pork may have salted it sufficiently.

Form the stuffing into a thick roll, place on the meat and roll it up tightly. Tie securely with string at frequent intervals and sew up the ends with thin string.

Heat the pork dripping in the *cocotte* and colour the veal and bones on all sides over a gentle heat to avoid burning the fat. When well browned pour away the excess fat and add onions and bouquet garni. Add 3 tablespoons hot water, cover, and place over a low heat. When simmering, reduce the heat to very low and cook for 1½ hours. After the first 30 minutes, turn the *falette* over twice during the next hour. Do not remove the lid except to turn the meat and add a tablespoon of hot water if necessary.

When ready to serve, place the *falette* on a warm serving dish, cover with foil and place in a hot oven with the door ajar.

Remove the bones from the pan, scrape the bottom with the back of a fork to release the browned juices and add another tablespoon of hot water. Allow to bubble for a moment and pour into a heated sauceboat. Surround the meat with *pommes sautées*. Carve at table. Serve with a medium dry white wine such as an Anjou Montlouis or Anjou rosé, or a good medium dry cider.

Filet de veau farci

Stuffed fillet of veal

TO SERVE SIX

INGREDIENTS
50 g (2 oz) salted butter
1.5 kg (3 lb) rolled and tied fillet of veal
1 large veal knucklebone, chopped in pieces
2 tablespoons brandy

Stuffing
150 g (5 oz) mushrooms
juice of ½ a lemon
150 g (5 oz) chicken livers
40 g (1½ oz) unsalted butter
pinch of salt
100 g (4 oz) brown breadcrumbs
¾ teaspoon dried marjoram
black pepper
1½ tablespoons brandy

The delicate flavour of veal is greatly enhanced either by dry white wine or brandy. Herbs must be used with great discretion when included in a veal recipe, or their flavour can dominate that of the meat. But a subtle blending of these ingredients can make a very delectable dish, as in this recipe suitable for entertaining.

Bring the butter to foaming stage in a large *cocotte* or heavy iron braising pot and as it begins to colour add the veal and bones and brown them well on all sides. Use a low to medium heat to avoid burning the butter. When these ingredients are well coloured, cover, reduce the heat to very low and cook until tender, for about 1½ hours, lifting the lid as little as possible to avoid any loss of condensation. Meanwhile prepare the stuffing.

To make the stuffing

Wipe the mushrooms with a damp cloth, trim the stalks, chop, sprinkle with lemon juice and set aside. Trim the chicken livers and slice off any parts stained yellow. Melt half the butter in a sauté pan over a gentle heat and cook the livers until just sufficiently firm to chop but no more. Remove with a slotted spoon, chop finely and set aside. Add the remaining butter to that in the pan and when melted, add the mushrooms and sprinkle with salt. Cook, covered, until softened and the juice is rendered. Then add breadcrumbs, marjoram, livers, pepper and a little more salt if necessary. Mix well and sauté together for 10 minutes. Remove the pan from the heat. Warm 1½ tablespoons of brandy in a small heavy saucepan over a low heat, pour over the mixture in the sauté pan, ignite and baste until the flames die down. Mix well and keep the stuffing hot by covering with a lid.

When the meat is cooked remove the string and carve into 8–12 slices, not quite severing them at the bottom, spread a tablespoonful of stuffing between each slice and reshape the meat by tying a string around it lengthways. Remove the bones from the pan, and replace the meat. Warm the remaining two tablespoons brandy and pour over the meat. Ignite immediately, baste the meat until the flames die down, cover, increase the heat to medium and simmer for 15 minutes to reheat thoroughly. When ready to serve place the veal on a heated serving dish, carefully remove the string, cover with foil and keep hot in the oven.

Pour 3 tablespoons of boiling water into the pan, scrape the bottom with the back of a fork to release and incorporate the browned meat juices. Season, allow the juices to bubble for a few moments and pour into a heated sauceboat.

Garnish the veal with sprigs of watercress and serve with hot game chips. A dry Anjou, or Vouvray or a Muscadet, a good claret such as St Emilion or Côtes de Beaune, or a rosé, an Artois or Tavel, will be equally appreciated with this fine dish.

Pain de veau

Veal loaf

TO SERVE SIX

INGREDIENTS

- 50 g (2 oz) wholemeal bread
- 3 tablespoons double cream
- 75 g (3 oz) onions
- 1 clove garlic
- 3 tablespoons chopped parsley
- salt and black pepper
- pinch of nutmeg
- 1 tablespoon olive oil
- 550 g ($1\frac{1}{4}$ lb) shoulder of veal or pie veal
- 550 g ($1\frac{1}{4}$ lb) lean blade of pork
- 2 eggs (size 4)
- 3 tablespoons *chapelure* (*page* 54)
- 15 g ($\frac{1}{2}$ oz) butter

Heat the oven to 150°C, 300°F, Gas Mark 2. Soak the crumbled bread in cream and leave until required. Peel and roughly chop the onions and garlic and then chop them finely with the parsley, add the breadcrumb mixture and season lightly with salt, pepper and nutmeg. Heat the oil in a pan and add these ingredients. Cook together for 5 minutes, stirring frequently.

Trim both meats, removing any skin or membrane, cut in rough pieces and pass through the medium grid of the mincer. Mix well together and spread out on a board. Sprinkle with salt, freshly ground pepper and a generous seasoning of grated nutmeg. Mix together again and spread out. Cover evenly with the onion mixture and incorporate thoroughly. Beat the eggs and bind the meat with them. Form into a large loaf. Sprinkle generously with *chapelure*, dot with butter, place in a buttered dish and bake for $1\frac{1}{2}$ hours. Serve with *sauce tomate* (*see page* 18) and *gratin dauphinois* (*see page* 166). Serve with a light white wine.

Ris de veau normande

Sweetbreads with calvados and apples

TO SERVE SIX

INGREDIENTS

- 1 kg (2 lb) calves' or lambs' sweetbreads, fresh or frozen
- 2 litres ($3\frac{1}{2}$ pints) water
- 175 g (6 oz) onions, peeled and sliced
- bouquet aromatique (*page* 216)
- salt, 6 peppercorns
- 3 shallots
- 100 g (4 oz) butter
- black pepper
- 5 tablespoons Madeira
- 2 tablespoons calvados
- 150 ml ($\frac{1}{4}$ pint) double cream
- 3 Cox's apples
- 1 tablespoon potato flour

If the sweetbreads are frozen place in the refrigerator for 24 hours, then remove to thaw to room temperature. If fresh, leave in cold water for 1 hour before cooking.

Make a *court-bouillon* of the water, onions, the bouquet aromatique, 1 teaspoon salt and the peppercorns, and simmer in a large uncovered pan for 30 minutes. Then blanch the sweetbreads in this liquid for 20 minutes over a very gentle heat. Strain, reserving a teacup of the *court-bouillon*, and place the sweetbreads in cold water. When cold remove the membrane and dry on kitchen paper.

Peel and finely chop the shallots. Melt 50 g (2 oz) butter in a *sauteuse* or large frying pan and add the shallots. Cook until soft but do not colour them. Add the sweetbreads and when firm on the outside but not coloured, add salt and pepper, cover, and leave for 20 minutes over a very low heat. Then moisten with the Madeira, calvados, double cream and 2 or 3 tablespoons of *court-bouillon*, mix well, bring slowly to simmering point, draw the pan from the heat, cover and leave to macerate for 10 minutes.

Meanwhile wash, wipe and core the apples but do not peel them. Cut into rings 1 cm ($\frac{1}{2}$ in) thick. Melt the remaining 50 g (2 oz) butter until foaming and cook the apples in this until tender but not coloured, and keep hot. Remove the sweetbreads from the pan with a slotted spoon and keep warm between two plates over a saucepan of hot water.

Mix the potato flour with a little cold water until smooth and whisk it into the sauce a teaspoonful at a time away from the heat. Bring the sauce back to boiling point after each teaspoonful has been added. When the sauce has the consistency of cream thick enough to coat a wooden spoon, add no more thickening. Season to taste, return the sweetbreads to the sauce and simmer for 3–4 minutes until hot.

To serve, arrange the sweetbreads in a mound in the centre of a deep, heated serving dish, pour the sauce over them and surround with the apple rings.

This dish of great refinement deserves a wine worthy of it – such as a burgundy, Gevrey-Chambertin or a white Bordeaux, Grand crus de Sauterne.

Foie de veau à l'orange

Calves' liver cooked in orange juice

TO SERVE SIX

INGREDIENTS
3 large oranges
100 g (4 oz) butter
6 slices calves' or lambs' liver, cut into 2 cm (½ in) thick slanting slices
salt and ground allspice

The liver must be cut in slanting slices, not chopped off vertically.

Working over a large plate to catch the juice, remove the peel and pith from 2 of the oranges with a sharp knife, cutting down to the pulp in one operation. Cut out each section from between the membrane and set aside. Reserve the juice and add it to the juice of the third orange. Strain and set aside. Heat a large iron frying pan or a *sauteuse*, dry, over a medium low heat for a few moments. Add 75 g (3 oz) of butter and as soon as it starts to foam add the slices of liver, reduce the heat to minimum and cook very gently for no more than 2 minutes on each side. It must remain soft with no outer crust, and pink inside. Liver continues cooking by its own heat when removed from the pan. Arrange on a heated serving dish and keep hot covered with a plate.

Increase the heat to medium, deglaze the pan with the orange juice, incorporating the meat residue by scraping it up with the back of a fork, season lightly, allow to bubble, then add the orange sections. Tip the pan to and fro allowing the hot juice to flow over the fruit. This must be done quickly. Remove the sections with a fork and place them round the meat. Remove the pan from the heat, whisk in the remaining 25 g (1 oz) butter cut into small pieces and pour over the liver. Serve without delay with either buttered noodles (*see page* 162) or small new potatoes. Serve with champagne or blanc de blanc.

Ris de veau normande; foie de veau à l'orange

Poulet
9,95 F

Poultry and game

The theory that cooking is an art is borne out by the knowledge that many of France's artists, writers and painters have turned their talent to cooking and writing about food. Alexandre Dumas provided a great deal of fascinating information, both culinary and literary in his *Dictionnaire de la Cuisine*. He pointed out that chicken came to the west from India. Then the Romans, sophisticated in matters of food, living, laws and colonizing even in the first century B.C., learned from natives of the island of Cos how to fatten chickens by keeping them in a dark place and feeding them with barley flour mixed with milk. This practice was so enthusiastically adopted by the people that the senators were forced to pass a law prohibiting the raising of chickens in the open streets. The Gauls, when colonized by the Romans, were just as quick to learn and through the centuries these methods have been perfected until areas such as Bresse, La Flèche, Crèvecoeur and other less romantically named places are internationally famous for the free range birds that they produce.

While it is hard to believe that every restaurant in France claiming *poulet de Bresse* on its menu has bought at source, when presented with an authentic capon simply roasted in fresh butter and garnished with watercress and game chips, the fortunate diner cannot mistake this memorable dish for anything else. The French have, however, many interesting ways of cooking poultry of less glamorous origin.

Poulet aux trente gousses d'ail

Chicken cooked with thirty cloves of garlic

TO SERVE SIX

INGREDIENTS
- 2 kg (4 lb) chicken
- 30 cloves garlic
- 1 sprig each or ½ teaspoon dried rosemary, thyme, savory and basil
- 1 bayleaf
- 4 tablespoons olive or corn oil
- salt, black pepper, grated nutmeg
- 1 tablespoon cognac

Pommes de terre à la provençale
- garlic residue (*see above*)
- 6 medium-sized potatoes
- 4 large tomatoes, preferably Mediterranean variety
- salt and pepper
- parsley for garnishing

This ancient country recipe can be recommended to gourmets intrigued by the muted flavour of garlic produced by long slow cooking.

Wipe the chicken inside and out with a cloth wrung out in boiling water. Cut into ten pieces – two drumsticks, two thighs, two wings, and two breasts, halved. Peel the garlic cloves of their outer skin but leave the last fine one intact. Place the herbs in the bottom of a large *cocotte*, arrange the garlic in one layer over them and sprinkle evenly with oil. Place the chicken joints on top, add salt, freshly ground black pepper and a generous flavouring of grated nutmeg. Cover and place over a very low heat and cook for 1½–2 hours, lifting the lid as little as possible, but during this time 2 or 3 tablespoons of hot water may be added if necessary.

After 1½ hours, remove the *cocotte* from the heat, pour the cognac over the bird, ignite with a match and when flaming, cover immediately with the lid. Leave to impregnate for a few minutes.

To serve, lift out the chicken with a slotted spoon and arrange on a heated serving dish. Garnish with buttered noodles or *Riz créole* (*see page* 163). Cover with foil and keep hot.

Strain the sauce into a bowl, reserving the garlic residue to make the potato dish (*see below*). Deglaze the bottom of the pan with a tablespoon of hot water, working the meat residue into it with the back of a fork. Pour the sauce back into the *cocotte*, mix well, allow to bubble for a moment and pour into a heated *gras-maigre* sauceboat. Serve with a full-flavoured white wine such as Graves, Pouilly-sur-Loire or a Montrachet.

Pommes de terre à la provençale
(Mediterranean potato dish)
Use the garlic residue to prepare a very savoury potato dish to eat with the remaining cold chicken or other cold meat.

Peel and thickly slice the potatoes and peel the tomatoes. Remove the seeds, and roughly chop the flesh. Remove the herbs from the garlic residue, place in a *cocotte* with the potatoes and tomatoes and add just sufficient water to reach the level of the vegetables but not to cover. Season well with salt and freshly ground pepper and cook over a brisk heat, uncovered, for 20–25 minutes or until the potatoes are cooked and the greater part of the liquid has evaporated. Garnish with chopped parsley and serve very hot.

Poulet aux trente gousses d'ail with pommes de terre à la provençale made from the remaining chicken and garlic residue

Poulet chasseur

Chicken cooked with vermouth and tomatoes

TO SERVE SIX

INGREDIENTS
- 1.5–2 kg (3–4 lb) chicken
- 3 shallots
- 6 small onions
- 50 g (2 oz) butter
- 2 tablespoons olive oil
- 75 ml (3 fl oz) dry vermouth or dry white wine
- salt and pepper
- 1 bouquet garni
- 1 bayleaf
- 225 g (8 oz) tin peeled tomatoes
- 225 g (8 oz) button mushrooms
- 1 tablespoon chopped parsley

Wipe the chicken inside and out with a cloth wrung out in boiling water. Cut into ten pieces (two thighs, two drumsticks, two wings and two breasts cut in halves). Peel and finely chop the shallots and peel the onions but leave them whole. Melt the butter in a large *sauteuse*, add the oil and heat together for a moment. Place the chicken in one layer in the pan and over a medium heat brown the pieces on both sides, skin side down first for 5–8 minutes. After the first side is browned add the onions to colour them a little and the shallots after a further 2–3 minutes when the rest of the ingredients are nearly ready, so that the shallots melt but do not colour.

Remove the pan from the heat, add the vermouth or dry white wine and when warm ignite with a match. Tip the pan to and fro until the flames die down, add salt, pepper, bouquet garni and bayleaf and, replace the pan over a very low heat. Simmer for 5 minutes in order to reduce the liquid to half.

Drain the tomatoes and roughly chop and set aside. Add the juice to the pan and mix well. Cover and leave for 1 hour to cook gently without lifting the lid. Wipe the mushrooms with a damp cloth and trim them. Add the mushrooms and tomatoes to the pan. Cover and cook for a further 30 minutes until the chicken is tender and the sauce thickened and reduced. When finished there should not be a great deal of sauce but it will be well flavoured.

To serve, sprinkle with chopped parsley, place chicken on to a heated serving dish and pour the sauce over it. Serve with *purée de marrons* (*see page* 160).

Serve with the same white wine as that used in the cooking or with Blanc de blancs if vermouth is used.

Poulet vallée d'Auge

Chicken cooked with apple brandy

TO SERVE SIX

INGREDIENTS
275 ml ($\frac{1}{2}$ pint) veal stock (*page* 13)
1.8 kg (4 lb) chicken
3 shallots
50 g (2 oz) unsalted butter
1 dessertspoon corn oil
3 tablespoons Calvados
salt, black pepper or allspice
1 small sprig thyme
150 ml ($\frac{1}{4}$ pint) double cream
2 teaspoons potato flour

Simmer the veal stock briskly in a small pan to reduce by half and set aside.

Wipe the chicken inside and out with a cloth wrung out in boiling water. The bird can then either be cut into pieces and cooked in a *sauteuse* or left whole and cooked in a large *cocotte*..

Peel and finely chop the shallots. Melt the butter over a low heat, add the oil, heat gently and brown the bird on all sides. This should take about 15 minutes. When not quite fully coloured add the shallots. When they colour slightly pour the Calvados over the chicken, allow the alcohol to evaporate for a moment, draw the pan from the heat and ignite with a match. Shake the pan and cover before the flames die down. Season, add the thyme and reduced veal stock, cover again, return to the heat and cook gently over a very low heat for 1–1$\frac{1}{2}$ hours, depending on whether the chicken is whole or cut.

When tender remove the bird to a heated serving dish and keep hot. Allow the juices to bubble and reduce slightly, draw the pan from the heat and beat in the cream, reheat very gently but do not boil. If a thicker sauce is preferred the juices may be thickened at this stage by adding the potato flour worked to a smooth cream with a tablespoon of cold water. Add to the pan juices and heat gently until thick. Pour the sauce over the bird and serve immediately.

This is a fine dish and deserves a fine claret, for instance Château Margaux, or if white wine is preferred, a Barsac.

Poularde à l'alsacienne

Chicken stuffed with foie gras, chicken livers and cooked in white wine and brandy

TO SERVE SIX

INGREDIENTS
- 2 kg (4 lb) free-range chicken
- 100 g (4 oz) chicken livers
- 25 g (1 oz) butter
- 75 g (3 oz) fresh breadcrumbs
- 75 g (3 oz) boiled ham
- 75 g (3 oz) foie gras
- salt and black pepper
- 1 tablespoon olive or corn oil
- 150 ml ($\frac{1}{4}$ pint) Riesling

Sauce
- 150 ml ($\frac{1}{4}$ pint) Riesling
- 75 g (3 oz) foie gras
- 2 teaspoons potato flour
- 150 ml ($\frac{1}{4}$ pint) double cream
- 2 tablespoons brandy
- salt and black pepper

Wipe the chicken inside and out with a cloth wrung out in boiling water. Remove the pieces of fat from inside the bird and reserve them. Trim all the livers, slicing off any parts stained yellow, and remove all fat from the ham.

In a small frying pan melt the butter and when foaming colour the breadcrumbs to the blond stage, stirring frequently. Chop together the livers, ham, foie gras, chicken fat, breadcrumbs and any fat surrounding the foie gras. Season well, mix thoroughly and stuff the bird, reserving a little stuffing for over the wishbone. Sew up the cavity, fold over the neck skin underneath the bird and tie back between the wings.

Heat the oil in a large *cocotte* and brown the bird on all sides. Sprinkle with salt and freshly ground pepper, add the Riesling to the pan, shake to mingle the liquids, cover and cook over a very low heat for $1\frac{1}{4}$–$1\frac{1}{2}$ hours. Test by pricking the thickest part of the thigh with a long-pronged cooking fork. When tender remove the bird to a heated serving dish, remove strings and keep hot.

To make the sauce remove the fat from the pan juices first with a large metal cooking spoon and then by drawing bands of absorbent kitchen paper over it until quite clear. Add the Riesling and allow to bubble over a medium heat until reduced by half. Meanwhile crush the foie gras with a fork and force through a fine sieve, if not in purée form. Mix the potato flour into the cream until smooth. Draw the pan away from the heat, add the cognac, cream and purée of foie gras, beating them in until smooth. Return to very low heat and bring to the first bubble, beating constantly. Correct the seasoning if necessary. Mask the chicken breast with a little sauce and serve the rest in a heated sauceboat.

Traditionally this recipe is served garnished lavishly with *Nouilles au beurre* (*see page* 162), a small quantity of which, sautéd in melted butter until crisp when crumbled over the garnish, form a dressing of contrasting consistency.

Serve with a lightly chilled Riesling.

Poussins, beurre à l'ail

Poussins with garlic butter

TO SERVE SIX

INGREDIENTS
- 3 poussins or spring chickens – 450 g (1 lb) each
- salt
- 2 teaspoons lemon juice
- $1\frac{1}{2}$ tablespoons olive oil
- freshly ground black pepper

Beurre à l'ail
- a small clove of garlic
- $\frac{1}{2}$ teaspoon salt
- 2 teaspoons lemon juice
- freshly ground black pepper
- 100 g (4 oz) softened butter
- 4 tablespoons finely chopped parsley

Wipe the poussins inside and out with a cloth wrung out in boiling water. With a sharp knife split them along the breast bone into halves. Place cut side downwards on a chopping board and flatten with two or three sharp blows with the side of a cleaver. If a cleaver is not available beat with back of a large wooden spoon until quite flat. Stir $\frac{1}{2}$ teaspoon of salt into the lemon juice until dissolved and beat in the olive oil until cloudy. Brush both sides of the birds lightly with this mixture, sprinkle with freshly ground pepper and set them aside. Make the garlic butter.

Heat the grill to maximum, or the oven to 220°C, 450°F, Gas Mark 9.

Place the birds, cut side uppermost, on the grill tray, about 10 cm (4 in) below the element, or on a wire rack in the oven. Cook for 12 minutes on the cut side, turn the pieces over, sprinkle lightly with salt to crisp the skin and cook for a further 10–12 minutes until well browned and tender.

Arrange on a very hot serving dish, pour the pan juices over them, garnish with sprigs of parsley and place a pat of garlic butter on each portion. Serve immediately with the remaining garlic butter handed separately.

Either a dry white wine or a full-bodied burgundy may be served with this dish.

Beurre à l'ail (Garlic butter)
Crush the garlic to a pulp with the salt. Work it into the softened butter, adding the lemon juice at the same time. When these ingredients are thoroughly blended, work in the finely chopped parsley until smooth. Place in the refrigerator until firm enough to shape into a thick roll about 3 cm (1 in) in diameter, and cut into 12 thick slices and chill again until hard.

Poussins aux oignons

Poussins cooked with onions

TO SERVE SIX

INGREDIENTS

- 900 g (2 lb) medium-sized onions
- 3 poussins or spring chickens – 450 g (1 lb) each
- 4–5 tablespoons olive oil or chicken or duck fat
- salt and black pepper
- 1 sprig thyme
- 1 bayleaf

Peel and slice the onions finely. Wipe the birds inside and out with a cloth wrung out in boiling water. With a sharp knife split them along the breastbone into halves.

Melt 2 tablespoons of oil or fat in a *sauteuse* and when hot sauté the birds over a medium heat, colouring them to the blond stage. Shake the pan frequently to prevent sticking. Remove the poussins with a slotted spoon and keep hot.

Add another 2 tablespoons of oil or fat to the pan and cook the onions over a low heat for about 20 minutes to the transparent stage. When they have coloured lightly add the birds, season with salt and freshly ground pepper, add the herbs, cover and cook gently until tender, for a further 40 minutes, shaking the pan frequently and stirring the onions several times. Care must be taken to prevent them from burning.

Serve with *Pommes lyonnaise* (*see page* 166) and a bottle of very full-bodied red burgundy.

Filets de dinde au plat

Turkey breasts with herbs

TO SERVE SIX

INGREDIENTS
175 g (6 oz) onions
1 clove garlic
2 tablespoons chopped fresh parsley
$\frac{1}{2}$ teaspoon dried thyme
75 g (3 oz) butter
1 kg (2 lb) turkey breasts
salt and black pepper
150 ml ($\frac{1}{4}$ pint) dry white wine

Heat the oven to 200°C, 425°F, Gas Mark 7. Peel the onions and garlic and chop finely with the parsley. Add the dried thyme. Mix well and cover the bottom of a large buttered *gratin* dish with this mixture.

Dot with 25 g (1 oz) of butter cut into small pieces. Season the meat on both sides with salt and freshly ground pepper, work the remaining 50 g (2 oz) butter to a soft cream and cover the breasts thickly with it. Arrange closely together over the onion mixture, buttered-side uppermost, pour the wine down the sides of the dish and place in the oven. When the surface turns golden, baste with the juices and herbs, lower the heat to 180°C, 350°F, Gas Mark 4, and simmer for a further 30–40 minutes, until tender, basting frequently. Serve immediately. If the dish has to wait before being served cover with foil to prevent the meat drying. Serve with *purée de pommes de terre* or with *pommes sautées* (*see page* 168).

Either white (a Meursault, Graves or Sancerre) or red wine (Volnay or Fleurie) can be served with this dish. Alternatively Champagne is suitable.

Pigeons aux petits pois

Pigeons cooked with young peas

TO SERVE SIX

INGREDIENTS
6 young plump pigeons
150 g (5 oz) butter
1 teaspoon flour
275 ml ($\frac{1}{2}$ pint) rich veal stock (*page* 13)
16 very small onions (pickling size)
200 g (7 oz) lean streaky bacon, cut in one piece
150 ml ($\frac{1}{4}$ pint) dry white wine
675 ($1\frac{1}{2}$ lb) small shelled peas
1 firm lettuce heart
1 teaspoon sugar
1 bouquet garni
salt and black pepper

Have the pigeons cleaned and singed. Tie the wings and legs to the body, passing the string across the back. Melt a teaspoon of butter in a small pan over a medium heat and work in the flour. Remove the pan from the heat, add the veal stock all at once, whisk until smooth, return to the heat and bring to boiling point. Lower the heat and simmer until the stock has reduced by a third and is slightly thickened. Set aside until required.

Peel the onions and blanch them in boiling salted water for 5 minutes. Drain and dry them. Remove the rind from the bacon, and cut the meat into small thick strips or *lardons*. Melt half the remaining butter to the blond stage in a *sauteuse* and colour the *lardons* lightly then add the onions so that both bacon and onions are coloured golden brown at the same time. Remove with a slotted spoon and add the rest of the butter to the fats in the pan. When it froths, brown the pigeons on all sides, remove and drain.

Deglaze the bottom of the *sauteuse* with the wine and reduced veal stock, scraping up the meat residue with the black of a fork. When well incorporated replace the pigeons, the *lardons* and the onions together with the shelled peas, the shredded lettuce, sugar, bouquet garni and seasoning. Cover and simmer over a very low heat until the birds are tender.

If a *sauteuse* is not used prepare the ingredients in a large iron frying pan and finish cooking in a casserole in the oven preheated to 150°C, 300°F, Gas Mark 2 for $1\frac{1}{2}$ hours.

To serve, place the birds in a mound in the centre of a heated serving dish and pour the sauce, onions and peas around them. Serve with small new potatoes.

Serve a Meursault or Muscadet for those who prefer white wine, a Chinon, Volnay or Bourgueil for those who would rather drink red wine.

Pigeons aux petits pois

Canard aux navets

Duck with turnips

TO SERVE FOUR–SIX

INGREDIENTS
2 kg (4 lb) duck
675 g ($1\frac{1}{2}$ lb) young turnips
12 very small onions (pickling size)
1 dessertspoon castor sugar
150 ml ($\frac{1}{4}$ pint) white wine
150 ml ($\frac{1}{4}$ pint) veal or chicken stock (*pages* 12–13)
bouquet garni
1 sprig parsley
salt and black pepper

How to carve a duck

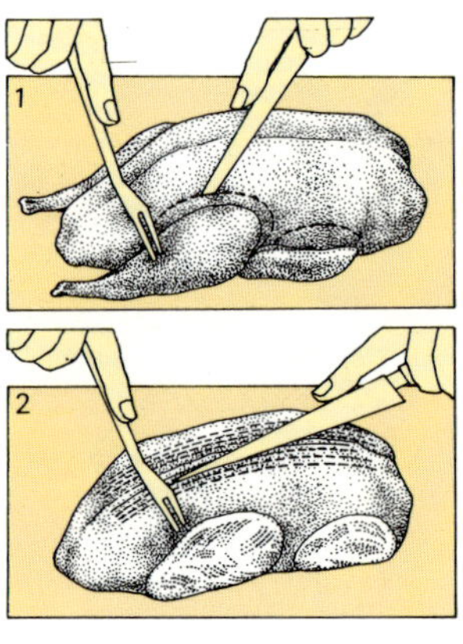

Canard aux navets is a country dish prepared when young ducks and small purple-skinned turnips are at their best. It is a delicious combination and recognized as one of the classics of French cooking.

Heat the oven to 190°C, 375°F, Gas Mark 5. Wipe the duck inside and out with a cloth wrung out in boiling water. Dry thoroughly and pierce the breast skin horizontally in several places with a long-pronged kitchen fork without piercing the flesh. Rub the skin all over with salt, and place in a buttered casserole or deep roasting tin, breast side down, and put in the oven. After 30 minutes drain off the rendered fat and turn breast side uppermost. Continue cooking for a further 10 minutes, drain and cook for 10 minutes, then drain for the last time.

Reduce the heat to 180°C, 350°F, Gas Mark 4, and continue cooking for $1\frac{1}{2}$ hours until the duck is tender and the skin crisp and puffed. Meanwhile peel the turnips and blanch them in boiling, salted water over a medium heat for 5 minutes. Peel the onions. Drain the turnips well, dry and add to the duck with the onions. Sprinkle the vegetables with sugar and allow them to brown on both sides. Mix the wine and stock and pour two-thirds into the casserole. Add the bouquet garni, parsley and seasoning.

After $1\frac{1}{2}$ hours when the duck and vegetables are tender, remove them from the oven, carve the duck (*see diagram*), and place on an ovenproof serving dish with the vegetables arranged in small groups around it. The duck can also be carved later at table if preferred. Return to the oven to keep the skin crisp and vegetables hot.

Remove the herbs from the casserole and add the carving juices. Remove the fat first with a large metal serving spoon and then by drawing bands of kitchen paper across it until quite clear. Deglaze with the remaining wine and stock, working the browned juices into it with the back of a fork. Place over a medium heat and after bubbling fast for a few minutes to reduce, pour into a heated *gras-maigre* sauceboat and serve immediately. This dish must be served very hot.

All dry white wines are suitable to serve with this dish, Montrachet, Pouilly-Fuissé, Vouvray or Champagne Nature.

Canard au poivre vert

Duck cooked with green peppercorns

TO SERVE FOUR–SIX

INGREDIENTS
- 2 ducklings – 1 kg (2 lb) each or 1 large duck – 2 kg (4 lb)
- 2 shallots
- 50 g (2 oz) butter
- 150 ml ($\frac{1}{4}$ pint) dry white wine
- 4 tablespoons brandy
- 1 small bottle green peppercorns, obtainable from delicatessen shops
- 1 tablespoon potato flour or plain flour
- 150 ml ($\frac{1}{4}$ pint) double cream
- salt and pepper

Poivre vert, the fresh green peppercorns, sold in bottles or frozen in small sachets impart a deliciously exotic flavour to duck and chicken. Unfortunately they are not available everywhere but for gourmets who take the trouble to find them, here is a good recipe.

Heat the oven to 190°C, 375°F, Gas Mark 5. Wipe the ducklings inside and out with a cloth wrung out in boiling water. Pierce the breast skin horizontally in several places with a long-pronged cooking fork without piercing the flesh. Place in a buttered *cocotte* or braising pan, breast side down, with no other fat and cook for 30 minutes. Pour off the rendered fat, turn the ducklings over, replace in the oven and after 15 minutes reduce the heat to 180°C, 350°F, Gas Mark 4. Continue cooking and after 10 minutes, pour off the fat again, repeat after a further 10 minutes.

Remove the ducklings from the *cocotte*, reserving the juices. Place on a large meat plate, remove the legs with their skin, peel off the skin from the rest of the birds, remove the wings, and carve the breast meat in long slivers parallel to the bone. Pour the juices on the plate into a small bowl and set aside. Keep the meat hot covered with foil and cut the carcasses into small pieces with strong kitchen or game scissors.

Peel and finely chop the shallots and melt them in a small pan with 25 g (1 oz) of butter. When the shallots are transparent add them, with the pieces of carcass, to the juices in the *cocotte*. Place over a gentle heat and when they start to colour add the white wine and brandy. Remove the pan from the heat, ignite and when flaming, cover and braise for 20 minutes over a medium heat. Pour the contents of the pan through a sieve into a bowl, deglaze the pan with 2 tablespoons of boiling water, scraping up the meat residue with the back of a fork and add this to the bowl. Leave for a few minutes in a cool place for the fat to rise and remove it thoroughly, first with a large metal cooking spoon and then with bands of absorbent kitchen paper drawn over the surface.

Measure out 1 tablespoon of green peppercorns, drain and chop them roughly. Pour the sauce into a small pan, add the peppercorns and place over a gentle heat. Mix the potato flour with a little cold water, stir it into the cream and add little by little to the sauce, whisking until smooth. Simmer as slowly as possible and skim if froth rises to the surface. Season to taste.

Wash and dry the *cocotte*, place the meat and reserved juices in it, pour on the boiling sauce, cover and keep hot. Brown and crisp the skin of the legs by placing them under a hot grill for a few minutes. Serve the ducklings arranged in the centre of a deep serving dish with the sauce poured over them and garnished with the crisply grilled legs. A good vintage burgundy is most suitable to serve with this dish.

Canard aux raisins

Ducklings cooked in Muscadet with white grapes

TO SERVE FOUR–SIX

INGREDIENTS
100 g (4 oz) butter
2 small ducklings – about 1 kg (2 lb) each
salt and black pepper
4 shallots
4 tablespoons brandy
450 g (1 lb) white seedless grapes
150 ml (¼ pint) Muscadet
2 tablespoons double cream (optional)

Heat the oven to 200°C, 400°F, Gas Mark 6. Melt 50 g (2 oz) butter in a *cocotte* or small, deep, roasting tin over a low heat, place the ducks breast side down and leave for 5 minutes or long enough to make the flesh firm without colouring. Turn the birds breast side up, pierce the skin several times horizontally with a long-pronged cooking fork without piercing the flesh to enable the fat to flow out. Sprinkle with salt and freshly ground pepper, add 4 tablespoons water and transfer the *cocotte* to the oven and cook, uncovered, for 35 minutes, turning the ducks once again. Reduce the heat to 150°C, 300°F, Gas Mark 2, and cook breast side uppermost for a further 1¼ hours or until tender. The ducks are cooked when the leg twists off easily.

Remove the legs, keep the rest hot, covered with foil, in the oven with the heat turned off and the door ajar.

Pour the juices into a wide-topped bowl and remove the fat thoroughly, first with a large metal cooking spoon and then by drawing bands of absorbent paper over the surface until it is clear. Peel and finely chop the shallots. Wash out the *cocotte*, pour the juices back and add the shallots and 25 g (1 oz) butter, cut into small pieces. Cook for 3–4 minutes over a medium heat, stirring constantly. Place the legs in this sauce, sprinkle the brandy over them, remove the pan from the heat, ignite the brandy, cover immediately and leave for 10 minutes to marinate.

Meanwhile wash and dry the grapes, remove them from the stalks and cut into halves. Crush enough of them through a fine sieve to make 150 ml (¼ pint) of juice. Add this juice and the Muscadet to the pan, replace over a gentle heat and simmer for 20 minutes.

Meanwhile carve the ducks, removing the wings, and the breasts in whole pieces and not in slivers. Reserve the juice. Heat the remaining 25 g (1 oz) butter in a wide-based pan over a gentle heat, add the rest of the grapes and cook until transparent, but no more.

Remove the legs from the pan, sieve the juices and remove any excess fat again if necessary. Return the juices to a clean pan, and correct the seasoning. Add all the meat, the juices left after carving, and the grapes in the pan. Reheat gently until simmering. If cream is used it can now be stirred in a little at a time.

Serve immediately, with the duck arranged in the centre of a very hot serving dish with the grapes and juice poured around it. Garnish with thick finger-length croûtons sautéd in butter until light golden brown.

A claret is most suitable to serve with duck, but in this case tradition can be broken by serving a bottle of Muscadet such as Sèvres et Maine.

Canard au vermouth

Duck cooked in vermouth and orange

TO SERVE FOUR–SIX

INGREDIENTS
- 2 kg (4 lb) duck
- 5 large oranges
- 150 ml ($\frac{1}{4}$ pint) sweet vermouth
- salt, black pepper, powdered ginger

Heat the oven to 190°C, 375°F, Gas Mark 5. Wipe the duck inside and out with a cloth wrung out in boiling water. Pierce the breast skin horizontally in several places with a long-pronged cooking fork without piercing the flesh. Place in a buttered *cocotte*, breast side down with no fat. Cook in the oven for 30 minutes and then pour off the rendered fat. Turn breast side up, continue cooking and after a further 15 minutes reduce the heat to 180°C, 350°F, Gas Mark 4, pouring off the fat twice more at 10 minute intervals.

Meanwhile squeeze the juice from 3 oranges, peel the fourth by cutting off the peel and pith in one operation with a sharp knife, and reserve the last orange for garnishing. Mix half the orange juice with half the vermouth. Remove the duck from the oven, insert the peeled orange and 1 tablespoon of vermouth into the body, pour over it the orange juice and vermouth mixture. Sprinkle with salt, pepper and a pinch of ginger and continue cooking for about $1\frac{1}{2}$–2 hours depending on the age of the bird until the flesh is tender and the skin puffed and crisp.

When cooked remove the duck to a large meat plate and cut into serving pieces, with the skin carefully retained. Place the meat on a serving dish skin side uppermost and return to the oven to keep the skin crisp. Reserve all the juices. Remove the fat from the pan residue first by passing a large metal cooking spoon over the surface and then by drawing bands of kitchen paper over it. Deglaze with the remaining orange juice and vermouth, add the carving juices and scrape the base of the pan with the back of a fork to incorporate the meat residue. Bring to boiling point, allow to bubble for a few moments and pour into a heated *gras-maigre* sauceboat.

Garnish the duck with thin slices of unpeeled orange and serve immediately with *pommes Anna* (*see page* 166).

Serve with either claret (Graves, Médoc or Pomerol) or burgundy (Nuits St George or Musigny).

Lapin aux pruneaux

Rabbit with prunes

TO SERVE SIX

INGREDIENTS
20 large prunes
150 ml ($\frac{1}{4}$ pint) Madeira
1.3 kg (3 lb) domestic or hand-raised rabbit
150 g (5 oz) boiled ham, cut in one slice
50 g (2 oz) butter
1 tablespoon corn oil
salt and black pepper

Domestic or hand-raised rabbit, appreciated just as much as a free-range chicken, is served in innumerable ways in France. It is cooked with prunes in the north, with mustard and cream by Parisians, and with garlic and herbs in Provence.

One hour before cooking remove the stones from the prunes with a sharply pointed knife and place in the Madeira in a stoppered jar. Cut the rabbit into serving pieces and wipe with a damp cloth. Cut the ham into cubes without removing the fat.

Place a *sauteuse* over a slow to moderate heat and in it melt 25 g (1 oz) of butter, add the oil and when the butter froths colour the rabbit to the blond stage on all sides. Add the ham and cook until just firm, but no more. Season well. Drain the prunes from the Madeira and dilute it with 3 tablespoons cold water. Pour over the rabbit. Place the prunes on top, cover, reduce the heat to minimum and cook for 45 minutes. Test by stabbing with a sharply pointed knife and if not tender cook for a further 15–20 minutes. This will depend on the age of the rabbit.

Remove the meat from the pan and arrange on a heated serving dish, garnish with the prunes and keep hot. Heat the sauce until the first bubble appears, remove the pan from the heat and beat in the remaining 25 g (1 oz) butter, cut into small pieces. Pour over the rabbit and serve immediately.

Serve with boiled potatoes and a fruity white wine such as a Coteaux de la Loire or Montlouis.

Râble de lapin à la moutarde

Saddle of rabbit cooked with cream and mustard

TO SERVE SIX

INGREDIENTS
- 1.8 kg (4 lb) domestic or hand-raised rabbit
- 5 tablespoons strong French mustard
- 225 g (8 oz) thin barding fat or fat green streaky bacon
- 75 ml (3 fl oz) dry white wine
- salt and pepper
- 275 ml (½ pint) double cream

Heat the oven to 200°C, 400°F, Gas Mark 6. Remove the legs of the rabbit where they are attached to the saddle by sticking in the point of a boning knife at the joints and twisting it, then cut through without damaging the body. Cut off the tail. Remove the front legs and upper part above the rib cage (*see diagram*). Hit along the backbone sharply with the back of a large wooden spoon to facilitate carving. Wipe all the meat with a cloth wrung out in cold water, dry and cover thickly with mustard. Tuck the front and back legs into the rib cage and cover the entire saddle with barding fat or bacon held in place with wooden toothpicks, and place in a long ovenproof dish.

Place in the oven and colour on all sides, turning several times. Pour away any excess fat. Moisten with the wine and add salt and pepper. Reduce the heat to 180°C, 350°F, Gas Mark 4 and continue cooking for 45 minutes, basting frequently. Remove the bacon, add the cream and mix in the juices, scraping them up from the base of the dish with the back of a fork. Reheat until the first bubble appears.

Cut the saddle into serving pieces with game scissors, replace in the dish in the original shape, arrange the legs around it and baste with the sauce. Place in the oven to heat through and serve immediately with *purée de marrons* (*see page* 160) and game chips (obtainable in packets).

As mustard is no more conducive to savouring a fine wine than are onions, serve a robust Beaujolais with this very delectable dish, or the same white wine as that used in the cooking.

How to prepare a saddle of rabbit

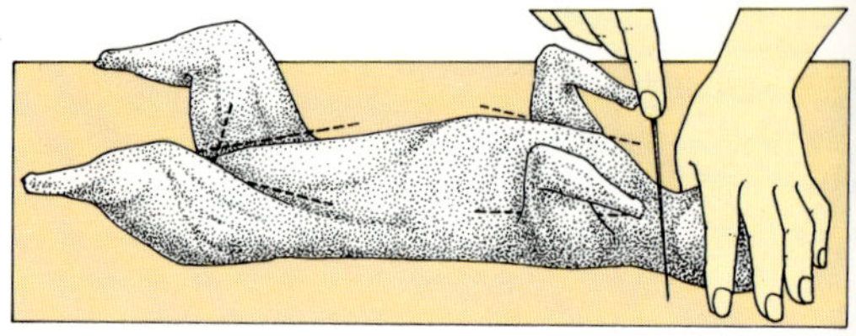

Gibelotte de garenne

Marinated rabbit casserole

TO SERVE SIX

INGREDIENTS
- 1.8 kg (4 lb) large wild rabbit or 2 small ones
- 225 g (8 oz) green streaky bacon, cut in one piece
- 2 tablespoons flour
- 225 g (8 oz) tomatoes, preferably large Mediterranean variety
- 350 g (12 oz) button mushrooms
- 50 g (2 oz) butter
- 12 very small onions (pickling size)
- 1 teaspoon sugar

Marinade
- 3 shallots
- 3 medium-sized onions
- 500 ml (18 fl oz) dry white wine
- 1 tablespoon olive oil
- black pepper and 4 cloves
- 1 bouquet garni
- 1 sprig thyme

Peel the shallots and peel and halve the 3 onions. In an earthenware or other non-metallic dish beat 1 teaspoon of salt into the wine until dissolved. Beat in the oil and add freshly ground black pepper, 4 cloves, bouquet garni, thyme, shallots, and the onions, and stir well.

Cut the rabbit into serving pieces and wipe them with a damp cloth. Place in the marinade – which should cover the meat – and leave in a cool place, but not refrigerated, for at least 6 hours.

Remove the rabbit, drain and dry on kitchen paper, reserving the marinade. Cut the bacon into *lardons* about the size of the little finger and in a *cocotte* placed over low heat, cook them in their own rendered fat until golden brown. Remove with a slotted spoon and set aside. Colour the pieces of rabbit to the blond stage in the fat, sprinkle with flour, leave to colour a little more deeply, moving the meat around to prevent burning. Pour in all the marinade and should it not cover the meat completely, add sufficient warm water for it to do so.

Skin the tomatoes, remove the seeds and roughly chop the flesh. Add it to the dish.

Increase the heat and bring rapidly to boiling point, reduce the heat to very low and simmer as slowly as possible for 45 minutes. Then add the *lardons*. Meanwhile wipe the mushrooms with a damp cloth, melt 25 g (1 oz) of butter in a pan, add the mushrooms, sprinkle with salt and cook them whole, for 5 minutes. When their juices have been rendered and reabsorbed add them and the cooking butter to the meat and simmer for a further 30 minutes.

Peel the small onions and cook in the remaining 25 g (1 oz) butter. After 5 minutes when they are half-cooked, sprinkle them with sugar, glaze and colour to the golden stage before adding to the rabbit 5 minutes before serving.

Remove the herbs, and the larger onions used in the marinade, and serve the *gibelotte* immediately with potatoes boiled in their skins. Serve with the same wine as that used in the marinade.

Top: râble de lapin à la moutarde; *bottom:* gibelotte de garenne

Faisans en cocotte

Pheasants in red wine

TO SERVE SIX

INGREDIENTS
- 2 pheasants
- 25 g (1 oz) butter
- 2 tablespoons corn oil
- 75 ml (3 fl oz) port
- 2 level tablespoons flour
- 1 bottle of good claret
- 225 g (8 oz) streaky bacon, cut in one piece
- 18 very small onions (pickling size)
- 2 cloves garlic, peeled and crushed
- 1 sprig fresh thyme or ½ teaspoon dried
- 1 bayleaf
- 8 juniper berries
- black pepper

This recipe is particularly suitable when the age of the birds is doubtful.

Cut the pheasants into serving pieces with game scissors. Melt the butter in a *cocotte* or braising pan over a low heat, and when foaming add the oil and the pieces of pheasant and colour until golden brown. Meanwhile heat the port in a very small pan until hot to the touch of a knuckle-joint, pour over the pheasant, and remove the *cocotte* from the heat. Ignite the port. Baste and shake the pan until the flames die down, return to the heat, sprinkle with flour, and work it in with a wooden spoon. Then add the wine gradually, whisking the sauce constantly.

When smooth add the raw bacon, cut into finger-sized *lardons*, the whole onions, the garlic, thyme, bayleaf and lightly crushed juniper berries. Season liberally with freshly ground black pepper, but little or no salt will be needed after the bacon is added. Cover and place over a very low heat for 1½ hours, lifting the lid as little as possible. After 1¼ hours remove the lid and allow the sauce to reduce if there is too much.

Serve garnished with long narrow croûtons, lightly browned in butter and *Choux de Bruxelles en purée* (*see page* 153). Serve with the same claret as that used in the cooking.

Lièvre à la betterave

Hare cooked with beetroot

TO SERVE SIX

INGREDIENTS
- 1.8 kg (4 lb) hare
- 175 g (6 oz) fat streaky bacon, cut in one piece
- 100 g (4 oz) butter
- 675 g (1½ lb) cooked beetroot
- salt and pepper
- 2 tablespoons tarragon vinegar
- 15 g (½ oz) flour
- 150 ml (¼ pint) double cream

Marinade
- 500 ml (18 fl oz) dry white wine
- salt and pepper
- 1 sprig thyme and 1 sprig rosemary or ½ teaspoon dried of each
- 1 bayleaf
- 1 large sprig parsley

Cut the hare into serving pieces and wipe with a cloth wrung out in cold water. Cut the bacon into *lardons* the size of a thick match. Make holes in the saddle and back legs with a metal skewer, and push the *lardons* into them. Mix the ingredients for the marinade in a large earthenware or other non-metallic dish and place the meat in it in one layer. If the liquid does not cover add more wine. Leave for 48 hours, turning occasionally.

Heat the oven to 180°C, 350°F, Gas Mark 4.

Melt 75 g (3 oz) of butter in a large iron frying pan or *sauteuse* until foaming. Add the pieces of hare taken from the marinade and colour to the blond stage.

Meanwhile simmer the marinade in a small pan over a medium heat until reduced by a third. Transfer the hare to a casserole or *cocotte* and strain the marinade over it. Cover, place in the oven and cook for 1–1½ hours until tender. About 20 minutes before serving peel the beetroot, cut into thick slices and then into dice. Melt the remaining 25 g (1 oz) butter in a wide-based pan and when foaming add the beetroot, seasoning and tarragon vinegar to taste. Do this at the last moment so that the beetroot will maintain a good colour when served.

Remove the hare from the *cocotte* and place on a heated serving dish with the beetroot around it. Keep hot. Whisk the flour into the cream until smooth and deglaze the *cocotte* quickly with this mixture, scraping up the meat residue with the back of a fork to incorporate it into the sauce. Season and allow to bubble for a few moments over a very low heat. Pour a little of this sauce over the hare and serve immediately with the rest of the sauce served separately in a heated sauceboat. The same wine as that used in the cooking is usually served but a full-bodied red wine may take its place if preferred.

Left: lièvre à la betterave; *right;* lièvre à la crème

Lièvre à la crème
Hare in cream

TO SERVE SIX

INGREDIENTS
- 1.8 kg (4 lb) young hare
- 200 g (7 oz) gammon, cut thick
- 40 g ($1\frac{1}{2}$ oz) butter
- 3 shallots, peeled
- 2 tablespoons white wine vinegar
- 150 ml ($\frac{1}{4}$ pint) dry white wine
- salt and black pepper
- 275 ml ($\frac{1}{2}$ pint) double cream
- 1 dessertspoon potato flour

This recipe is most suitable for a young hare. If it is not young, cook the saddle only. The remainder can be used for pâté.

Cut the hare into serving pieces and wipe with a damp cloth wrung out in cold water. Remove the rind from the gammon and cut into short narrow *lardons*. Melt the butter in a large *cocotte* until foaming over a low heat and colour the meat on all sides until golden brown. Before turning the meat over on to the second side, add the *lardons* and the shallots. The *lardons* and shallots should be coloured to the blond stage by the time the pieces of hare are well coloured.

Moisten with the vinegar and most of the wine, reserving 2 tablespoonsfull and season lightly with salt and generously with freshly ground black pepper. Cover, lower the heat to minimum and braise slowly for $1\frac{1}{2}$ hours. If the juices reduce too much during the cooking add a little more wine. When the meat is tender place the pieces of hare on a heated serving dish and keep hot. Remove the *cocotte* from the heat and add the reserved wine to deglaze the base of the pan scraping up the meat residue with the back of a fork to incorporate it into the sauce. Beat in the cream gradually. Mix the potato flour with a tablespoon of water, add to the pan, return to a low heat and beat until smooth and slightly thickened. Allow to bubble very slowly for a few moments and then mask the hare with this sauce.

Serve with *Pommes sautées* (*see page* 168) or jacket potatoes. Serve with either the same white wine as that used in the cooking or if red is preferred, with a Macon or Beaujolais.

Perdreaux aux choux

Partridges cooked with cabbage

TO SERVE SIX

INGREDIENTS
- 225 g (8 oz) lean pickled belly pork
- 100 g (4 oz) carrots
- 100 g (4 oz) onions
- 2 cloves
- 1.2 kg (3 lb) firm-hearted green cabbage
- 4 tablespoons pork fat or pure lard
- 1 old partridge
- bouquet garni
- 275 ml ($\frac{1}{2}$ pint) white wine
- 3 tablespoons cognac
- salt, black pepper and grated nutmeg
- 3 young partridges
- 8 strips of fat, streaky bacon or 175 g (6 oz) back fat, cut into thin slices
- 50 g (2 oz) butter
- 225 g (8 oz) country pork sausages

Most of the best game recipes hail, naturally, from the country, but in all parts of France, town and country alike, one of the most appreciated is partridge cooked with cabbage. This is an ideal autumn dish for a weekend lunch party. The recipe can be cooked successfully with two of last year's partridges and no young birds. In this case when the casserole birds are cooked they are cut into serving pieces with game scissors and placed on top of the cabbage with the other meats.

Wash the pickled pork in several changes of cold water and dry well. Cut into thick slices. Peel and slice the carrots into quarters lengthwise. Peel the onions and cut them into halves; stick the cloves into one of them.

Quarter the cabbage, remove the core and cut into 3-cm (1-in) thick slices. Blanch in boiling, salted water for 10 minutes and drain well, making sure the slices remain intact.

Melt 1 tablespoon pork fat or lard in a large *cocotte* or braising pan placed over a medium heat. Add the old partridge and the slices of pickled pork and colour to the golden brown stage. Add the cabbage, carrots, onions, bouquet garni, and moisten with the wine and brandy. Season lightly with salt, freshly ground pepper and a generous sprinkling of freshly grated nutmeg. Cover, reduce the heat to very low and leave to simmer as slowly as possible for 2 hours.

Heat the oven to 200°C, 400°F, Gas Mark 6. Cover the breasts of the young birds with thin slices of back fat or strips of fat streaky bacon. Melt the butter in a roasting tin and roast the young birds for 18 minutes. Meanwhile sauté the sausages in a buttered pan until brown and keep hot. When cooked, cut the young birds into halves along the breastbone and keep hot together with the juices. Remove the bouquet garni, pickled pork, and old partridge from the *cocotte*, slice off the meat from the bird into small pieces and mix them into the cabbage. Transfer the cabbage with its juices and meat to a deep earthenware serving dish. Cut the pork and sausages into serving pieces and arrange them on top. Place the young roasted birds alongside and pour their juices over them. Cover and place in the oven in a *bain-marie* for 30 minutes before serving.

This dish is always served with a choice red wine, either a Côtes-du-Rhône, for instance a Châteauneuf-du-pape, or if burgundy is preferred, a Chambertin or Nuits St Georges.

Gigue de chevreuil

Haunch of venison

TO SERVE SIX

INGREDIENTS
1.8–2.3 kg (4–5 lb) haunch of young venison
225 g (8 oz) back fat or fat streaky bacon, cut thick
100 g (4 oz) butter at room temperature

Marinade
2 bottles full-bodied red wine
6 lumps sugar
1 dessertspoon black peppercorns
3 cloves
6 bayleaves
1 teaspoon curry powder
3 fresh or dried sage leaves
1 sprig rosemary
1 sprig thyme
$\frac{1}{2}$ teaspoon freshly grated nutmeg
salt
$\frac{1}{2}$ teaspoon cayenne pepper

Compôte de poires
3 large pears
150 ml ($\frac{1}{4}$ pint) red wine
150 ml ($\frac{1}{4}$ pint) water
1 bayleaf
pinch of cinnamon
2 tablespoons sugar

Venison, being almost devoid of fat, needs to be marinated for a week or so to ensure tenderness. This method also enhances its flavour.

To make the marinade
Put the wine into an enamel-lined pan with the sugar, herbs, seasoning and spices and simmer for 30 minutes. Cool. Place the meat in an earthenware, or other non-metallic, vessel just large enough to hold it. When the marinade is cold, strain and pour it over the meat. Leave covered for 8–10 days according to taste, turning the meat over twice a day.

When ready to cook, drain the meat and reserve the marinade. Lard the meat by cutting the fat or thick bacon into narrow strips and pushing them through the meat with the grain, not against it, using a larding needle (*see page* 97). Cut off the *lardons* not too close to the surface in order to leave little tufts. Spread the butter thickly over the top and sides of the meat.

Heat the oven to 190°C, 375°F, Gas Mark 5. Place the meat in a deep earthenware casserole, just large enough to hold it. Pour over enough strained marinade to cover and reserve the rest. Cook for $1\frac{1}{4}$ hours, basting frequently. Then test for tenderness by piercing with a metal skewer and cook for a further 15–30 minutes, if necessary.

Meanwhile make a *sauce poivrade* (*see page* 17) using the remaining marinade. Add the juices and marinade from the meat when it is cooked and drained, and keep hot until required.

To serve, carve the meat into medium-thick slices and arrange on a heated serving dish garnished with a *compôte de poires*. Pour a little sauce over the meat and serve the rest separately in a heated sauce-boat. Serve with *purée de marrons* (*see page* 160) and with the same full-bodied wine as that used in the marinade.

Compôte de poires (Pear compôte)
Peel, halve and core the pears. Cut each one into 6 slices. Put the rest of the ingredients into a wide-based pan. Bring to boiling point over a medium heat. Stir and simmer until the sugar is dissolved. Add the pears, reduce heat to low, cover, and simmer for 15 minutes until the fruit is soft. Remove lid, increase the heat and reduce liquid to about 1 tablespoonful. Serve hot or cold.

Vegetables
and salads

Vegetables

It is strange that in a country of such big meat-eaters as France, vegetables should be so carefully and deliciously prepared that they are usually served as a separate course and frequently as a main course.

This careful preparation begins with the choice of the vegetables themselves. To satisfy the French housewife they must be picked small, when very young and at their most tender. They are then prepared and cooked the same day but, once prepared, they are *never left soaking in cold water until required.* This habit destroys not only their fine flavour but also the vitamin content of vegetables. The one exception is potatoes which must, in some cases, have their starch content drawn out by cold water in order to give the dish its correct consistency. There are two methods of cooking vegetables that are typically French: the *sauté* method, i.e. tossing vegetables in foaming butter or hot olive oil and the method of cooking *à la française* which uses no water at all (or in some cases only a very little) replacing it with lettuce leaves and onions to provide the necessary moisture.

Many of the more exotic French vegetables, until recent years unknown in the English market, are now readily available. The following ways of cooking and serving them, though perhaps unfamiliar, are typically French.

Artichauts caillaux

Stuffed artichoke hearts

TO SERVE SIX

INGREDIENTS
- 6 large globe artichokes
- 50 g (2 oz) butter
- salt and black pepper
- 175 g (6 oz) button mushrooms
- 3 tablespoons chopped parsley
- 200 g (7 oz) lean boiled ham, cut thick
- 425 ml (¾ pint) thick *sauce mornay* (*page* 16)
- curry powder
- 50 g (2 oz) freshly grated *gruyère* cheese

This is a recipe for which very large Brittany artichokes are essential as only the heart is used. This makes a memorable first course for a dinner party especially when a plainly cooked main course, such as roast chicken, is to follow. In this case the *Artichauts caillaux* can be prepared well in advance and put into a hot oven 30 minutes before serving.

Cut off the artichokes' stalks as closely as possible, wash in salted water, plunging them up and down head first, and cook in a large panful of salted boiling water for 30–40 minutes. When an outside leaf pulls away easily, they are cooked. Drain upside down until cold, remove the leaves and choke, scraping this off with the side of a fork and leaving the hearts clear. Reserve the leaves as they provide a delicately flavoured omelette filling when the soft flesh on the tip is scraped off and reheated with a little butter and seasoning.

Butter a large gratin dish and place the hearts in it well spaced out. Season with salt and pepper.

Peel the mushrooms, trim the stalks and chop medium fine. Melt 25 g (1 oz) of butter in a small pan and when foaming add the mushrooms, sprinkle them with salt and cook over a slow heat until the juice flows and is then re-absorbed. As the mushrooms start to turn colour add the parsley and mix well without further cooking. Remove all fat from the ham and cut the lean into small dice, add to the mushrooms, mix well, add freshly ground black pepper and set aside.

Heat the oven to 180°C, 350°F, Gas Mark 4. Make the *sauce mornay*, keep hot in a *bain-marie* and mix in just enough curry powder to give a subtle hint of its presence – not more than 1 teaspoonful. Add sufficient *sauce mornay* to the ham and mushrooms to form a stiff mixture and heap in a mound on top of the artichoke hearts. Sprinkle with *gruyère* cheese and dot with flecks of the remaining butter. Return the rest of the *sauce mornay* to the *bain-marie* to keep hot.

Place the gratin dish in the oven to heat the contents thoroughly and brown lightly on top, pour the rest of the hot sauce around the artichokes and serve straight away.

Top : aubergines à la ménagère; *bottom :* artichauts caillaux

Aubergines à la ménagère

Aubergines, country style

TO SERVE SIX

INGREDIENTS
6 medium-sized aubergines
fine salt
4 tablespoons olive oil
2 cloves garlic
1 kg (2 lb) large tomatoes
½ teaspoon thyme
1 bayleaf
freshly ground pepper
1 tablespoon chopped parsley
100 g (4 oz) *gruyère* cheese

In spite of the relatively high cost of the aubergines this dish as a meal in itself is not too expensive. This is a delicious accompaniment to grilled chops, steak or fish. As a main course for lunch or supper, it will serve four people. Serve with crisp French bread and a full-bodied red wine.

Peel the aubergines, cut them into thick slices, sprinkle on both sides with salt and place between two large plates with a weight on top to draw off the water. Leave for at least 30 minutes. Drain well, wash quickly under running cold water and dry on kitchen paper.

Heat the oven to 230°C, 450°F, Gas Mark 8. Heat half the olive oil in a large iron frying pan and cook the aubergines, colouring them only slightly on each side. Add the rest of the oil when necessary. Drain the slices in a colander as they are cooked, reserving the oil rejected by the aubergines on cooling. When they are all cooked add this oil to that remaining in the pan. Peel the outer skin of the garlic but retain the fine inner skin. Add the cloves to the pan and colour to the golden stage so that they will flavour the oil. Remove with a slotted spoon. Skin and remove the seeds from the tomatoes, cut into pieces and add the tomatoes, with the thyme and crumbled bayleaf. Stir well. Cook, uncovered, over a medium heat for 20 minutes until reduced and thickened. Add salt, pepper and the chopped parsley. Mix well and pour half the mixture into a large gratin dish. Arrange the slices of aubergine on top, scatter half the grated cheese over them, cover with the remaining tomato mixture and finally with the rest of the cheese. Place in the oven and cook for 45 minutes until bubbling and the cheese forms a golden brown crust.

Betteraves à la crème

Beetroot in cream

TO SERVE SIX

INGREDIENTS

- 9 small round cooked beetroot
- 25 g (1 oz) butter
- salt and allspice
- 2 tablespoons tarragon vinegar
- 275 ml ($\frac{1}{2}$ pint) double cream
- 1 tablespoon chopped fresh tarragon or 1 teaspoon dried

Beetroot, when served hot, can be a very good winter vegetable, and an interesting alternative to the usual limited choice of root varieties.

Heat the oven to 150°C, 325°F, Gas Mark 3. Skin the cooked beetroot, cut them into halves horizontally and place them cut side down in a large buttered gratin dish. If they are medium-sized, cut into thick slices and arrange them in rows, overlapping. Sprinkle with salt and freshly ground allspice. Dot with flecks of butter and sprinkle with tarragon vinegar.

Season the cream, beat in the fresh or dried tarragon and pour this over the beetroot. Cover with foil and bake for 30 minutes until both vegetable and cream are hot. Serve immediately.

Betteraves aux oignons

Beetroot with onions

TO SERVE SIX

INGREDIENTS

- 225 g (8 oz) onions
- 100 g (4 oz) butter
- 675 g ($1\frac{1}{2}$ lb) cooked medium-sized beetroot
- salt and black pepper
- 150 ml ($\frac{1}{4}$ pint) double cream

Peel and slice the onions as finely as possible. Melt the butter in a *cocotte* over a low heat, and when foaming add the onions, stir well to coat with butter and *sauté* until lightly coloured.

Meanwhile skin the beetroot and cut into thick slices, quarter them and mix into the onions. Season, cover and leave over a very low heat for 15 minutes, taking care that the onions do not colour deeply. When ready to serve, pour in the lightly seasoned cream, mix well, heat the ingredients for a few minutes without boiling and serve immediately.

Cooking vegetables à la française

Cooking vegetables without water whenever possible is a method greatly favoured by French cooks, amateur and professional alike. Experts contend that the delicate flavour of tender young vegetables is best preserved by cooking them in their own juices and in a tightly covered pan, which creates the necessary additional moisture through condensation.

A cast-iron pan makes this method simple but the same effect can be achieved by using the heaviest pan available placed over an asbestos mat with a sheet of greaseproof over the rim and the lid forced down tightly over it. The old country method of placing a deep soup-plate full of water over the pan instead of a lid serves the same purpose admirably.

The following vegetables can be cooked *à la française :* carrots, garden peas, small broad beans and green beans.

Carottes nouvelles à la française

TO SERVE SIX

INGREDIENTS
1 bunch spring onions
1 firm-hearted lettuce
50 g (2 oz) butter
salt
2 large bunches spring carrots
black pepper and sugar
2 tablespoons chopped parsley and chives, mixed

Choose spring onions with large bulbs, remove the roots and cut off all green parts, leaving the bulbs whole. When chopped very finely the green stems can be used in place of chives.

Refresh the lettuce (*see page* 170), take off all edible outer leaves and cut the heart into quarters. Butter a heavy pan thickly with 25 g (1 oz) of butter and line with the large lettuce leaves. Add the heart, onions and salt.

Top, tail and scrape the carrots, leaving them whole and place in one layer over the vegetables in the pan. Season lightly, sprinkle with sugar, add the rest of the butter cut into small pieces, and 3 tablespoons cold water. Cover closely and place the pan over a low heat for 3–4 minutes. As soon as the contents start to sing, reduce the heat to very low, shake the pan but do not uncover and cook for 20 minutes, shaking the pan occasionally. By this time the carrots should be tender but still faintly crisp. Replace the lid and cook for a further 3–5 minutes if necessary.

Pour the contents of the pan into a heated serving dish, scatter with chopped herbs and serve immediately.

Purée de carottes

TO SERVE SIX

INGREDIENTS
1.4 kg (3 lb) carrots
75 g (3 oz) onions
75 g (3 oz) butter
550 g ($1\frac{1}{4}$ lb) potatoes
4–5 tablespoons double cream
salt, pepper and sugar
2 egg yolks (size 2)

When carrots can no longer be classed as spring vegetables they can be presented very effectively in the following way.

Peel the carrots and cut into thick slices. Blanch them for 10 minutes in boiling salted water. Drain well. Peel and finely slice the onions. Melt 25 g (1 oz) of butter in a heavy pan over a low heat, add the onion and carrots, cover and cook slowly for 15 minutes until the carrots are tender when pierced with a sharply pointed knife. Neither of the vegetables should colour.

Meanwhile peel the potatoes, cut into quarters and cook in salted water until tender. Drain and dry with kitchen paper. Pass the carrots, onions and potatoes through the mouli-légumes until reduced to a smooth purée. It may be necessary to do this twice.

Melt 25 g (1 oz) of butter in the pan, add half of the purée and 2 tablespoons of cream and beat with a whisk over a low heat, adding more purée and more cream until all the ingredients are incorporated and the mixture is light. Add more salt, plenty of pepper and a generous pinch of sugar. Mix well, add a large tablespoonful of purée to the egg yolks, beat in the remaining 25 g (1 oz) of butter and mix thoroughly into the purée. Serve immediately.

Carottes nouvelles à la française; purée de carottes

Céleris en branche, sauce fines herbes

Celery with herbs

TO SERVE SIX

INGREDIENTS

3 medium-sized heads of celery
100 g (4 oz) butter
1 dessertspoon chopped fresh tarragon or 1 teaspoon dried
1 tablespoon chopped parsley
150 ml ($\frac{1}{4}$ pint) dry white wine
salt and black pepper
150 ml ($\frac{1}{4}$ pint) beef or chicken bouillon
chapelure (*page* 54)

Céleris en branche, sauce fines herbes; céleris-raves en purée

Remove outside stalks and leaves of celery, wash thoroughly and cut down to 10 cm (4 in) long. The rest can be used for soup (*see page* 32). Split the hearts into halves lengthways and cook in boiling salted water for 10 minutes. Drain well, and arrange in a buttered gratin dish, cut side uppermost.

Heat the oven to 180°C, 350°F, Gas Mark 4. Meanwhile put the herbs in a small saucepan with the wine and simmer gently for 20 minutes, uncovered. Add salt, pepper and the *bouillon*. Mix well, pour over the celery, sprinkle thickly with *chapelure*, dot with butter and bake for 25–30 minutes.

Céleris-raves en purée

Celeriac purée

TO SERVE SIX

INGREDIENTS

1 kg (2 lb) celeriac
275 ml ($\frac{1}{2}$ pint) beef *bouillon* (*page* 12)
450 g (1 lb) floury potatoes
100 g (4 oz) butter
salt, and black pepper
150 ml ($\frac{1}{4}$ pint) hot milk

Peel the celeriac and cut into small chunks. Cook in bouillon for 10 minutes until just tender. Drain and reduce to purée in the mouli-légumes. Peel and cut the potatoes into pieces the same size as the celeriac and cook in salted water until tender when pierced with a knife. Drain and purée in the mouli-légumes.

Butter a large pan, add the two purées, season and mix very thoroughly. Place over brisk heat, add 50 g (2 oz) of butter cut into small pieces and, beating constantly, add the hot milk gradually to bring the purée to a firm cream-like consistency.

When the first bubbles appear, serve immediately with the rest of the butter beaten in at the last moment.

If any of this purée is left over it can be mixed with *vinaigrette* (*see page* 22) and chopped fresh herbs, garnished with quartered hard-boiled eggs, chilled and served as a first course.

Champignons au paprika

Mushrooms with paprika

TO SERVE SIX

INGREDIENTS

2 large green peppers
oil for brushing
350 g (12 oz) large tomatoes, preferably Mediterranean variety
675 g (1½ lb) button mushrooms
juice of 1 lemon
50 g (2 oz) butter
100 g (4 oz) finely chopped onions
salt and black pepper
1 tablespoon paprika
1 teaspoon potato flour
4 tablespoons double cream

Halve the peppers and remove seeds and white intersections. Brush with oil and place under a preheated grill until the skin blisters. It can then be peeled off easily. Chop the peppers into dice. Peel and remove the seeds from the tomatoes. Cut them into dice the same size as the peppers. Trim the stalks of the mushrooms and wash quickly in cold water to which half the lemon juice has been added. Drain and dry them.

Heat the butter in a large frying pan over a low heat until foaming and add the onions. Cook gently for a few minutes, stirring occasionally. Add the rest of the lemon juice to the mushrooms, mix them into the onions and sprinkle with salt. Increase the heat and cook until the mushrooms have rendered and re-absorbed their juices. Add the diced peppers, sprinkle with paprika, cook for 5 minutes, season well with salt and pepper and add the tomatoes. Cook for 3–4 minutes, stirring constantly. Mix the potato flour into the cream, add to the pan, reduce the heat and allow to thicken, stirring constantly. Serve immediately.

Choux de Bruxelles en purée

Brussels sprouts purée

TO SERVE SIX

INGREDIENTS

1.3 kg (2½ lb) small brussels sprouts
100 g (4 oz) butter
450 g (1 lb) potatoes
salt and black pepper

Trim the brussels sprouts. Remove tough outer leaves, slice off the stalk and cut a cross in the base with a sharply pointed knife. Throw them into cold salted water as soon as they are trimmed, drain and place in a large pan. Cover with cold water, add salt and bring to boiling point over a high temperature. When half cooked and still firm in the centre, drain well and leave to cool a little. Melt 50 g (2 oz) of butter in the hot pan, cut the sprouts into halves and finish cooking in foaming butter over a low heat, but do not allow them to colour.

Meanwhile peel the potatoes, cut into quarters and cook in salted water until tender. Drain and reduce to purée in a mouli-légumes, and then purée the sprouts. Mix the sprout purée and the butter juices into the potato purée with a wooden spatula until thoroughly incorporated. Season well. Melt the remaining 50 g (2 oz) of butter in a large pan until foaming and beat in the mixed purées until very hot. Beat thoroughly until light.

Arrange in a mound in a heated serving dish, make a criss-cross pattern on the surface with a fork and serve immediately.

Pain de chou-fleur

Baked cream of cauliflower

TO SERVE SIX

INGREDIENTS

1 large cauliflower
425 ml (¾ pint) *sauce béchamel* (*page* 14)
40 g (1½ oz) butter
salt, black pepper, paprika
3 eggs (size 2)
2 heaped tablespoons concentrated tomato purée
sauce tomate (*page* 18)
3 tablespoons chopped parsley

Remove all outer leaves and stump of the cauliflower, make a cross-cut in the root end with a knife and wash well in cold, salted water. Place stalk-end down in a deep pan, pour boiling water over, add salt and cook for 25 minutes until the root is tender when pierced with a knife. Drain well and leave in the colander until quite dry. Reduce to purée in the mouli-légumes.

Heat the oven to 200°C, 400°F, Gas Mark 6. Make the *sauce béchamel* and reduce until very thick. Beat in 25 g (1 oz) of the butter and the cauliflower purée, add salt and plenty of freshly ground black pepper and paprika. It should be highly seasoned. Beat 2 whole eggs with the yolk of the third (setting the white aside) and beat them into the *sauce béchamel* with the tomato purée. Mix thoroughly. Beat the egg white to a stiff peak and fold in. Pour into a buttered charlotte mould and bake in a *bain-marie* in the oven for 35 minutes. Meanwhile heat the tomato sauce until boiling, then reduce the heat and keep hot, simmering slowly. Add the parsley 5 minutes before serving and stir well.

To serve, pass a knife around the inside of the charlotte mould, place a heated serving dish on top, invert and turn out the *pain de chou-fleur* on to the dish. Pour a little *sauce tomate* over the surface and the rest around it. Serve immediately.

Courgettes nature

TO SERVE SIX

INGREDIENTS
175 g (6 oz) onions
1 kg (2 lb) small courgettes
25 g (1 oz) butter
salt and black pepper
1 tablespoon chopped parsley

Peel, slice and chop the onions coarsely. Wipe the courgettes with a damp cloth and remove a thin slice from each end. Cut them into slices about 1 cm ($\frac{1}{2}$ in) thick. Butter the base of a cast-iron pan with 15 g ($\frac{1}{2}$ oz) of butter, add the onion in one layer and sprinkle with salt. This seasoning is important because it causes the onions to render their juice and thus provide part of the necessary moisture. Arrange the courgettes over them, add freshly ground black pepper and a little more salt and seal the pan by placing a sheet of greaseproof paper over the rim and forcing the lid down over it. Place the pan over a low heat, using an asbestos mat if an ordinary pan is used.

After 3–4 minutes when the moisture of the ingredients starts to bubble very faintly, reduce the heat to very low and cook for a further 10 minutes without removing the lid, shaking the pan occasionally and tossing the contents. By this time the courgettes should be cooked yet still slightly crisp in consistency. Do not overcook them but if necessary replace the lid and cook for a further 5 minutes.

Pour the contents of the pan into a heated serving dish, sprinkle with chopped parsley and serve immediately.

Courgettes nature; cresson à la crème

Cresson à la crème

Watercress cooked with cream

TO SERVE SIX

INGREDIENTS
8 large bunches watercress
75 g (3 oz) butter
6 tablespoons double cream
salt and black pepper

This is a delicious vegetable to serve with bland roast meats such as veal or pork.

Wash the watercress in several changes of cold water but do not leave it soaking. Shake it free of moisture, cut off the large coarse stalks and discard them. Cook the leaves and tender stalks in a large panful of boiling salted water for 5 minutes, no more. Drain well in a colander and pass quickly under cold running water, just long enough to make them sufficiently cool to handle. Press out all moisture, squeezing the watercress between the palms. Melt the butter until foaming in a *cocotte* or wide-based pan placed over a low heat, add the watercress and simmer for 10 minutes, stirring occasionally. Pour in the cream, season to taste, stir well and reheat until the first bubble rises. Correct the seasoning and serve immediately.

Endives braisées

Braised chicory

TO SERVE SIX

INGREDIENTS
- 1.4 kg (3 lb) medium-sized heads of chicory
- 100 g (4 oz) butter
- 1 dessertspoon oil
- salt and black pepper

The vegetable known as chicory in England and as endive in France needs careful preparation and a few hints to keep it free from bitterness and white in colour when cooked. To ensure this do not leave chicory soaking in cold water, but cook it immediately, generously covered with boiling salted water to which two or three thick slices of lemon and a large crust of bread have been added. When braised in butter without any previous blanching, as in the recipe below, chicory has even more flavour.

Melt the butter and oil in a *cocotte* or large braising pan over a low heat. Cut a slice from the root end of the chicory and remove any discoloured outer leaves. As each one is trimmed turn it in this mixture and when they are all coated, arrange them in one layer in the pan. Season, cover and cook over a very low heat until easily pierced with a knife, for about 1–1½ hours according to size. Shake the pan occasionally and turn them over so that when cooked they are tender and golden. This is the classic accompaniment to either roast or sautéd veal (*see page* 118).

Endives au gratin

Chicory cooked with cheese

TO SERVE SIX

INGREDIENTS
- 1.3 kg (3 lb) small to medium heads of chicory
- 1 lemon
- 1 large crust of bread
- 15 g (½ oz) butter
- *sauce béchamel* (*page* 14)
- 200 g (7 oz) *gruyère* cheese in one piece
- 150 ml (¼ pint) double cream
- 2 heaped tablespoons concentrated tomato purée
- salt and black pepper

Cut a slice from the root end of each head of chicory and remove any discoloured outer leaves. Throw the chicory at once into a large panful of boiling salted water in which the thickly sliced lemon and the crust have been placed. These prevent the chicory from discolouring. Cook over a medium heat until tender for about 35–40 minutes. Drain well in a colander, discard the bread, then place in a clean kitchen cloth and gently squeeze out all excess moisture.

Heat the over to 190°C, 375°F, Gas Mark 5. Butter a large gratin dish and arrange the chicory in it, head to tail. Season well with salt and pepper. Prepare the *sauce béchamel*. Grate about three-quarters of the *gruyère* cheese (it will have much more flavour if bought in the piece) and beat it into the *sauce béchamel*. Pour this over the chicory and scatter the rest of the cheese, cut into small dice, over the top. Season the cream and beat in the tomato purée. Cover the ingredients with this mixture, and put the dish into the oven for 25–30 minutes until bubbling and well coloured on the surface.

Epinards à la crème

Spinach in cream

TO SERVE SIX

INGREDIENTS
- 2 kg (4 lb) fresh or frozen spinach (leaf not purée)
- 100 g (4 oz) butter
- salt and black pepper
- 275 ml (½ pint) double cream or *sauce béchamel* (*page* 14)
- grated nutmeg

Wash the spinach in several changes of cold water and remove the centre rib. Wash again and shake to remove excess moisture. Place in a large pan with no water except that which clings to the leaves. Cover and place over a medium heat for 5 minutes. As soon as the spinach starts to soften, stir well and cook, uncovered, for 10 minutes turning it occasionally with a wooden spatula. Do not overcook. Drain as soon as it is tender. If left in the hot water it will discolour.

If frozen spinach is used, drop it into a small quantity of salted boiling water as instructed on the packet and when tender drain immediately.

When sufficiently cool to handle, squeeze out all moisture between the palms and chop roughly. Melt the butter in the same pan, add the spinach and dry thoroughly over a medium heat tossing and stirring occasionally. Season with salt and plenty of freshly ground black pepper.

Season the cream or *sauce béchamel* with grated nutmeg to taste and mix thoroughly into the spinach, turning it over and stirring over a low heat until very hot.

Turn the contents of the pan into a heated serving dish and garnish with long croûtons cooked in foaming butter until crisp and golden (*see page* 33). They can be garlic-flavoured if preferred.

Epinards en gâteau

Baked spinach

TO SERVE SIX

INGREDIENTS
675 g ($1\frac{1}{2}$ lb) spinach
350 g (12 oz) pickled belly pork
3 shallots
2 tablespoons pork dripping or pure lard
2 tablespoons chopped parsley
1 teaspoon dried thyme
1 bayleaf
50 g (2 oz) flour
3 eggs (size 3) plus 3 extra yolks
225 ml (8 fl oz) milk
salt and black pepper

Heat the oven to 220°C, 425°F, Gas Mark 7. Wash the spinach thoroughly in several changes of water. Drain, and dry in a kitchen cloth. Cut the spinach into strips with scissors.

Wash the pork under running cold water, dry, remove the rind and chop the rest finely. Peel and slice the shallots finely. Melt the pork dripping or lard in a large pan placed over a brisk heat, stir in the spinach, stirring it constantly with a wooden spoon until soft. As soon as it wilts add the shallots, parsley, thyme, and the bayleaf crumbled into small pieces. Mix well and draw the pan from the heat. Add the chopped pork and mix again. Beat the flour into the eggs and extra yolks and mix thoroughly. Beat well and stir in the milk. Season with pepper but do not add salt before tasting the mixture.

Pour into a large buttered gratin dish and bake for 40 minutes, watching the surface carefully so that it does not colour too deeply. Place a sheet of foil lightly over if necessary. Test by pressing the centre with a finger. It should be set when cooked.

Leave to cool for about 10 minutes before serving. This dish should be served just warm either as a course by itself or with roast or grilled meat, preferably pork (*see page* 108).

Clockwise: endives au gratin; épinards en gâteau; épinards à la crème

Fenouils braisés

Braised fennel

TO SERVE SIX

INGREDIENTS

8 small heads of fennel
2 level tablespoons flour
75 g (3 oz) butter or 2 tablespoons duck or chicken fat
2 tablespoons chopped herbs – chives, parsley and fennel tops
salt and black pepper

Cut off the root end of the fennel and any of the feathery leaf tops that may be faded, reserving some of the fresh ones for garnishing. Place a large panful of boiling salted water over a medium heat and beat in the flour mixed to a smooth cream with half a teacupful of cold water. When simmering steadily, blanch the fennel for 10–15 minutes or until it can be barely pierced with a knife point, but is not cooked through. Remove to a colander, refresh under cold running water for a moment, dry and cut into quarters.

Melt the butter or other fat in a *cocotte* over a low heat and when hot, *sauté* the fennel, turning the pieces over and shaking the pan from time to time. Season with pepper, a little more salt, cover and braise over a gentle heat for minutes until tender.

Pour the contents of the *cocotte* with its juices into a heated serving dish and sprinkle with herbs. Serve immediately.

Haricots verts au beurre

French beans in butter

TO SERVE SIX

INGREDIENTS

1.3 kg ($2\frac{1}{2}$ lb) very small French beans
75 g (3 oz) butter
2 tablespoons finely chopped parsley
salt and black pepper

In French cooking green beans are always left whole. For this reason, they are picked and sold when very small indeed. Home-grown green beans of any variety, even runner beans, can be cooked whole in the French way if picked when no more than 7 cm (3 in) long.

Wash the beans quickly under running cold water and drain immediately. Remove top and tail; they should be small enough to have no strings.

Prepare a large panful of boiling salted water and throw in the beans when the water is boiling steadily. Cook for about 15 minutes depending on size but they should be slightly crisp in texture when served.

Drain thoroughly, put the butter into the hot pan and back on the heat. When foaming, add the beans, season well, sprinkle with parsley and toss until they are hot and coated with the butter and parsley. Empty the contents of the pan into a heated dish and serve immediately.

Haricots verts à la crème (French beans in cream)
Add 4 tablespoons double cream to the beans after they have been tossed in butter, and mix carefully before serving.

Haricots verts aux échalottes (French beans with shallots)
Add 3 finely chopped shallots to the butter in the pan, allow them to heat and become transparent, but do not cook through. Stir in the parsley, add the beans when well drained, reheat and toss for a minute before serving.

Haricots verts à la française

TO SERVE SIX

INGREDIENTS
2 firm-hearted lettuce
1.4 kg (3 lb) French beans
3 bunches spring onions
100 g (4 oz) butter
fine salt
1 teaspoon sugar
75 ml (3 fl oz) cold water
4 large sprigs parsley
8 large sprigs chervil (optional)

For this recipe the beans must be minute. Wash and refresh the lettuce (*see page* 170) and leave until required.

Wash the beans quickly under running water and drain. Remove top and tail. Cut off the roots of the onions and all green parts, which can be used in place of chives in other dishes. Trim the bulbs removing the outer skin if damaged, but leave whole.

Butter a very large heavy pan, line it with the outer edible leaves of lettuce, add the hearts cut into quarters, the onions, salt and 50 g (2 oz) of butter, cut into small pieces. Place the beans on top, season and sprinkle with sugar and pour in the water. Tie the herbs together with a long string, place them in the pan and tie the other end to the pan handle. Cover tightly and place over a gentle heat. After 3–4 minutes when the moisture of the ingredients starts to bubble very faintly, reduce the heat to low and cook for 45 minutes. Test with a long-pronged cooking fork. When ready to serve the beans should be slightly crisp.

To serve, remove the herbs, and correct the seasoning if necessary. Carefully stir in the rest of the butter cut into small pieces and pour the contents of the pan into a large heated serving dish.

Top : haricots verts au beurre; *bottom :* haricots verts à la française

Laitues braisées

Braised lettuce

TO SERVE SIX

INGREDIENTS
8 firm-hearted garden lettuce
fine salt
black pepper
100 g (4 oz) butter
75 ml (3 fl oz) beef *bouillon* (optional) (*page* 12)

When home-grown lettuce are over-plentiful they can be cooked in the following way to produce a very delicately flavoured hot vegetable. This dish is served in Vichy as a diet dish, and even without the meat stock it is delicious.

Remove the damaged leaves from the lettuce. Fill a large bowl with cold water, add a handful of cooking salt and plunge the lettuce, head first, up and down to remove grit. Change the water and repeat the process. Shake carefully to remove excess moisture, cut off a slice across the root end and set the lettuce aside, head downwards, to drain.

Melt 50 g (2 oz) of the butter in a *sauteuse* or other wide-based heavy pan and, gathering the leaves closely around the heart, pack the lettuces tightly together in the pan, heads uppermost. Pour the *bouillon* down the sides of the pan. This is included for additional flavouring only. Season lightly. When the pan is tightly covered, the lettuce will produce sufficient liquid themselves for cooking even if stock is not used. Cover closely, place over a low heat and cook for about 25–30 minutes, without removing the lid.

Heat the oven to 200 °C, 400 °F, Gas Mark 6. Lift out the lettuce carefully so that they remain whole and drain in a colander. When cool enough to handle, gently squeeze out moisture between the palms, arrange in a heated, buttered serving dish and place in the oven. Reduce the liquids in the pan by fast simmering, beat in the remaining butter cut into small flecks and pour over the lettuce. Serve immediately.

Purée de marrons

Chestnut purée

TO SERVE SIX

INGREDIENTS
1.4 kg (3 lb) chestnuts
275 ml (½ pint) milk or chicken or veal stock (*page* 12)
fine salt
15 g (½ oz) sugar
1 stalk celery
75 g (3 oz) butter

Heat the oven to 200 °C, 400 °F, Gas Mark 6. Slash the rounded side of each chestnut with a sharp knife and place them in a roasting tin well spread out. Add just enough cold water to cover the bottom of the tin and put into the oven for 8 minutes. The two skins will then peel off easily.

When peeled cook them in the milk or stock with salt, sugar and the stalk of celery left whole. Simmer over a medium heat (low heat if milk is used) until tender when pricked with a fork.

Remove the celery, drain and reserve the liquid. Reduce the chestnuts to a purée in a mouli-légumes or pound through a sieve. If an electric blender is used a little liquid will need to be added.

Melt a small piece of butter in the pan, add the purée and beat in sufficient hot liquid to obtain a firm mixture. Add the rest of the butter cut into small pieces beating constantly with a wooden spatula. Test for seasoning, add more if required and serve very hot. Serve with *gigue de chevreuil* or pheasant (*see page* 145).

Top: oignons glacés; *bottom*: navets glacés

Oignons glacés

Glazed onions

TO SERVE SIX

INGREDIENTS
6 large flat Dutch onions
6 cloves
50 g (2 oz) butter
275 ml ($\frac{1}{2}$ pint) *bouillon* (*page* 12)
salt and pepper
6 lumps sugar
1 dessertspoon castor sugar

When the large flat Dutch onions are obtainable they make a delicious dish to serve with pork as an alternative to the usual apple sauce.

Peel the onions and stick a clove into the root end of each one. Butter a large *sauteuse* or shallow braising pan with 25 g (1 oz) butter; place the onions in it root end downwards, and season with salt and pepper. Add enough *bouillon* to reach the level of the onions but not to cover them. Dot with small pieces of butter and place over a very low heat, uncovered. Cook very slowly for about $1\frac{1}{2}$ hours until the onions are tender when pierced with a long-pronged cooking fork, taking care not to break them. If during cooking time the liquid reduces too rapidly, add a little more *bouillon*.

When tender place a lump of sugar on each onion, sprinkle with castor sugar and place under a medium-hot grill to glaze. Watch carefully and remove as soon as the sugar colours, or it will burn. Serve with the reduced and caramelized juices from the pan.

Navets glacés

Glazed turnips

TO SERVE SIX

INGREDIENTS
1.4 g (3 lb) small young turnips
50 g (2 oz) butter
1 tablespoon castor sugar
salt and black pepper
150 ml ($\frac{1}{4}$ pint) *bouillon* (*page* 12)

Peel the turnips and cut them into halves horizontally. Cook in sufficient cold water to cover for 15 minutes after boiling point is reached.

Butter a *sauteuse* or other wide-based pan thickly with 25 g (1 oz) butter. Drain the turnips thoroughly, place them cut side down in the pan, sprinkle evenly with sugar, season with salt and freshly ground pepper and pour the *bouillon* down the side of the pan. Spread the remaining butter over a large circle of greaseproof paper and place this over the vegetables, tucking it down around them, and place over a medium heat. When boiling point is well established reduce the heat to low and continue cooking until the liquid is reduced to about 2 tablespoonsful. Serve very hot with the remaining juices.

Poireaux en purée

Leek purée

TO SERVE SIX

INGREDIENTS
675 g (1½ lb) leeks
450 g (1 lb) floury potatoes
pinch of salt
black and white pepper
150 ml (¼ pint) hot milk
25 g (1 oz) butter
150 ml (¼ pint) double cream

Remove root and any damaged leaves from the leeks, and cut off the tough green part, leaving 3 cm (1 in) of the edible part. The rest of the green can be used for soup (*see soupe aux poireaux, pommes de terre, page* 37). Slash the leeks down and crossways as far as the white part and plunge them up and down, cut-end foremost, in a bowl of tepid water to loosen the grit. Cut into short lengths and cook in boiling salted water until tender. Drain well in a colander and when cool squeeze out excess moisture between the palms before setting aside.

Meanwhile peel the potatoes, cut them into even pieces and cook in cold, salted water until just tender. Do not over cook them. Drain well.

Heat the milk in a small pan. Pass both vegetables through the mouli-légumes into the hot, dry saucepan which has been rubbed over with buttered paper. Season lightly with salt and highly with black and white pepper, and place the pan over low heat. Beat the purée vigorously while adding the hot milk and butter a little at a time. When incorporated and the purée is light, add the cream in the same way. When thoroughly hot, pile into a heated dish, dot with flecks of butter and serve immediately.

Nouilles au beurre

Noodles in butter

TO SERVE SIX

INGREDIENTS
350 g (12 oz) noodles
salt
50 g (2 oz) butter
black pepper

Nouilles à la crème
1 egg yolk
4 tablespoons double cream

Drop the noodles into a large panful of fast boiling, salted water and cook for 10 minutes. Cook for a further 2–3 minutes if necessary but do not cook them too soft. They must still be firm when bitten. Drain immediately in a colander and put the hot pan back over a low heat, add a little butter and as it melts tip in the noodles and season with salt and freshly ground black pepper. Turn the noodles over and over until they are hot and well coated with melted butter. Pour into a heated dish and serve immediately. To keep hot place the dish over a pan half full of hot water and cover with a buttered greaseproof paper.

Nouilles à la crème (Noodles with cream)
Cook the noodles as indicated above and turn them in the butter. Beat the egg yolk into the cream, season, and over a low heat stir this into the pan with the noodles for a few moments. Turn them over again and pour into a heated serving dish.

Riz créole; nouilles au beurre

Riz créole

Creole rice

TO SERVE SIX

INGREDIENTS
juice of 1 lemon
1 tablespoon salt
350 g (12 oz) long-grained rice
50 g (2 oz) butter
1 tablespoon oil
black pepper

Plain-boiled rice as an accompaniment to meat dishes or as a basic ingredient for salads, must be dry and fluffy with the grains separated. The following method will produce the desired result.

Choose a very large pan in which to cook the rice, as the more water used the better. Butter the rim inside to prevent the rice from boiling over, fill to three-quarters with boiling water, add the strained lemon juice and 1 tablespoon salt and place over a medium high heat. Pour in the rice gradually so that the water does not stop boiling and cook for exactly 8 minutes. Test: the centre should be slightly firm between the teeth. If not, continue boiling for a further 2–3 minutes, but 13 minutes at the most will be sufficient time for cooking most varieties of rice.

Meanwhile heat the oven to 160°C, 325°F, Gas Mark 3. Butter a large shallow dish thickly, add half the butter and all the oil and place in the oven. Having tested the rice, pour into a colander, drain and hold under running cold water for 3–4 minutes to wash thoroughly, then drain well and empty into the buttered dish turning the rice over and over to coat it with melted butter. Put into the oven and turn the rice over from time to time to dry out the moisture. In 30 minutes it will be hot and the grains free of moisture and well separated. Season well with salt and pepper, mix in the rest of the butter and serve at once.

If required to wait, place a buttered greaseproof paper lightly on top and place low down in the oven.

When cooking *riz créole* as a salad ingredient, dry the rice in 2 tablespoons of oil only, and no butter.

Petits pois à la française

TO SERVE SIX

INGREDIENTS
- 1 bunch large spring onions
- 1 firm-hearted lettuce
- 50 g (2 oz) butter
- salt, black pepper, sugar
- 1.4 g (3 lb) small fresh green peas

Remove roots and green stems from the onions leaving the bulb whole. Wash and trim the lettuce, remove the edible outer leaves and cut the heart into quarters. Butter a large heavy pan thickly, line with large lettuce leaves, add the heart, onions and salt. Add a few flecks of butter and the peas. Cover tightly by placing a piece of greaseproof paper over the rim and forcing the lid down over it. Place over a low heat. Use an asbestos mat over a gas flame if it is difficult to control at a low temperature.

After 3–4 minutes when the ingredients will start bubbling, reduce the heat to very low and cook for 20 minutes without uncovering the pan, but tossing it occasionally to turn over the contents. Test the peas and if not quite cooked replace the lid and cook for another 2–3 minutes. Correct the seasoning, stir in the rest of the butter and pour into a heated dish. Serve immediately.

Fèves fraîches à la française

When broad beans first come into season and the outer skin is very tender they are delicious cooked as above.

Frozen peas and beans can also be cooked *à la française* by adding them frozen to the pan, after it has been prepared as indicated above.

Pommes de terre à l'ail

Potatoes with garlic and cheese

TO SERVE SIX

INGREDIENTS
- 150 g (5 oz) streaky bacon, thickly cut
- 2 tablespoons olive or corn oil
- 1 kg (2 lb) potatoes, thinly sliced
- salt and black pepper
- 100 g (4 oz) grated *gruyère* cheese
- 3 cloves garlic
- 1 tablespoon chopped parsley
- 2 tablespoons double cream

English red-skinned potatoes named Desirée are the variety nearest to the waxy French potatoes used in the following dishes.

This dish can be served either as a lunch or supper dish, with a green salad.

Wipe out a heavy cast-iron *cocotte* with an oiled paper. Cut the bacon into 1-cm ($\frac{1}{2}$-in) wide strips, and over a medium heat cook until crisp and golden coloured, then add the oil and a first layer of potatoes. Season well with salt and pepper and cover with a layer of grated cheese. Continue filling the dish with alternate layers of seasoned potatoes and cheese until the dish is full. Sprinkle with finely chopped garlic and parsley. Cover the dish and place over a low heat. Cook for 30 minutes shaking the dish occasionally but do not stir the contents. When the potatoes are tender when pierced with a pointed knife, pour the cream over the surface, replace the lid and cook for a further 3–4 minutes.

Serve the gratin immediately either in the dish or turned out on to a heated serving dish, crusted side uppermost.

Serve a strong red carafe wine with it.

Pommes Anna

TO SERVE SIX

INGREDIENTS
1 kg (2 lb) small waxy potatoes
150 g (5 oz) butter
salt and black pepper

Heat the oven to 190°C, 375°F, Gas Mark 5. Peel the potatoes and slice them thinly. Thickly butter a deep charlotte mould and line the sides with potato slices placed closely together and attached firmly to the butter. Cover the bottom also and sprinkle lightly with salt, freshly ground pepper and flecks of butter, cover with another layer of potatoes, seasoning and butter and so on until the tin is three-quarters full. Cover with buttered paper and cook for 45 minutes or until tender when pierced with a sharply pointed knife.

To serve, pass the blade of a knife around the inside of the tin, hold a heated plate over it and invert, giving a sharp tap as the plate is set down to turn out the contents. The inside should be soft and the outside crust crisp and golden brown.

Gratin dauphinois

TO SERVE SIX

INGREDIENTS
1.3 kg (3 lb) waxy potatoes
275 ml (½ pint) milk
salt and pepper
grated nutmeg
75 g (3 oz) butter
275 ml (½ pint) double cream
1 clove garlic
150 g (5 oz) grated *gruyère* cheese

This is a delicious combination of potatoes, cream and cheese.

Heat the oven to 160°C, 325°F, Gas Mark 3. Peel the potatoes, wipe clean with a damp cloth and cut them into thin slices. Do not wash or soak them in water as this would remove the starch essential to the correct consistency of the dish.

Pour the milk into a large saucepan, season with salt, freshly ground pepper and nutmeg to taste and add the butter cut into small pieces. Place over a medium heat, beat with a birch whisk and bring slowly to boiling point, add the potatoes and the cream gradually, reduce the heat and simmer very slowly for 10 minutes, stirring frequently. Rub a large gratin dish with the cut clove of garlic, butter it generously and pour in the potato mixture. Scatter the cheese on top and bake very slowly for 1½ hours until a crisp brown crust has formed. Serve immediately.

Pommes de terre au lard

Potatoes cooked with bacon

TO SERVE SIX

INGREDIENTS
300 g (12 oz) lean streaky bacon, cut in one piece
15 very small onions (pickling size)
1.3 kg (2½ lb) waxy potatoes
50 g (2 oz) butter
25 g (1 oz) flour
salt and black pepper
500 ml (18 fl oz) *bouillon*
275 ml (½ pint) white wine
a bouquet garni

Remove the rind from the bacon and cut the meat into small thick *lardons*. Blanch in boiling water for 5 minutes. Remove with a slotted spoon and set aside. Peel and blanch the onions in the same water for a further 5 minutes, drain and set aside with the *lardons*.

Peel the potatoes and leave them, whole, in a wet cloth until required. Place a large *cocotte* over a low heat and melt the butter. Work in the flour, season and remove the *cocotte* from the heat. Add all the *bouillon* at once. Beat with a birch whisk until smooth. Replace on the heat, beat in the wine and when well mixed add the bouquet garni, onions, *lardons*. Cut the potatoes into thick chips and add them to the cocotte as they are cut. Stir well, add a little more seasoning if necessary, cover, reduce the heat to very low and cook very slowly for about 45 minutes.

This is an excellent dish of potatoes to serve with grilled meat, or with green salad, as a supper dish.

Pommes lyonnaise

TO SERVE SIX

INGREDIENTS
1 kg (2 lb) waxy potatoes
225 g (8 oz) onions
40 g (1½ oz) butter
40 g (1½ oz) pork fat
salt and black pepper
2 tablespoons chopped parsley

Peel and slice the potatoes very thinly. Peel and slice the onions medium-fine. Heat the oven to 180°C, 350°F, Gas Mark 4. Melt the butter and pork fat in a large iron frying pan over a medium-low heat and add the onions, cooking them for 4–5 minutes until transparent before adding the potatoes. Season well. Turn them over occasionally with a wooden spatula and when they have coloured to the blond stage, mix in the parsley. Empty the contents of the pan into a large oval gratin dish and cook very slowly in the oven for at least 1 hour or until browned and crusted on the surface and melting underneath.

Top: pommes Anna; *centre:* gratin dauphinois; pommes de terre au lard; *bottom:* pommes lyonnaise

Purée de pommes de terre

Mashed potatoes

TO SERVE SIX

INGREDIENTS
1.3 kg ($2\frac{1}{2}$ lb) floury potatoes
350 ml (12 fl oz) milk
100 g (4 oz) butter
salt, white and black pepper

Perfect mashed potatoes are, according to many French experts, one criterion by which to judge a good cook. This is a popular dish but not unless it is presented very white, very fluffy, very smooth and very hot. The dish must always be served as soon as it is ready. Like a soufflé *Purée de pommes de terre* cannot wait. If necessary it must be waited for.

Peel the potatoes, cut the large ones into quarters so that they are all of equal size, and place in a large pan with enough cold water to cover. Add salt and bring to boiling point over a medium heat, then reduce to low and simmer, uncovered, until just tender. Meanwhile heat the milk in a small pan.

Drain the potatoes into a colander. Rub a pan with a buttered paper. Pass the potatoes through a mouli-légumes into the hot pan. Put the pan back over a very low heat and beating vigorously add first the butter, cut into small pieces and then the boiling milk a little at a time. Add a little more salt and plenty of both peppers, beat until very hot but do not allow the purée to boil again or it will become discoloured. Heap into a very hot dish and serve without delay.

Pommes de terre sautées

Sauté potatoes

TO SERVE SIX

INGREDIENTS
1 kg (2 lb) medium-sized waxy potatoes
salt and pepper
75 g (3 oz) butter, pork and/or chicken fat mixed or
50 g (2 oz) butter and 1 tablespoon corn or olive oil
2 tablespoons chopped parsley for garnishing

Scrub the potatoes until clean. Boil them in their skins in enough salted water to cover until just tender when pierced with a sharply pointed knife. Do not over-cook them. Leave until completely cold.

Peel the potatoes and cut into fairly thick slices and season highly. Place a large iron frying pan, dry, over a medium heat for a minute, add the fats and when the butter froths add the potatoes and turn them over thoroughly with a wooden spatula to coat with fat. Continue cooking, shaking the pan to prevent the contents sticking, lifting them up when turning them over with a flick of the wrist, so that they fall back into the pan. When they are browned, slightly crumbled and crisp, sprinkle with chopped parsley and serve immediately.

Top : purée de pommes de terre; *bottom :* pommes de terre sautées; Tian du midi

Tian du midi

TO SERVE SIX

INGREDIENTS
1.3 kg ($2\frac{1}{2}$ lb) waxy potatoes
100 g (4 oz) onions
2 large Mediterranean tomatoes
100 g (4 oz) Parmesan cheese
3–4 tablespoons olive oil
$1\frac{1}{2}$ teaspoons dried thyme or *herbes du midi*
salt and black pepper

Herbes du midi are a mixture of Mediterranean herbs difficult to reproduce elsewhere. They are, however, obtainable in all kitchen equipment shops and give the authentic flavour to this very appetizing vegetable and cheese pancake known in Provençal dialect as a *tian*.

This is a delicious dish, usually served in the Midi after a hearty soup. When a bowl of fresh apricots or peaches follows, this makes an excellent menu for a summer's evening.

Peel the potatoes and cut into thin slices, throw them into a bowlful of cold water to cover and leave until required.

Peel and slice the onions very finely and skin the tomatoes. Grate the cheese. It will have much more flavour if bought in the piece and grated as required.

Drain the potatoes and dry them very thoroughly in a thick kitchen cloth. This is important. Heat the oil in a large iron frying pan over a medium heat and arrange the potatoes in layers with seasoning, sliced onions, cheese and a sprinkling of thyme or *herbes du midi* between each one. Increase the heat slightly and cook, shaking the pan constantly and loosening the sides with a palette knife, until the bottom crust has formed. This will take about 30 minutes. Cover and continue cooking for a further 15 minutes.

Slice the tomatoes very thinly. (Those of the right variety will have a firm centre without liquid and will therefore not need to be seeded and drained. If large domestic tomatoes are used, slice, de-seed and drain them beforehand.) Place them over the top layer of potatoes, season and add a light sprinkling of herbs, cover and cook for 25 minutes, keeping the crusted underside free of the pan by shaking it occasionally and loosening again when necessary.

When ready to serve, pour a few drops of olive oil under the *tian*, increase the heat, tip and shake the pan to loosen and crisp the contents underneath, place a large heated serving plate over the pan and invert. Serve immediately.

Salads

Green salads are an important item on the French menu and the art of making them depends on preparing the lettuce, curly endive, escarole, batavia or other leaf vegetable so that when served it is very crisp, dry and thinly coated with dressing. When the leaves are wet the dressing soaks in and the salad is limp. To achieve perfection any salad not coming directly from the garden to the kitchen must be refreshed as indicated below.

To refresh a salad
This procedure consists of cutting a slice from the root of the lettuce and placing it root-end down in 3 cm (1 in) of cold water in a washing-up bowl. The bowl must be large enough to hold the leaves spread out without touching the water. If left in a cool place for at least 1 hour all the outer leaves, however limp they were before, will have drunk their fill through the root and become so crisp that very little will be wasted.

Fill the bowl with clean cold water and add 1 tablespoon salt. Remove any damaged outer leaves and holding the lettuce by the root-end plunge it head first up and down in the water to flush out the grit. Repeat the process and when clean shake out excess moisture. Pick off the edible leaves carefully and if necessary wash again under running water, shake well and place on a clean kitchen towel. Gather up the corners and swing the towel round several times. A wire basket can also be used for this purpose. Take out the lettuce leaves and place in a large plastic bag, close tightly with a wire band and refrigerate until required. Treated in this way leaf salads will keep fresh, dry and crisp for 3 days.

To dress the salad
Mix the vinaigrette chosen (*see page* 22) in a large salad bowl, cross the wooden serving spoon and fork in the bottom and lightly heap on top of them the lettuce leaves, torn into large pieces. Do not cut with a knife. Place the bowl in the refrigerator until required. (This salad can remain there to advantage for 2 hours or more.) When ready to serve, and not before, turn the salad over very lightly and delicately until the leaves are coated with dressing and serve immediately.

Always use a very large salad bowl so that the contents can be turned over easily without bruising. In this way they will remain dry and crisp.

A dozen or so leaves of young tender spinach added to a green salad gives a welcome new flavour. If sorrel is obtainable it is even better. Either vegetable should have the centre rib removed, and then be washed and dried, torn into pieces and mixed in with the rest.

For those who like a subtle aroma of garlic in a green salad rub a cut clove around the salad bowl. For those who like

Salade d'endives, de haricots blancs and haricots verts

a more definite flavour add garlic *vroûtons* (*see page* 33). A clove peeled, crushed and beaten into the vinaigrette gives a very strong flavour indeed.

Salade d'endives

Chicory salad

TO SERVE SIX

INGREDIENTS
vinaigrette à la crème (*page* 22)
2 large Cox's apples
1 large head celery
225 g (8 oz) chicory
24 walnut halves
100 g (4 oz) cooked beetroot
salt and black pepper
1 teaspoon lemon juice

Mix the *vinaigrette* in a large salad bowl and, as the ingredients for the salad are prepared, turn them in the dressing to prevent them from discolouring.

Peel, core and thinly slice the apples, chop the celery coarsely, cut off a slice from the root-end of the chicory, remove any damaged outer leaves, wipe with a damp cloth and cut into fairly thick, round slices. Mix these ingredients and the walnuts into the dressing. Cut the beetroot into large dice and add last of all. Correct the seasoning, adding a little more lemon juice to sharpen the flavour if necessary.

Salade de haricots blancs

White haricot bean salad

TO SERVE SIX

INGREDIENTS
3 medium-sized tomatoes
40 g ($1\frac{1}{2}$ oz) black olives
1 clove garlic
vinaigrette (*page* 22)
6–8 tablespoons cooked white haricot beans
3 large hard-boiled eggs

The following appetizing salad can be made from white haricot beans left over from the *Epaule d'agneau aux haricots blancs* (*see page* 102).

Pour boiling water over the tomatoes, leave for 3 minutes and then plunge them into enough cold water to cover. Skin and halve them and remove their seeds. Turn them upside down to drain.

Cut the flesh from the olives in strips and place them in a salad bowl. Peel and crush the garlic and beat into the *vinaigrette*. Cut the tomato flesh into pieces and add to the bowl, together with the beans, and eggs, cut into 8 sections. Pour the *vinaigrette* over these ingredients, season well and turn carefully with the salad fork and spoon to coat with dressing.

Salade de haricots verts

French bean salad

TO SERVE SIX

INGREDIENTS
1 kg (2 lb) small french beans (*haricots verts,* bush beans or very small runner beans)
vinaigrette (*page* 22)
1 dessertspoon chopped fresh tarragon
salt and black pepper
75 g (3 oz) *gruyère* cheese

Top and tail the beans. They should not be large enough to have strings. Place a large pan quarter full of salted water over a high heat and bring to boiling. Throw in the beans and cook rapidly for about 15 minutes after boiling point has been re-established. When cooked, they should be tender but still firm and slightly crisp. Drain without delay and when quite dry and still warm, toss with the *vinaigrette* and tarragon in a salad bowl large enough to allow them to be turned easily. Season to taste. When cold mix in the *gruyère* cheese, cut into small dice.

Salade au lard des Ardennes

Ardennes salad

TO SERVE SIX

INGREDIENTS
450 g (1 lb) escarole, curly endive, batavia or young dandelions
450 g (1 lb) small waxy potatoes
225 g (8 oz) streaky bacon, cut in one piece
2 tablespoons olive oil
4 tablespoons red or white wine vinegar
25 g (1 oz) butter
black pepper

This salad is claimed to be the one salad in which vinegar does not adversely affect the bouquet of wine as the alcohol evaporates on heating. For this reason it is known in Anjou as *salade amie du vin.*

Wash, trim and dry the escarole, bataria or curly endive and tear into pieces. If young dandelions are obtainable trim the root but do not remove it, as it holds the leaves together, then wash and dry.

Scrub the potatoes and boil them in their skin until tender. Peel and cut into large dice. Remove the rind from the bacon and cut the meat into cubes. Place in a large frying pan and cook until crisp and coloured, turning over the cubes to brown them evenly. Heat the oil in a large pan, add the potatoes and prepared salad. Add the vinegar to the crisp bacon cubes, mix well and when boiling hot pour over the contents of the pan. Add butter and plenty of pepper and heat for a few minutes turning the ingredients carefully without breaking the potatoes. Transfer to a heated salad bowl and also heat the plates.

Serve very hot at the beginning of a meal, as in the Ardennes.

Salade aux noisettes

Hazelnut salad

TO SERVE SIX

INGREDIENTS
75 g (3 oz) raisins
225 g (8 oz) rice (*page* 163)
3 tablespoons mild curry powder
2 tablespoons oil
75 g (3 oz) whole hazelnuts
1 tin small garden peas
salt and black pepper
mayonnaise (*page* 21)
juice of ½ a lemon

Put the raisins into a small bowl and cover with warm water. Set aside for 1 hour.

Cook the rice (*see page* 163), beating the curry powder into the boiling water before adding the rice, and dry as suggested but use 2 tablespoons of oil only. Allow to cool. Preheat the oven to 160°C, 325°F, Gas Mark 3. Spread the hazelnuts out on a baking sheet, and place in the oven for about 10 minutes, until the brown skin rubs off easily between the fingers.

Drain the raisins and the peas. Place the rice in a large salad bowl and mix in the nuts, peas and raisins. Season well and mix. Make the mayonnaise and add sufficient lemon juice to give it a sharp flavour. Pour this over the other ingredients and turn over carefully until blended. Chill lightly for not more than 1 hour before serving.

Opposite, from top to bottom: Salade aux noisettes, salade de pommes de terre, salade de poulet aux amandes

Salade de pommes de terre

Potato salad

TO SERVE SIX

INGREDIENTS
675 g (1½ lb) waxy potatoes
vinaigrette (*page* 22)
salt and black pepper
2 tablespoons chopped fresh herbs such as chives, parsley and/or mint

Scrub the potatoes and remove any blemishes. Place in a large pan with enough cold water to cover and boil over a medium heat until just tender when pierced with a sharp pointed knife. Do not boil fast or they will disintegrate on the outside before the centre is cooked and they must remain very firm.

Meanwhile make the *vinaigrette* in a bowl large enough to allow room for turning the potatoes without breaking them. Drain and peel the potatoes. Cut into thick slices, season well and turn in the dressing while still hot. Leave to cool completely. Correct the seasoning and sprinkle with chopped fresh herbs before serving.

To vary the flavour, pour 75 ml (3 fl oz) dry white wine over the hot potatoes before turning them in the *vinaigrette,* or add 1 tablespoon finely chopped onion or shallot to the *vinaigrette* before adding the potatoes.

Salade de poulet aux amandes

Chicken almond salad

TO SERVE SIX

INGREDIENTS
50 g (2 oz) slivered almonds
salt and black pepper
1 bunch watercress
1 large celery heart
450 g (1 lb) cold chicken
juice of $\frac{1}{2}$ an orange
mayonnaise (*page* 21)

Put the almonds on a fireproof plate, sprinkle with salt and grill under a medium heat until slightly browned. Set aside to cool and to become crisp.

Wash and trim watercress, removing the coarse stalks before shaking in a kitchen towel to dry. Reserve a few sprigs for garnishing. Wash and clean the celery but do not remove the tender green leaves. Dry and chop coarsely.

Remove skin and bones from the chicken, cut into slivers and season with salt and pepper. Mix chicken, watercress, celery and nuts in a large salad bowl. Beat the orange juice into the mayonnaise and mix into the salad. Garnish with sprigs of watercress and chill lightly before serving.

2F50
3F00
FROMAGE FERM

Cheeses

The great Colette, doyen of gastronomers as well as luminary of the literary world, wrote, 'If I had a son in search of a wife I would say to him "Beware of a girl who loves neither wine, nor truffles, nor cheese, nor music"'. Sound advice indeed, for France is a country of cheeses. Every *département*, every region, and many villages even, have their own speciality, and a woman who guards the reputation of her table is as proud of having a good cheese merchant as she is of having a good butcher. This importance stems from the affinity that exists between wine and cheese. The bouquet of a fine burgundy is never so well appreciated as when a perfect Camembert provides the background flavour. Hence the preference in France for cheese and fruit instead of a sweet dish at the end of a menu and on occasion, when both are served, this is the reason for the cheese being presented before the *crème au chocolat*, contrary to our own habit. In this way the wine served with the main course is finished with its most suitable complement.

There are over 400 varieties of cheese listed in France and many more that are not listed. While relatively few are imported into Britain, the number we have to choose from is considerable and those named here are the most widely available.

The ability to select a good cheese is a matter of experience, but the following indications can be a guide.

To test a soft, ripened cheese like Camembert, wrap the forefinger in cling film and press the centre lightly. It should be supple, but not soft and sunken.

To preserve cheese, keep in a cool dark place but do not refrigerate. After returning it to the box, stop the cut sides of a ripened cheese with long thin strips of bread crust.

To preserve hard cheese like *gruyère* or goat, wrap it in cheesecloth wrung out in white wine – 3 tablespoons will be sufficient.

Some of the most widely available French cheeses:

1. Banon
2. Bleu de Bresse
3. Boursin
4. Brie
5. Camembert
6. Cantal
7. Carré de l'est
8. Chèvre

Banon (1) Provence
A small ewe's milk cheese, also made of goat's milk or cow's milk according to season, and wrapped in chestnut leaves bound with rafia. The crust should be slightly oily in appearance and the interior firm but supple. Serve with either rosé or light red wine.

Beaufort Savoie
A cow's milk cheese of the *gruyère* family, but it should have hardly any 'eyes' and taste a little less salty than *gruyère* proper. Can be used also in cooking. Serve with a young Beaujolais or the fruity white wines of Savoie.

Bleu de Bresse (2) Pays de l'Ain
A small cylindrical cheese made of rich cow's milk, high in fat content. The crust should be smooth and blue and the interior creamy and blue veined, supple when pressed but not soft. If the crust is reddish-grey, do not buy. Serve with Côtes-du-Rhône or Beaujolais.

Bondon Normandie
A small cylindrical cheese made from cow's milk. It should have a smooth, rather downy white crust and be supple to touch, smooth and creamy inside. Smells faintly of mushrooms. Serve with light fruity red wines.

Boursin (3) Normandie
A small cylindrical full-fat soft cheese made of enriched pasteurized cow's milk and aromatized with herbs. Can also be garlic or pepper-flavoured. It should be white and well formed, without crust, tender yet not too soft and should smell of herbs. Serve with any good strong red wine.

Brie (4) Ile-de-France
This ever-popular ripened, soft cheese is made of cow's milk, sometimes pasteurized, sometimes not, according to area. The crust should be smooth and white and have occasional downy patches sprinkled with faint red colouring. The interior should be pale yellow, evenly supple and creamy, never runny. It should bulge slightly with pressure. Avoid it if the centre is white, chalky or too liquid. Serve with good burgundy or claret.

Camembert (5) Normandie
This is made of either untreated cow's milk and called *camembert fermier* or of pasteurized milk and called *camembert pasteurisé*. *Fermier* is the better of the two but less easy to find. A good Camembert should have a level surface and be white with downy patches – the *fermier* is flecked with red specks, but not the *pasteurisé*. They should both be supple to the touch but, above all, not runny. The interior should be evenly creamy yellow, not white or chalky. Avoid both of them if the surface has sunk or shows black patches. Honour a perfect Camembert with a good burgundy (such as Nuits St Georges, Corton), a claret, or Côtes-du-Rhône.

Cantal (6) Auvergne
A hard pressed cheese made from cow's milk. It should have a faintly grey crust without fissures and have a nutty flavour. It is also used for cooking. Serve with all light fruity red wines such as Beaujolais or Côtes-du-Rhône.

Carré de l'est (7) Champagne, Lorraine, and other eastern *départements*
A small square cheese made of pasteurized cow's milk, rich in fat content. This soft, ripened cheese, of the Brie type in consistency, should have a white downy crust and prove supple to light pressure but not soft. Serve with a light burgundy or claret.

Chabichou Poitou
This small goat's milk cheese, shaped like a cone with its point removed, should have a white crust when unwrapped from its paper and smell quite strongly. *Chabichou fermier* (farmhouse *chabichou*) and *chabichou laitier* (dairy *chabichou*), the former not wrapped, should both have a fine blue-grey crust with reddish streaks. The very piquant flavour marries well with the light red wine of Poitou.

Chèvre à la feuille, chèvre long, chevret (8) Poitou, Savoie, Anjou, Auvergne
These are a few of the many goat's milk cheeses made all over France. They should have a fine, thin white or greyish crust, never thick and dried up. A well-chosen goat's cheese makes an excellent background flavour for dry or semi-dry white wines and rosé, Pouilly fuissé or Sancerre, Muscadet – or Anjou rosé.

Comté Franche-Comté, Jura, Vosges
A form of *gruyère* made of cow's milk. It is a large cheese, like a millstone, and should have a slightly domed surface, smooth crust and widely spaced eyes never smaller than a cherry. It is used also for cooking, i.e. fondu, gratin, *croque-monsieur*. Serve with the light fruity reds or rosés of the Jura or Savoie.

Coulommiers (9) Ile-de-France
A cow's milk cheese usually eaten fresh and salted. A good one should have a white crust slightly downy, with a greyish tinge. The crust often has reddish patches. Inside it should be supple, homogeneous and faintly yellow. Serve with Côtes-de-Beaune or any light red wine.

Crémets Nantais, crémets d'Anjou, coeurs à la crème (10) Anjou, Ile-de-France
These small, unsalted, fresh, soft cheeses made of rich cow's milk are of different shapes according to the region in which they are made, but most often they are heart-shaped. They have no crust and are eaten as dessert, sprinkled with sugar and sometimes served with cream.

Edam français (11) Flandres, Bretagne, Savoie
Made of pasteurized cow's milk, should be firm but not rubbery, with a smooth red wax crust. Serve with light white or red wines such as Muscadet or Beaujolais.

Emmenthal français (12) Franche Comté, Bretagne, Savoie
A very large round cheese made of cow's milk. It is of the *gruyère* family but less pungent and less salty than the true *gruyère* made in Savoie, and is therefore not as good for cooking.

Excelsior (13) Normandie
One of the richest cheeses made from cow's milk and very high in fat content. It is a very good substitute for Camembert in hot weather when the latter tends to be over-strong. Test in the same way as Camembert, but serve with a light red wine, Fleurie, Chinon or young Beaujolais.

Fromage blanc (14) made in all areas
A cottage cheese made from skimmed cow's milk. Of crumbling texture, it is used mainly instead of cream for family menus. Beaten with sufficient cold milk to form a thick Devonshire cream consistency, it can be served with all seasonal soft fruit. Serve with medium and sweet white wines such as Sauternes.

Gouda français (15) Flandres
A very mild cow's milk cheese of the Edam type. It is, however, of a different shape – a small wheel and not a round ball as is Edam. It should have the same characteristics as Edam français and be served with the same wines.

Gruyère français (16) Savoie, Franche Comté, Pays de l'Ain
This cow's milk cheese is made, at its best, on the Swiss borders of France and is as good as Swiss *gruyère* in all ways. This is the best cheese for cooking and used in sauces, gratins, and fondus. Buy in a whole piece and grate as required to obtain full flavour. When cooked, true *gruyère* retains its taste much more than Emmenthal and Comté do, although they too are of the *gruyère* family. The interior should be creamy yellow with few, quite small holes, and it should taste fruity, and sometimes salty. Serve with light white wines of Neufchâtel or with Muscadet, also with light red wines.

Monsieur (17) Normandie
A small ripened cheese, cylindrical in shape, made of enriched cow's milk high in fat content. The crust should be white flecked faintly with red, the interior supple and creamy with quite a penetrating odour. Avoid this cheese if the crust is dried out or has too many red flecks. Serve with robust red wines of Bordeaux, Burgundy or Côtes-du-Rhône.

Petit Suisse (18) made all over France
A non-salted full-fat cheese that can be served as it is bought, or used to make *fromage blanc* (*see facing page*).

Pont l'Eveque (19) Normandie
A rich soft ripened cow's milk cheese of the Camembert type. It should have a golden yellow crust and the interior should be soft but not runny. It has a pronounced odour, but if the crust is hard and greyish, avoid it. Serve with a robust burgundy or Côtes-du-Rhône.

Port Salut (20) made all over France
A semi-hard cheese made of pasteurized cow's milk, it was originally a product of the monasteries. It should have a smooth crust, tender interior and a slightly sweet taste. Serve Port Salut with either red or white wine.

Reblochon (21) Savoie
This small cylindrical cheese is made from cow's milk and is presented on a thin sheet of wood. It should have a white but faintly pinkish crust, a very supple interior, with a rather sweet taste. Serve with a light wine, either white or red.

Roquefort (22) Aquitaine
This ewe's milk cheese is one of the finest that France produces. The crust should be greyish in colour, the interior ivory yellow evenly veined with blue and be of a very rich creamy consistency. Avoid one that is white and chalky. Roquefort can also be used crumbled into *vinaigrette* for a salad dressing or used in a *Croque-monsieur (see page* 52). Serve with very good bottles of red wine, Châteauneuf-du-Pape, Château Margaux, Château Léoville Las-Cases.

Roquefort cheese is one of the oldest cheeses of France and is said to have originated when a local shepherd boy left his snack of bread and curd cheese in a cave when sheltering from the winds of that arid region. Then, unable to find the spot where it was hidden, he forgot it until several months later when it was found in a moment of desperate hunger, eaten for lack of something better, declared excellent in spite of the mould, and thereby hangs the tale.

This story could be true, for even today Roquefort is made with special bread-crumbs mixed into the curd of ewe's milk.

9. Coulommiers
10. Coeur à la crème
11. Edam
12. Emmenthal
13. Excelsior
14. Fromage blanc
15. Gouda
16. Gruyère
17. Monsieur
18. Petit Suisse
19. Pont l'Evêque
20. Port Salut
21. Reblochon
22. Roquefort

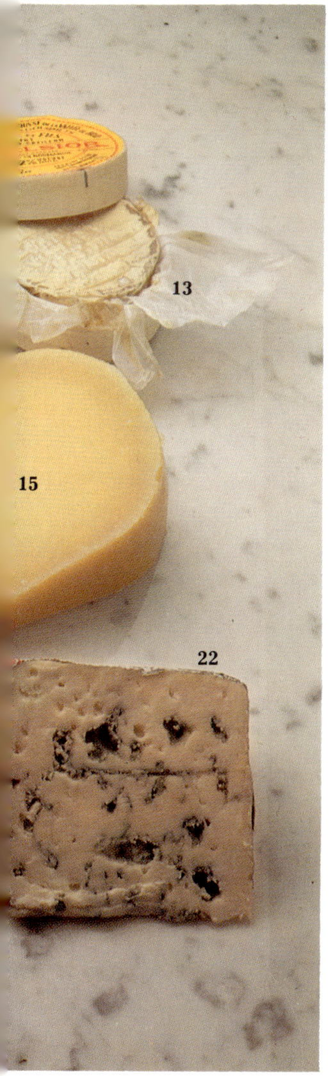

CHOCOLAT MENIER
CHOCOLATE
MEDAILLES
DIPLOMES D'HONNEUR
CHOCOLATE
FOR COOKING AND EATING
CHOCOLAT MENIER

Crèmes, crêpes, compôtes and entremets

Pudding is a word that has no equivalent either in the French language, or in French menus. If a sweet course is served at all, the place of the pudding is taken by cold confections of the egg-and-milk variety, or *compôtes* of fruit poached in syrup, and on special occasions by fruit tart or by cold *entremets* of great refinement. These, as their names indicate, were originally small sweet morsels, or even water ices, served between the many meat courses of court dinners to afford breathing space and stimulate the appetite.

With changing customs and fewer courses the *entremets* fell from favour and down to the end of the menu without changing its name or nature.

Crèmes

Crème anglaise à la vanille

TO SERVE SIX

INGREDIENTS
- 1 litre ($1\frac{3}{4}$ pints) full-cream milk
- 1 vanilla pod
- 100 g (4 oz) granulated sugar
- 4 egg yolks (size 2) plus 1 egg white
- pinch of salt

Crème anglaise is used both as a basic ingredient for many *entremets* and as a sweet sauce in place of cream.

Heat the milk, vanilla pod and sugar together in a medium-sized saucepan, stirring occasionally over a gentle heat until boiling point is reached and the sugar is dissolved. Allow to cool. Beat together the yolks and extra white with a pinch of salt and strain the milk into them through a fine sieve. Reserve the vanilla pod. Wash out the saucepan and rinse with cold water. Beat the egg/milk mixture for 2–3 minutes, strain it back into the pan, stand this in a *bain-marie* and place it over a medium heat. Keeping the water at simmering point, cook until the mixture coats the back of a wooden spoon. It must be stirred constantly but do not allow it to boil. When thick pour into a serving bowl and sprinkle the surface lightly with castor sugar to prevent a skin forming. Chill before serving.

When dried the vanilla pod can be wrapped in foil and used up to four times. After the first time it should be slit open and bent before use to increase the aroma.

As the *crème anglaise à la vanille* and many of the other *crèmes* use egg yolks only, *crème aux blancs d'oeufs* and *crème instantanée* are interesting ways of using up the egg whites instead of making meringues.

Crème à la vanille; crème aux blancs d'oeufs with langues de chat

Crème bachique

TO SERVE TWELVE ⚜

INGREDIENTS
- 575 ml (1 pint) sweet white wine (Sauternes preferably)
- 1 teaspoon finely chopped lemon peel
- 1 3-cm (1-in) cinnamon stick
- pinch of salt
- 16 egg yolks (size 3)
- 50 g (2 oz) castor sugar
- 150 ml ($\frac{1}{4}$ pint) sweet Sauternes
- 4 tablespoons brandy
- butter for coating the mould
- sugar for coating the mould
- 1 tablespoon each of chopped angelica, candied apricots, candied pineapple, candied orange peel, drained maraschino cherries
- 225 g (8 oz) strawberries
- 225 g (8 oz) raspberries
- a 1-litre (2-pint) fluted jelly mould

This recipe was popular with Parisian hostesses in Edwardian times and recalls the tenor of those days not only by its refinement but by the lavishness of its ingredients. It is a recipe for a very special occasion.

Heat the oven to 180°C, 350°F, Gas Mark 4. In an enamel-lined pan gently heat 575 ml (1 pint) of Sauternes with the chopped lemon peel, cinnamon and a pinch of salt. As boiling point is reached remove the pan from the heat and set it aside.

In a large bowl beat the egg yolks and sugar until the sugar is dissolved. Beat in the 150 ml ($\frac{1}{4}$ pint) of Sauternes and the unheated brandy. Strain the hot Sauternes through a fine sieve into this egg mixture and beat thoroughly with a wire whisk. Strain again.

Butter the mould and coat thickly with sugar. Spread the candied fruits over the sugar and pour in the mixture very carefully. Place the mould in a *bain-marie* and bake for 45–60 minutes or until the centre is firm. If it colours during cooking, cover with a sheet of foil. When cooked allow to cool completely and chill for at least 5 hours.

Shortly before serving crush the strawberries and raspberries with a fork, sprinkle with sugar, mix well, and set aside.

To unmould, loosen the sides of the mixture with a sharply pointed knife and placing the serving dish on top, gently invert, setting the dish down with a soft tap. Pour the fruit around it and serve immediately with a bottle of the same Sauternes as that used in the recipe.

Crème aux blancs d'oeufs

TO SERVE SIX

INGREDIENTS
- 500 ml (18 fl oz) milk
- 150 g (5 oz) castor sugar
- 10 egg whites
- 4–5 tablespoons Kirsch, Cointreau or brandy

Heat the milk and sugar in a very large pan, stirring occasionally until the milk boils and the sugar is dissolved. Remove from the heat to cool. Meanwhile beat the egg whites to a soft peak. Add the liqueur or brandy to the sweetened milk and fold in the egg whites with a wooden spatula. Return the pan to a low heat and cook for 15–20 minutes until very thick and light brown in colour. Pour into a deep serving dish and when quite cold place in the refrigerator for 1 hour before serving with *sacristans* (*see page* 200).

Crème au café

TO SERVE SIX

INGREDIENTS
500 ml (18 fl oz) milk
175 g (6 oz) granulated sugar
75 ml (3 fl oz) very strong black coffee
5 egg yolks (size 2)
pinch of salt
275 ml ($\frac{1}{2}$ pint) double cream

Boil the milk and sugar together, stirring occasionally until the sugar is dissolved, remove the pan from the heat and add the black coffee.

Beat the egg yolks in a large bowl with a pinch of salt and pour in the milk mixture. Beat thoroughly with a whisk. Wash out the pan and rinse with cold water and pour back the eggs and milk. Stand the pan in a *bain-marie* placed over a medium heat and stir the mixture with a wooden spoon until thick, keeping the water at simmering point. Do not allow it to boil fast or the *crème* will curdle. When thick remove from the heat and strain through a fine sieve into a bowl. When cold fold in the cream until thoroughly incorporated and pour into the serving dish. Chill for at least 1 hour before serving. Serve with *tuiles aux amandes* (*see page* 200).

Crème au chocolat

TO SERVE TWELVE

INGREDIENTS
225 g (8 oz) cooking chocolate
500 ml (18 fl oz) milk
8 egg yolks (size 3)
100 g (4 oz) granulated sugar
150 ml ($\frac{1}{4}$ pint) double cream

Preheat the oven to 180°C, 350°F, Gas Mark 4. Cut the chocolate into very small pieces and melt it in a saucepan without water and over a very gentle heat. When melted add the milk and bring to boiling point, whisking the chocolate into the milk until incorporated.

In a large bowl beat together the egg yolks, sugar and cream with a birch whisk. Continue beating for several minutes. Now add the boiling milk very gradually, stirring constantly. Pour into small 8-cm (3-in) diameter ramekins.

Half-fill a large roasting tin with hot water and place the ramekins in it, transfer to the oven and bake for 25 minutes or until the centre of the *crème au chocolat* is firm to the touch. Cool and chill lightly before serving. Serve with *cigarettes russes* (*see page* 200).

Crème aux noisettes

TO SERVE SIX

INGREDIENTS
75 g (3 oz) hazelnuts or almonds
1 litre ($1\frac{3}{4}$ pints) full-cream milk
200 g (7 oz) granulated sugar
1 teaspoon cornflour
6 egg yolks (size 2)
4 tablespoons bitter chocolate powder
4 dessertspoons instant coffee powder
100 ml (4 fl oz) double cream

Place the hazelnuts on a baking sheet and put under a hot grill until the brown skin is easily rubbed off between the fingers. Chop coarsely and set aside. If almonds are used, grill until lightly coloured and chop coarsely.

Boil the milk with half the sugar, stirring occasionally until the sugar is dissolved. In another pan put the rest of the sugar with two tablespoons of cold water and place over a medium heat until the sugar melts, bubbles and finally starts to turn colour. Do not stir but swirl this mixture round the pan until the sugar turns to caramel, and when nut colour immediately pour in the boiling milk, remove the pan from the heat and stir until the caramel has dissolved.

Stir the cornflour into the egg yolks and beat together until smooth, and when the milk is cool mix them together. Place the pan in a *bain-marie* half-full of simmering water and cook the mixture until it coats the back of a wooden spoon. It must be stirred constantly. When thick, remove the pan from the heat, stir in the chocolate and coffee powders, allow to cool a little and fold in the cream and nuts. Pour into a deep serving dish and chill well before serving. Serve with *langues de chat* (*see page* 200).

Crème au café, au chocolat, and aux noisettes with tuiles aux amandes

Crème instantanée

TO SERVE FOUR

INGREDIENTS
3 egg whites
3 tablespoons castor sugar
3 tablespoons apricot jam
1 desertspoon brandy

Beat the egg whites to a soft peak, add the sugar gradually and beat until a stiff peak is obtained. Mix the apricot jam and brandy and fold into the meringue with a wooden spatula until well incorporated. Heap into 4 tall glasses and serve immediately with *sacristans* (*see page* 200).

Crêpes aux bananes

Banana pancakes

TO MAKE TWELVE

INGREDIENTS

Pâte à crêpes

100 g (4 oz) flour
1 egg (size 2) plus 1 extra yolk
pinch of salt
1 teaspoon sugar
4 tablespoons milk
2 tablespoons cold water
2 tablespoons melted butter

Filling

6 bananas
175 g (6 oz) butter
3 tablespoons castor sugar
5 tablespoons rum

Sieve the flour into a mound in a mixing bowl and make a well in the centre. Break the egg into it, add the extra yolk and a pinch of salt and the sugar and mix with a wire whisk. Add the milk and cold water to form a very fluid batter. Melt the butter and when liquid mix into the batter. Leave the mixture in a cool place for at least 1 hour before use; but the best results are obtained when it is left overnight. Heat the oven to 200°C, 400°F, Gas Mark 6. Skin the bananas and halve them lengthways. Melt 100 g (4 oz) butter in a frying pan and when foaming cook over a low heat until they start to soften. Do not allow the butter to colour deeply. Sprinkle with sugar and 3 tablespoons rum and put the pan into the oven. Baste from time to time until the fruit is caramelized and browned.

Stir the batter well before use, and if it has thickened while standing add a further 2 or 3 tablespoons cold water. The pancakes must be very thin, therefore the batter must be almost as liquid as water.

Heat a small frying pan (16–18 cm or 6–7 in diameter base) over a medium heat, wipe it round with a buttered paper, and pour a large tablespoon of batter into it, quickly turning the pan so that the mixture runs evenly over the bottom. Cook for 1 minute, shaking the pan to loosen the pancake, turn it over and cook the other side for 1 minute. When ready place each pancake between two soup plates over a pan of simmering water until the batter is all made up. Wrap each half banana in a pancake and arrange side by side in a buttered gratin dish. Dot with flecks of butter and sprinkle with sugar and the rest of the rum. Bake for 10 minutes and serve immediately. The pancakes may be served *flambéed* if desired. Heat 2 tablespoons of rum in a small jug placed in a *bain-marie*, pour over the pancakes at table, ignite and baste until the flames die away.

Crêpes aux bananes

Crêpes fourrées

TO MAKE TWELVE

INGREDIENTS
100 g (4 oz) flour
1 large egg plus 1 extra yolk
pinch of salt
1 teaspoon sugar
4 tablespoons milk
2 tablespoons cold water
2 tablespoons melted butter

Filling
crème pâtissière (*page* 197)
2 tablespoons Curaçao, Chartreuse verte or Kirsch

Sieve the flour into a mound in a mixing bowl and make a well in the centre. Break the egg into it, add the yolk and a pinch of salt and the sugar and mix with a wire whisk, adding the milk and the cold water to form a very fluid batter. Melt the butter and when liquid mix into the batter. Leave the mixture in a cool place for at least 1 hour before use but the best results are obtained when it is left overnight.

Stir the batter well before use, and if it has thickened while standing, add a further 2-3 tablespoons of cold water. The pancakes must be very thin, therefore the batter must be almost as liquid as water.

Heat a small frying pan over a medium heat, wipe it round with a buttered paper and pour a large tablespoon of batter into it, quickly turning the pan so that the mixture runs evenly over the bottom. Cook for 1 minute, shaking the pan to loosen the pancake, turn it over and cook the other side for 1 minute. When ready, place the pancake between two soup plates over a pan of simmering water until the batter is all made up.

Heat the oven to 200°C, 400°F, Gas Mark 6. Stir the liqueur into the *crème pâtissière* while it is still warm and leave to cool. Spread 2 tablespoons of this mixture in a thick strip on one half of each pancake, roll it up and place them side by side in a buttered gratin dish, sprinkle with sugar and reheat for 10 minutes in the oven. Serve without delay.

Compôtes

INGREDIENTS
to each 450 g (1 lb) fruit allow:
- 175 g (6 oz) granulated sugar
- 350 ml (12 fl oz) water
- flavouring (*see below*)

The French method of cooking fresh fruit produces the fruit at its best, both in flavour and appearance.

Apples and pears should be peeled, cored and either left whole or cut into halves or thick rings. Stone fruit such as apricots, peaches, plums, greengages, etc., should be wiped with a damp cloth, halved and stoned, or pricked at each end with a sharply pointed knife. Gooseberries should be washed, topped and tailed, then pricked and left whole.

Put the sugar and water into a pan (large enough to allow the fruit to rest on the bottom in one layer). Add the flavouring and bring slowly to simmering point over a gentle heat. Stir occasionally until the sugar has dissolved and the syrup boils and then put the fruit into the pan. When the liquid starts to simmer again cook slowly, without a lid, until the fruit is not quite tender when pierced with a knife point. Remove the pan from the heat, cover immediately and leave until cool. Serve warm in winter or slightly chilled (but not iced) in summer.

Raspberries and strawberries, after being placed in the boiling syrup, should be removed from the heat as soon as boiling point has been fully re-established. Swirl the pan around to cover the fruit with syrup and allow to cool without covering.

When cooking rhubarb in the French manner cut it into short lengths, add the fruit to the boiling syrup, and as the liquid starts to simmer steadily again, remove the pan from the heat, cover and leave until cold. The fruit will then remain whole.

To cook fruit in the oven
Heat the oven to 160°C, 325°F, Gas Mark 3. When fruit is cooked in the oven, make the syrup in a pan and when boiling pour it over the prepared fruit arranged in one layer in an ovenproof dish, cover and place in the oven. After about 10 minutes, when the syrup simmers again, cook for 5 minutes, turn off the oven and leave the door ajar. Leave the *compôte* until cold. Rhubarb must be removed from the oven when the syrup simmers again, and left uncovered to cool.

Flavourings
These are to be added to the sugar and water before cooking.
1. Apples may be flavoured with a vanilla pod, or with the strained juice of a lemon.
2. Gooseberries gain greatly in flavour when a large head of elder flower is cooked in the syrup.
3. Pears flavoured with 2 bayleaves have a delicious aroma and a pleasant pinkish tone. They can also be cooked using half red wine and half water to make the syrup and flavoured with a vanilla pod.
4. Prunes can also be treated in the same way as pears but flavoured with a short length of cinnamon stick or the thinly peeled zest of a lemon.
5. Rhubarb loses its astringency when cooked with the juice of a lemon and its zest added to the syrup.

Compôte d'hiver

TO SERVE SIX

INGREDIENTS
- 450 g (1 lb) dried apricots, peaches, pears and prunes, mixed
- 3 large oranges
- 3 large bananas
- juice of 1 lemon
- 1 tablespoon dark brown sugar

This simple dish is much appreciated when presented at the end of a dinner when duck, game or any rich meat course has been served.

Place the dried fruit in one layer in a large ovenproof dish. Squeeze and strain the orange juice and pour over the dried fruit. Cover with foil and leave overnight.

Heat the oven to 180°C, 350°F, Gas Mark 4. When ready to cook add a little cold water, just sufficient to barely cover the fruit. Peel and halve the bananas lengthways and turn them in the lemon juice to prevent them from discolouring. Arrange them in between the other fruit, sprinkle with the lemon juice and sugar, cover again with foil and bake for 1 hour. Serve warm.

Compôte (rhubarb); compôte d'hiver

Abricots fourrés

TO SERVE TEN

INGREDIENTS
- 450 g (1 lb) fresh ripe apricots or large dried ones
- 1 tablespoon lemon juice
- 225 g (8 oz) soft dark brown sugar
- 100 g (4 oz) pine kernels
- 225 g (8 oz) ground almonds
- 4 tablespoons Madeira
- 4 egg whites (size 2)
- $\frac{3}{4}$ teaspoon cream of tartar
- *crème anglaise à la vanille* (*page* 182)

This more elaborate recipe for cooking fruit makes a delectable sweet course for a dinner party after a plain roast-meat course. The large semi-dried apricots which need not be soaked are sold in Italian delicatessen shops. These are recommended for this recipe if fresh ones are not in season.

Wash and halve the fresh apricots and remove the stone with a sharply pointed knife. If dried ones are used, soak in warm water to cover until plump. Drain and discard the water.

Put the fruit in a large pan, spread out in one layer, add the lemon juice, cover and cook over a very low heat until the juice flows. Add 175 g (6 oz) of sugar, stir carefully until dissolved, cover and poach gently for 40 minutes. Remove the pan from the heat and allow apricots to cool.

Heat the oven to 150°C, 300°F, Gas Mark 2. Coarsely chop the pine kernels and mix them with the remaining sugar and half the ground almonds. Moisten with the Madeira and mix to a soft paste.

Drain the apricots and reserve the syrup. Arrange the fruit hollow side up in a large ovenproof dish in one layer. Fill with the nut paste, sprinkle with the rest of the ground almonds and the syrup. Beat the egg whites with the cream of tartar until stiff and glossy and spread over the fruit covering the surface completely and touching the sides of the dish. Bake for about 45 minutes or until the meringue is firm and set and lightly coloured. Serve immediately with the chilled *crème anglaise*.

Bavarois praliné

TO SERVE SIX

INGREDIENTS

Praline

almond oil
75 g (3 oz) granulated sugar
1 tablespoon cold water
75 g (3 oz) coarsely chopped almonds

Crème anglaise

350 ml (12 fl oz) milk
1 vanilla pod
pinch of salt
50 g (2 oz) sugar
3 egg yolks (size 2)
1 level teaspoon gelatine
1 level teaspoon cold water
250 ml (9 fl oz) double cream
3 tablespoons Kirsch

To make the praline

Brush a baking sheet or marble slab with almond oil. Melt 75 g (3 oz) sugar with a tablespoon of cold water in a saucepan over a medium heat. When it bubbles add the almonds, and watching carefully, cook until medium gold in colour. Then remove from the heat and swirl the mixture round the pan as the colour deepens and pour evenly on to the prepared oiled surface to cool. When cold remove with a sharp knife and crush in a mortar.

To prepare the crème anglaise

Heat the milk, vanilla pod, salt and sugar together in a medium-sized saucepan, stirring occasionally over a gentle heat until boiling point is reached and the sugar dissolved. Allow to cool. Beat together the egg yolks with a pinch of salt and strain the milk into them through a fine nylon sieve.

Reserve the vanilla pod (*see page* 182). Wash out the saucepan and rinse in cold water. Beat the egg and milk mixture together for 2–3 minutes and strain it back into the pan. Stand this in a *bain-marie* half-full of hot water and place it over a medium heat. Keeping the water at simmering point, cook the mixture until it coats the back of a wooden spoon. It must be stirred constantly but do not allow it to boil. Leave to cool a little and then stir in the gelatine dissolved in cold water. Strain through a fine sieve and leave to cool further. If the double cream is too liquid beat until fairly thick. Brush the mould with almond oil and set aside. When the *crème anglaise* is cold beat in the Kirsch, the whipped cream and the praline and pour into the mould. Freeze for 3 hours before serving.

Diplomate

TO SERVE TWELVE

INGREDIENTS
crème anglaise (*page* 192) made from 725 ml ($1\frac{1}{2}$ pints) milk, vanilla pod, 4 tablespoons granulated sugar, 6 egg yolks (size 4), and salt
50 g (2 oz) seedless raisins
25 g (1 oz) currants
4 tablespoons brandy, rum or Kirsch
275 ml (10 oz) boudoir biscuits
4–5 tablespoons redcurrant jelly
1 tablespoon each of angelica, orange peel, lemon peel, all chopped
1 tablespoon lemon juice
a $1\frac{1}{2}$-litre ($2\frac{1}{4}$-pint) charlotte mould

Make the *crème anglaise* (*see page* 192) and set aside to cool. Put the raisins and currants to soak in a little warm water. Cover the bottom of the mould with a circle of greaseproof paper. Pour 1 tablespoon of liqueur into a saucer, add an equal quantity of water and dip the biscuits *very lightly* into it before lining the bottom and sides of the mould with the biscuits, placed closely together. Dip the biscuits in the liqueur just to flavour them, not to soak or even wet them.

Drain the currants and raisins. Cover the biscuits in the bottom of the mould with successive layers of lightly spread redcurrant jelly, raisins, currants and candied fruit before adding another layer of *lightly* flavoured biscuits and so on until the mould is full, ending with a layer of biscuits. Measure out a quarter of the *crème anglaise*, add to it the rest of the liqueur and the lemon juice, mix well and pour this over the contents of the mould to fill it. Cover with a saucer slightly smaller than the diameter of the mould and placed rounded side down, add a weight and refrigerate for 12 hours.

To serve, pass a thin knife blade down the sides of the mould in several places, place the serving dish on top, invert and leave to unmould by itself. Mask with a little chilled *crème anglaise* and serve the remainder separately.

Bavarois praliné; diplomate with crème anglaise

Strasbourgeois

TO SERVE TWELVE

INGREDIENTS

Crème anglaise (unsweetened)

500 ml (18 fl oz) milk
1 vanilla pod
pinch of salt
6 egg yolks (size 4)

Strasbourgeois

2 teaspoons instant coffee
225 g (8 oz) unsalted butter
225 g (8 oz) granulated sugar
225 g (8 oz) ground almonds
3 tablespoons Kirsch or brandy
almond oil for brushing
225 g (8 oz) boudoir biscuits
crème anglaise à la vanille for serving (*page* 182)
a 1½-litre (2¼-pint) metal charlotte mould

As there are two quantities of *crème anglaise* to be made, the sweetened one for serving can be made well in advance (*see page* 182) and left to chill until required. The unsweetened one is used in making the *strasbourgeois* itself which is also prepared 24 hours before serving.

To make the crème anglaise

Heat the milk, vanilla pod and salt together in a medium-sized saucepan, stirring occasionally over a gentle heat until boiling point is reached and the salt dissolved. Allow to cool. Beat together the egg yolks with a pinch of salt and strain the milk into them through a fine sieve.

Reserve the vanilla pod (*see page* 182). Wash out the saucepan and rinse in cold water. Beat the egg and milk mixture together for 2–3 minutes and strain it back into the pan. Stand this in a *bain-marie* half-full of hot water and place it over a medium heat. Keeping the water at simmering point, cook the mixture until it coats the back of a wooden spoon. It must be stirred constantly but do not allow it to boil. Leave to cool a little.

To make the strasbourgeois

Dissolve the coffee in 2 tablespoons hot water and set aside. Cut the butter into small pieces, place in a warmed bowl and beat to a soft cream. Add the sugar and continue beating until smooth. Add the tepid *crème anglaise*, the ground almonds and coffee. Mix the liqueur with 1 tablespoon cold water.

Brush the mould over with a thin film of almond oil and closely line the base and sides with biscuits dipped *very lightly* into the liqueur. They must not be wet. Carefully pour in the prepared *crème anglaise* and refrigerate for 24 hours.

To serve, dip the mould into a bowl of cold water for a few seconds, dry well, loosen the contents around the sides with the point of a sharp knife, place the serving dish on top, invert and set down with a sharp tap. Mask with a little of the *crème anglaise à la vanille* and pour the rest around the *strasbourgeois*. Serve immediately with a sweet dessert wine.

Sorbet aux pêches

Peach sorbet

TO SERVE SIX

INGREDIENTS
450 g (1 lb) ripe peaches
2 ripe apricots
275 g (10 oz) sugar
2 tablespoons lemon juice
4 ripe peaches
150 g (5 oz) sugar
6 tablespoons cold water
Maraschino (optional)

Stone the 450 g (1 lb) of peaches and the apricots, cut into pieces and pass through a mouli-légumes. Add the first quantity of sugar and sufficient cold water to measure 1 litre ($1\frac{3}{4}$ pints). Stir until the sugar is dissolved. Work through a fine sieve with a wooden spoon and add the lemon juice to the purée obtained. Pour into a freezer container and freeze for 40 minutes. Remove, whip thoroughly with a silver fork (or a wooden one) and freeze for 6 hours.

Meanwhile, scald the 4 peaches with boiling water, plunge into cold water and skin them. Cut each one into 6 sections and set them aside.

Pour the second quantity of sugar into a wide-based pan, add the cold water and cook over a gentle heat until the sugar dissolves and the syrup starts to thicken. Place the peach sections in the pan, bring the syrup back to boiling point, remove the pan from the heat and leave to cool completely. Remove the fruit with a slotted spoon and divide between 6 tall glasses. Put into a cool place. Reduce the syrup by simmering until just enough remains to barely cover the fruit in the glasses. Keep cool.

To serve add a coffeespoon of Maraschino to each glass and place a scoopful of sorbet on top of the peaches. Serve immediately with either *cigarettes russes* or *langues de chat* (*see page* 200).

Sorbet de fraises et de framboises

Strawberry and raspberry sorbet

TO SERVE SIX

INGREDIENTS
450 g (1 lb) strawberries
450 g (1 lb) raspberries
200 g (7 oz) sugar
275 ml ($\frac{1}{2}$ pint) water (only if using fresh fruit)
juice of 2 lemons

Hull the fruit, liquidize or mash it and pass through a fine sieve to remove pips. Beat in the sugar until dissolved, add water and strained lemon juice and pour into a freezing container. Freeze for 40 minutes.

Remove and beat with a silver fork (or a wooden one) and freeze again for 4 hours. Serve in tall glasses with *cigarettes russes* (*see page* 200).

Sorbet aux pêches; sorbet de fraises et framboises with cigarettes russes

Gâteaux, petits gâteaux and tarts

Elaborate gâteaux are a treat served in France on special occasions, and particularly at christenings, first communions, engagements and wedding celebrations. *Petits gâteaux*, or biscuits of a rather special kind are served with the various dessert creams described in the previous chapter, and fruit tarts are served nearly always after Sunday lunch, but all of them have one thing in common. They are light, delicately flavoured and served in small quantities. As in music, the sweet high note that finishes a gastronomic symphony must be played with a delicate touch.

Gâteaux

Top : Paris–Brest;
bottom : choux au Cointreau

Paris-Brest

TO SERVE SIX

INGREDIENTS
Pâte à chou
75 g (3 oz) flour
150 ml (¼ pint) water
pinch of salt
50 g (2 oz) butter
25 g (1 oz) slivered almonds
3 eggs (size 3)
Filling
2 egg whites (size 3)
75 ml (3 fl oz) water
100 g (4 oz) sugar
100 g (4 oz) unsalted butter
50 g (2 oz) praline (*page* 190)
3 boudoir biscuits
3 tablespoons rum
icing sugar

To make the chou paste

Heat the oven to 220°C, 425°F, Gas Mark 7. Sieve the flour on to a folded paper and set aside.

Pour the water into a small saucepan placed over a medium heat, add a pinch of salt and the butter, cut into small pieces. When the water boils and the butter melts, remove from the heat, add the flour all at once and stir vigorously with a wooden spoon until smooth. Return to the heat and continue working the mixture until it leaves the surfaces of the pan clean. Add one egg and beat thoroughly before adding the second. Beat the third separately in a small bowl and add half, reserving the rest for glazing. Work the mixture very thoroughly and when supple and glossy allow to rest for 20 minutes. With a round icing nozzle, pipe the paste into a ring 22 cm (8½ in) in diameter on to a buttered baking sheet, brush with the remaining beaten egg and sprinkle with the almonds. Bake for about 15–20 minutes or until well risen and firm to touch. Cool on a wire rack.

To make the filling

Beat the egg whites to a stiff peak. Simmer the water and sugar in a small saucepan until a thick syrup forms—220°F on a sugar thermometer or to the stage when a fork dipped into it and held up, forms a thread. Slowly drip the boiling syrup into the egg whites, beating constantly as if making mayonnaise. Beat vigorously until the mixture is cold.

Cream the butter in a warm bowl until soft, add the crushed praline, mix well and fold in the cold egg white and syrup. Cut the *chou* ring through horizontally and pipe half the cream onto the bottom crust, using a plain round icing nozzle. Dip the biscuits into the rum and crumble them over the cream.

Cover the biscuits with the remaining cream piped into loops through a fluted nozzle. Cover with the other half of the *chou* ring and dust with icing sugar.

Choux au Cointreau

TO SERVE SIX

INGREDIENTS
Pâte à chou
150 g (5 oz) flour
275 ml (½ pint) cold water (less 2 dessertspoons)
pinch of salt
75 g (3 oz) butter
¼ teaspoon sugar
4–5 eggs (size 4)
Crème pâtissière au Cointreau
4 egg yolks (size 2)
100 g (4 oz) castor sugar
40 g (1½ oz) flour
½ litre (18 fl oz) milk
4–5 tablespoons Cointreau
icing sugar

To make the choux

Sieve the flour on to a folded paper and set aside. Put the water, salt, butter, and sugar into a heavy pan over a medium heat and bring to boiling point. When the butter has melted draw the pan from the heat, pour in the flour all at once and stir vigorously with a wooden spatula. Work the paste thoroughly until smooth, then return the pan to the heat, working until all moisture has evaporated and the mixture leaves the surfaces of the pan clean. The drier the paste the more eggs are required, the more eggs used the lighter the *choux*.

Add the eggs one at a time, working the mixture thoroughly in between each one. Beat the last egg separately in a small bowl and add it gradually to avoid making the mixture too liquid. When finished it should be thick, supple and glossy. Leave to rest for 20 minutes.

Heat the oven to 220°C, 425°F, Gas Mark 7. Butter and flour a baking sheet and drop onto it small knobs of paste the size of a walnut, and well spaced out. Bake for about 10–15 minutes or until well risen and firm to touch. Cool on a wire rack.

To make the filling

When cold make a slit along the side of each *chou* near the top and fill with the following mixture: In a large bowl beat the egg yolks, sugar and flour until smooth. Add the milk, stir and strain through a fine sieve into a heavy-based pan. Place over a medium heat and stir until the mixture thickens, which it will do rapidly so it must be watched carefully.

As it contains flour this cream can be simmered gently without the yolks coagulating. Cook gently until very thick, stirring all the time. Remove from the heat, stir in Cointreau to taste and cool completely before filling the *choux*.

Fill the choux with *crème pâtissière* using a round icing nozzle and dust with icing sugar before serving.

If a soft icing is preferred to plain icing sugar, mix the sugar with sufficient Cointreau to form a thick cream consistency and smooth it over the top of the *choux*, using a knife blade occasionally dipped in water. If preferred Grand Marnier, Curaçao or Kirsch can be used instead of Cointreau.

Crème frangipane

This filling is made by adding 50 g (2 oz) of ground almonds to the above recipe whilst the mixture is still hot and omitting the Cointreau.

Moka

TO SERVE SIX

INGREDIENTS

Génoise

4 eggs (size 2)
225 g (8 oz) castor sugar
225 g (8 oz) flour
15 g ($\frac{1}{2}$ oz) butter
20-cm (8-in) diameter sponge tin

Sirop au café

100 g (4 oz) granulated sugar
75 ml (3 fl oz) water
2 tablespoons very strong black coffee or extract
2 tablespoons rum

Crème au beurre

150 g (5 oz) granulated sugar
75 ml (3 fl oz) water
2 egg whites (size 2)
225 g (8 oz) unsalted butter
10 g ($\frac{1}{3}$ oz) vanilla sugar (*page* 217)
coffee essence
50 g (2 oz) grilled almonds

To make the génoise cake

Heat the oven to 160°C, 325°F, Gas Mark 3. Set a *bain-marie* of warm water over a low heat so that the water does not boil. Break the eggs into a bowl, add the sugar and place in the *bain-marie*. Beat with a wire whisk until double in volume and warm to the touch. Remove from the *bain-marie* and beat until cold.

Beat in the sifted flour and when smooth pour into the buttered tin. Bake for 18–20 minutes before opening the oven door. Test with a pointed knife blade which should come out clean. Remove from the tin and cool on a wire rack.

To make the sirop au café

Boil the sugar and water together over a medium heat for 5 minutes after boiling point is reached. Allow to cool a little before adding the coffee and rum.

To make the crème au beurre

Cook the granulated sugar and water until the syrup formed registers 220° on a sugar thermometer (or test by dropping a little of the syrup into cold water, a soft ball should form when rolled between the fingers).

Beat the whites to a stiff peak, slowly add the boiling syrup in a fine stream (as though making mayonnaise) beating constantly. Beat until the mixture is cold.

Soften the butter in a warm bowl until creamy, work in the vanilla sugar and fold in the egg whites. Add a few drops of coffee essence to colour.

Cut the *génoise* across horizontally and sprinkle the cut surfaces with the *sirop au café*. Spread the bottom half liberally with the *crème au beurre* and place the other half on top. Using a metal spatula dipped occasionally in water spread the side and top of the cake with the butter cream, reserving a little for decoration. Coarsely chop the grilled almonds and press them thickly around the sides of the cake. Pipe the remaining cream with a fluted nozzle into a design on top. Chill lightly for 12 hours before serving.

Dominique's gâteau au chocolat

TO SERVE SIX

INGREDIENTS
- 175 g (6 oz) plain dark chocolate
- 75 g (3 oz) almonds
- 175 g (6 oz) unsalted butter
- 4 eggs (size 2), separated
- 175 g (6 oz) sugar
- 75 g (3 oz) flour
- 1½ teaspoons baking powder
- 25 g (1 oz) blanched whole almonds
- icing sugar
- 20-cm (8-in) square cake tin

Heat the oven to 190°C, 375°F, Gas Mark 5. Break up the chocolate into pieces, place in a small bowl, standing in a *bain-marie* of hot water to melt.

Chop the almonds, medium fine. Melt the butter and beat into the egg yolks until creamy, add sugar and continue beating until dissolved. Sift the flour and baking powder together and add them to the egg mixture, beating until smooth. Add the melted chocolate and the chopped almonds, working them in thoroughly. Beat the egg whites to a stiff peak and *fold* them into the chocolate mixture carefully with a wooden spatula (*see page* 60). Do not stir them in.

Pour the mixture into the buttered and floured tin, smoothing the mixture slightly upwards towards the sides with a palette knife to ensure an even surface when baked. Bake for 45–50 minutes or until the centre is just firm to the touch and a metal skewer plunged into the centre comes out clean. Cool on a wire rack.

Split the blanched almonds into halves and cut each one into strips. Spike the surface of the cake with them and dust with icing sugar.

Cigarettes russes

INGREDIENTS
150 g (5 oz) unsalted butter
300 g (10 oz) vanilla sugar (*page* 217)
175 g (6 oz) flour
6 egg whites (size 3)
1 tablespoon double cream

The very thin crisp biscuits served in France with *crème au chocolat* and *crème au cafè* (*see page* 184) are also served with sweet dessert or sparkling wines. They are quickly made and keep well when stored in an airtight tin.

Make sure that all the ingredients are at room temperature, including the egg whites. Lightly butter a baking sheet.

Work the butter and sugar together in a warm bowl with a slotted spoon until creamy. Sieve the flour. Add the unbeaten egg whites, two by two. Beat the mixture well between each addition and continue beating, while adding the cream and lastly the flour. When the mixture is quite smooth, pipe small round discs about 2 cm (¾ in) in diameter and widely spaced on to the baking sheet. Bake for about 4 minutes until the large thin circles formed are lightly browned.

Quickly remove them from the tray with a sharp knife and wrap around a pencil or wooden spoon handle. Cool on a wire rack.

Langues de chat

INGREDIENTS
100 g (4 oz) butter
100 g (4 oz) castor sugar
100 g (4 oz) flour
2 egg whites (size 2)
10 g (⅓ oz) vanilla sugar (*page* 217)

Special baking tins for making *langues de chat* can be bought from most kitchen equipment shops but an éclair tin will give the traditional cat's tongue shape if only half filled with the mixture.

Heat the oven to 200°C, 400°F, Gas Mark 6. Lightly butter and flour a baking sheet.

Warm the butter in a bowl and beat until creamy. Add the sugar, beating constantly with a whisk, and then add the sifted flour. Beat the whites in a separate bowl until a soft peak forms and fold them into the sugar and butter mixture. Using a small round icing nozzle, pipe narrow 6-cm (2½-in) lengths on to the baking sheet, spacing them well apart to allow for spreading. Bake for 6–8 minutes. When they are cooked only the edges should be coloured. Cool on a wire rack.

Sacristans

INGREDIENTS
butter for the baking tin
375-g (13-oz) packet frozen flaky pastry
1 egg (size 2)
100 g (4 oz) finely chopped almonds
about 4 tablespoons castor sugar

Heat the oven to 220°C, 425°F, Gas Mark 7. Lightly butter a large baking sheet. Roll out the pastry into a rectangle 4 mm (⅛ in) thick. Brush lavishly with beaten egg and sprinkle liberally with sugar and chopped almonds. Cut down the length into two bands, each about 9 cm (3½ in) wide. Place one on top of the other, with the sugared side uppermost. Straighten the sides with a palette knife and cut into strips 1 cm (½ in) wide.

Pick up each one between the forefingers and thumbs of both hands, twist in opposite directions and place on the baking tin, pressing down the ends to stick the strip on to it.

Bake for 8–10 minutes until puffed, browned and caramelized on the edges. Cool on a wire rack. These *petits gâteaux* are best eaten fresh or within 2–3 days of baking. During this time store in an airtight tin.

Tuiles aux amandes

INGREDIENTS
75 g (3 oz) unsalted butter
100 g (4 oz) castor sugar
40 g (1½ oz) flour
juice and grated rind of ½ an orange
200 g (7 oz) slivered almonds

Heat the oven to 200°C, 400°F, Gas Mark 6. Butter a baking sheet. Place the butter, cut into small pieces, in a warm bowl. Work with a slotted spoon until creamy, add the sugar and work it until dissolved. Sift in the flour, and beat it in, add orange juice and rind and continue beating until smooth. Roughly chop the almonds and stir them in.

Drop teaspoons of the mixture on to the baking sheet. Leave them widely spaced as they will spread. Bake for about 4–5 minutes until the rim turns biscuit colour. Remove immediately from the sheet with a sharp knife and curl over a rolling pin to shape. Remove when cool and place on a wire rack until quite cold. These biscuits are very fragile and will only curl while hot. Store in an airtight tin.

Top: cigarettes russes; langues de chat; *bottom:* sacristans; tuiles aux amandes

Tarts

The bottom crust of a fruit tart has proved to be the Waterloo of many budding pastry-cooks, but each country has its method of combating the menace of a damp, half-cooked undercrust. Americans sprinkle it generously with equal quantities of flour and sugar before filling with fruit, English cooks brush it with unbeaten egg white but in French cooking the solution to the problem lies in the method by which the pastry itself is made.

The two pastries used for both sweet and savoury tarts are *pâte sucrée* (sugar pastry) and *pâte brisée* (short pastry).

All these amounts are sufficient for 25-cm (10-in) diameter tart tins with a loose base or 8 small ones 10-cm (4-in) in diameter.

Tarte aux cerises; tarte aux fraises

Pâte sucrée

Sugar pastry

INGREDIENTS
225 g (8 oz) flour
100 g (4 oz) butter cut into small pieces
75 g (3 oz) granulated sugar
pinch of salt
1 egg (size 3)

Sift the flour on to a folded paper and set aside. Drop the pieces of butter into a warm mixing bowl, add the sugar and a pinch of salt and work together with a wooden spatula until creamy. This pastry is not mixed with the fingertips. Break in the egg and work until smooth. Pour in the sifted flour and mix rapidly. Empty on to a floured board and work the ingredients together with one hand, gathering them up lightly with the fingers and pushing the mixture with the heel and palm of the hand to incorporate the flour (1). Do this only until a ball forms, about 4–5 times more.

Cut the pastry into 4 pieces, pile one on top of the other and push them down firmly together again (2). Do this 3 times. Leave the pastry to rest for 1 hour before use.

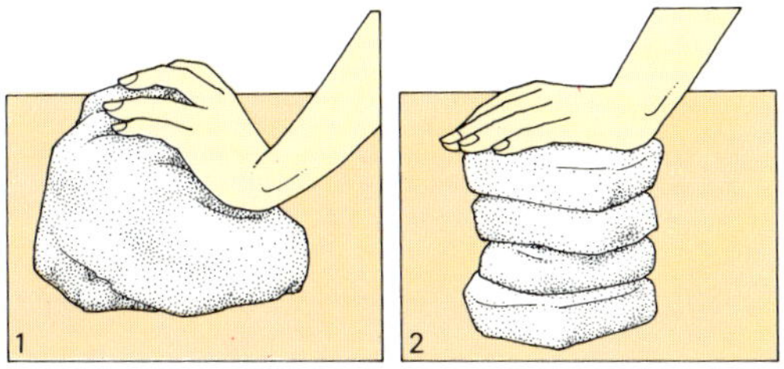

Tarte aux cerises

Cherry tart

TO SERVE SIX

INGREDIENTS
butter and flour for the baking tin
pâte sucrée (see above)
550 g ($1\frac{1}{4}$ lb) stoned cherries
100 g (4 oz) redcurrant jelly

Traditionally this tart is made with rather sour red cherries, and the contrast between their acidity and the sweetness of the jelly is a delicious finale to a rather rich dinner; alternatively firm black cherries can be used.

Heat the oven to 220°C, 425°F, Gas Mark 7 with a baking sheet inside. Lightly butter and flour the tart tin and set aside. Roll out the pastry on a floured greaseproof paper to a thickness of $\frac{1}{2}$ cm ($\frac{1}{4}$ in) and slide it into the tin. It will crumble but correct this by pressing the cracks together with the fingers. Trim off the pastry, leaving a rather thick edge and work this up a little between the fingers and thumb so that it stands $\frac{1}{2}$ cm ($\frac{1}{4}$ in) above the rim of the tin, keeping it as thick as possible. Prick the base evenly with a fork and chill for 30 minutes.

Beginning at the outside, fill the pastry with stoned cherries, arranging them in circles and crowding them together. Place on the baking sheet and bake for 20 minutes, then reduce the heat to 160°C, 325°F, Gas Mark 4 and cook for a further 20–25 minutes. Free the tart from the tin by pushing a sharply pointed knife down the sides, unmould and place on a wire rack. Melt the redcurrant jelly and when the tart is cold brush the fruit and pastry border liberally with it, pouring the remainder over the fruit.

Tarte aux framboises

Raspberry tart

TO SERVE SIX

INGREDIENTS
butter and flour for the baking tin
pâte sucrée (see above)
3 tablespoons redcurrant jelly
675 g ($1\frac{1}{2}$ lb) raspberries
icing sugar

Heat the oven to 200°C, 400°F, Gas Mark 6 with a baking sheet inside. Butter and flour the tin lightly and set aside.

Roll out the pastry on a floured greaseproof paper to $\frac{1}{2}$ cm ($\frac{1}{4}$ in) thick and slide it onto the tin. It will crumble but correct this by pressing the cracks together with the fingers. Prick the base with a fork, cover entirely with a circle of greaseproof paper, prick this too and fill with dried beans or peas. Place on the baking sheet and bake for about 15 minutes or until the pastry edge is firm enough not to fall inwards. If it has done so push it back into its original place.

Remove paper and beans and continue baking for a further 10 minutes without colouring any deeper than a medium biscuit colour. Cool for a few seconds, unmould and leave to cool completely.

Put the redcurrant jelly in a small bowl and stand it in a *bain-marie* to melt. To serve, brush the crust thickly with redcurrant jelly and fill with raspberries, closely arranged in circles beginning at the outside. Sprinkle the top liberally with icing sugar.

Tarte aux fraises (Strawberry tart)
Alternatively small strawberries can be used and, when arranged in the pie, glazed by brushing redcurrant jelly over them instead of sprinkling with icing sugar.

Pâte brisée

Short pastry

INGREDIENTS
100 g (4 oz) butter
225 g (8 oz) flour
1 egg yolk
pinch of salt
1 tablespoon cold water

Pâte brisée is used when making tarts with fruit of a very juicy nature such as plums. It is also used for savoury tarts, or *quiches*.

Soften the butter in a warm bowl and work to a cream. Sieve the flour into a mound, make a well in the centre and into it drop the yolk, salt and butter. Work them together with the fingers of one hand and when mixed gather in the flour, add a tablespoon of very cold water, and a second one if necessary, until a soft supple ball is formed. Put it immediately into the refrigerator to chill for 30 minutes.

Roll out the pastry, fold into four and roll out again. Chill again for 30 minutes before use.

Tarte aux pommes alsacienne

Alsatian apple tart

TO SERVE SIX

INGREDIENTS
pâte brisée (see above)
1 kg (2 lb) Cox's apples or other sweet apples
2 tablespoons granulated sugar
2 eggs (size 3)
75 g (3 oz) sugar
10 g ($\frac{1}{3}$ oz) vanilla sugar (*page* 217)
200 ml (7 fl oz) double cream

Heat the oven to 200°C, 400°F, Gas Mark 6. with a baking sheet inside.

Butter and flour the baking tin. Line the tin with the chilled *pâte brisée* and pass the rolling pin over the rim to trim off excess pastry. Chill again for 30 minutes.

Peel and core the apples and cut each one into 8 sections. Prick the bottom of the pastry evenly with a fork and fill the tin with apple sections, rounded side uppermost and in circles, working from the outside. Sprinkle lightly with sugar and bake for 30 minutes.

Meanwhile beat the eggs and both sugars together and stir in the cream until blended. Test the apples with a sharp-pointed knife and when just tender pour the flan mixture over them and cook until set, for about 10–15 minutes. Serve warm.

Polkas

TO MAKE TWELVE

INGREDIENTS
Pâte sucrée
225 g (8 oz) flour
100 g (4 oz) butter
75 g (3 oz) granulated sugar
2 pinches of salt
1 egg (size 3)
Pâte à chou
150 g (5 oz) flour
275 ml ($\frac{1}{2}$ pint) water (less 2 dessertspoons)
pinch of salt
75 g (3 oz) butter
$\frac{1}{4}$ teaspoon sugar
4/5 eggs (size 4)
Crème pâtissière
4 egg yolks (size 2)
100 g (4 oz) castor sugar
10 g ($\frac{1}{3}$ oz) vanilla sugar (*page* 217)
40 g ($1\frac{1}{2}$ oz) flour
500 ml (18 fl oz) milk
icing sugar and granulated sugar for decoration

This delectable cross between a tart and a *chou à la crème* combines *pâte sucrée*, *pâte à chou* and *crème pâtissière*. This delicious combination is called a *polka*, for no discoverable reason, and is a useful recipe for combining leftover quantities of any of these pastries. The quantities given here, however, start from scratch.

Make the *pâte sucrée* (*see page* 203) and leave in a cool place to rest for 30 minutes.

Make the *crème pâtissière* (*see page* 197) and leave to cool completely, then refrigerate until required.

Make the *pâte à chou* (*see page* 197) and set aside until needed.

Heat the oven to 200°C, 400°F, Gas Mark 6. Butter and lightly flour a baking sheet. Roll out the *pâte sucrée* and cut into 12 circles with an 8-cm (3-in) diameter fluted cutter. With a round icing nozzle pipe around the outside of each circle a ring of *pâte à chou* (the thickness of a little finger), leaving the centre clear. Cook for 20 minutes. During the last 10 minutes check to see that the surface colour is not colouring too fast. Cover lightly with foil if necessary. Cool on a wire rack.

To serve, dust each *polka* with icing sugar, fill the centre generously with *crème pâtissière* and carefully place a $\frac{1}{2}$ teaspoon of granulated sugar in a small heap in the centre. Hold a metal kitchen fork with an oven glove over a high gas flame or very hot electric ring and when extremely hot place the back and prongs of the fork on to the heap of granulated sugar. Leave it there long enough to caramelize and colour it golden brown.

SIROP DE
FRAISE
CREME DE CASSIS
DE DIJON

Jellies, jams, cordials, liqueurs and summer drinks

Gelée de groseilles à cru

Uncooked redcurrant jelly

INGREDIENTS
1.8 kg (4 lb) very ripe redcurrants
castor sugar

Certain jellies are important ingredients in French cooking, notably redcurrant jelly which is used in fruit tarts and also in the confection of more elaborate sweet dishes such as *diplomate* (*see page* 191). For these purposes an uncooked redcurrant jelly is preferred because it retains the full flavour of the ripe fruit. It is *essential* to use very ripe fruit for the uncooked method.

Do not wash the fruit but strip it from the stalks with the prongs of a fork into an earthenware bowl. Crush the grains gently with the end of a bottle, just enough to burst the skins, empty them into a jelly bag and allow to drip.

Weigh the juice and weigh out an equal quantity of castor sugar. Empty the juice into a wide, shallow earthenware bowl and add the sugar a little at a time, stirring constantly with a wooden spoon until it is completely dissolved. Pour into small jars immediately and seal. If the jars are small the jelly sets more easily.

Gelée de groseilles

Cooked redcurrant jelly

INGREDIENTS
1.8 kg (4 lb) redcurrants
75 ml (3 fl oz) water
1.8 kg (4 lb) granulated sugar
buttered paper

Quickly wash the redcurrants in a colander under running water and drain. There is no need to strip them from the stalk.

Put the fruit into a preserving pan with the water and place over a medium heat. Bring to boiling point, stirring occasionally. Remove from the heat, allow to cool and crush the fruit lightly with a wooden spoon. Empty into a jelly bag, hang it up and leave it to drain over a large bowl. If no jelly bag is available crush the fruit in a mouli-légumes and then drain through a fine nylon sieve, pressing out the juice with a wooden spoon.

Measure the juice and allow 1 kg (2 lb) sugar for 1 litre ($1\frac{3}{4}$ pints) juice. Lightly butter the inside of the preserving pan with a buttered paper (this reduces the scum) and empty in the juice and the sugar. Place over a gentle heat, stir to dissolve the sugar, and bring to boiling point. After boiling point is reached, boil for 5 minutes and test by dropping a few drops of jelly onto a cold plate. The surface should wrinkle when pushed with the finger. Leave to cool a little and then remove the scum with a slotted spoon or skimmer, and pour the jelly into small pots, filling them to the brim. The less air in the pots the better the contents will keep. Seal and leave for a minimum of 48 hours before use. Store in a cool place.

Gelée de groseilles (*left*) uncooked and (*right*) cooked

Confiture de framboises à cru

Uncooked raspberry jam

INGREDIENTS
1 kg (2 lb) ripe raspberries
1 kg (2 lb) castor sugar
1 teaspoon brandy or sherry

Heat the oven to 150°C, 300°F, Gas Mark 2. Hull the raspberries and place them in a wide earthenware bowl. Put the sugar into another bowl of the same size. Place both bowls in the oven and heat very slowly for about 20–30 minutes until both fruit and sugar are warm to the touch.

Remove from the oven and add the sugar to the fruit a little at a time, stirring carefully with a wooden spoon to dissolve the sugar without crushing the raspberries.

When the sugar is completely dissolved pour the jam into small pots and cover the surface with a disc of waxed paper dipped in brandy or sherry. Seal with jam covers. Stored in a dark cool place this jam will keep just as well as cooked jam while retaining the full fruit flavour.

Confiture de fraises

Strawberry jam

INGREDIENTS
1 kg (2 lb) strawberries
buttered paper
675 g ($1\frac{1}{2}$ lb) granulated sugar
juice of 1 lemon
1 teaspoon brandy or sherry

Do not wash the fruit, simply remove the hulls and wipe with a piece of damp kitchen paper. Butter the inside of the preserving pan very lightly with a buttered paper to reduce the scum, and place a single layer of strawberries in the bottom. Cover with a layer of sugar and continue layering the fruit and sugar, finishing with a layer of sugar. Cover and leave overnight.

By the next morning the sugar will have nearly all dissolved and made the juice flow freely from the fruit. Place the pan over a medium low heat and leave until the remaining sugar has dissolved. Shake the pan occasionally but do not stir as this damages the fruit. After 30 minutes increase the heat to medium high, add the strained lemon juice, shake the pan to distribute it and when rapid boiling point is reached cook for exactly 8 minutes, shaking the pan occasionally. Test by dripping a little of the syrup on to a cold plate. Allow to cool for 2–3 moments and if the surface wrinkles when pushed with the finger, the jam is cooked. If not, continue boiling for 3 minutes and test again, but do not overcook. Jam thickens as it sets.

Take the pan from the heat, remove the scum with a slotted spoon and leave for 30 minutes. Pour into small heated jars, cover the surface with a disc of waxed paper dipped in brandy or sherry and seal with jam covers. Store in a cool dry place.

Confiture de framboises à cru; confiture de fraises

Liqueurs, cordials and summer drinks

The pleasant informal habit of inviting friends after dinner for coffee, tisane, cakes and liqueurs still exists in France. In the provinces and the country the delectable liqueurs in question are very often home-made and are regarded as an aid to digestion. They are also used to flavour gâteaux, desserts, and even some savoury dishes. Fruit preserved in alcohol, and fruit cordials are also served and they occupy an important part of the country housewife's store cupboard. For the confection of some liqueurs and cordials wine is used and others are made with white eau-de-vie or white alcohol, also known as *alcool à fruits,* which varies in strength from 35 to 90° proof.

Cassis; Kir (in glass); Curaçao; vin à l'orange

Liqueur de cassis

INGREDIENTS
2 kg (4 lb) ripe blackcurrants
1 litre ($1\frac{3}{4}$ pints) 90° proof white alcohol
1 kg (2 lb) sugar
500 ml (18 fl oz) water

One of the best-known of these cordials is *liqueur de cassis* made from blackcurrants. It is used mainly for making a delicious, if heady, aperitif known as *Kir* and much appreciated in summer.

Strip the currants from the stalks with the prongs of a fork into a large wide-topped bowl. Crush gently with the end of a bottle until the skin bursts and pour the alcohol over them. Mix well and empty into a large glass jar with a well-fitting cork or ground-glass stopper. Place in a sunny window and leave for 8 days. Shake the bottle occasionally to mix the contents and give it a quarter turn each day so that all sides catch the sun.

Mix the sugar and water together and heat in a large pan over a gentle heat until boiling point is reached. Allow the syrup to bubble for 2–3 minutes and stir to make sure the sugar is completely dissolved. Leave until cold.

Pass the fruit and alcohol through a fine nylon sieve, pressing the blackcurrants with a wooden spoon to extract all the juice. Mix the juice with the syrup and pour back into the glass jar, seal well with wax and leave for a further 8 days. Filter through filter papers and bottle in 300-ml ($\frac{1}{2}$-pint) bottles. Leaving a half-empty bottle of alcohol after use causes the contents to deteriorate. It is therefore more economical to use the 300-ml ($\frac{1}{2}$-pint) size bottles which will make enough *Kir* for 6–8 people. Store in a cool dry place for 2 months before use.

To make Kir

Chill a bottle of dry white wine. Measure $1\frac{1}{2}$ tablespoons *liqueur de cassis* into each tall glass, three-quarters fill with chilled wine, stir well and serve immediately. A small ice cube may be added if desired.

Curaçao

INGREDIENTS
peel of 12–15 medium-sized oranges
1 litre ($1\frac{3}{4}$ pints) 65° proof rum
225 g (8 oz) sugar
275 ml ($\frac{1}{2}$ pint) water

Curaçao makes a delicious liqueur for a *diplomate* or *bavarois praliné* (*see pages* 190–191), or to serve after dinner with tisane or coffee.

Cut the peel of each orange into 8 sections and dry in the bottom of the oven until they are hard and brittle. Place in a wide-mouthed glass jar and add rum to cover. Add more dried peel or remove some to ensure that the quantity of rum used covers the peel. Cork tightly and leave on a sunny window sill for 6 weeks, turning the jar regularly to expose all sides to the sun.

Mix the sugar and water and heat in a large pan over a gentle heat until boiling point is reached. Allow the syrup to bubble for 3–4 minutes and stir to make quite sure the sugar is completely dissolved. Leave until cold. Strain the rum and orange peel through a nylon sieve and press the peel lightly with a wooden spoon before discarding it, mix with the syrup, filter through filter papers and bottle in small 300-ml ($\frac{1}{2}$-pint) bottles. Cork and seal tightly, and store in a cool dry place for 2 months before use.

Vin à l'orange

INGREDIENTS
6–8 thin-skinned oranges
1 bottle Muscadet, Vouvray, or Sancerre
150 g (5 oz) castor sugar
150 ml ($\frac{1}{4}$ pint) 65° proof rum

A less expensive cordial, just as delicious to serve after dinner as a digestive, is made with wine in the following way.

Wipe the oranges with a damp cloth, remove the peel in quarters and cut into strips as fine as possible—this is important. Measure out 150 ml ($\frac{1}{4}$ pint) wine from the bottle (this will not be needed). Push the orange peel down the neck with the handle of a wooden spoon. Add as many strips as possible until the wine reaches its full level. Cork tightly and leave on a sunny window sill for at least 3 months, turning the bottle regularly to expose all sides to the sun.

Empty out the wine and peel through a nylon sieve into a large earthenware bowl. Press the peel a little to extract all the wine and then discard the peel. Stir the sugar into the wine and continue stirring until it has completely dissolved. Add the rum, mix well and pour through filter papers. Bottle and cork tightly and leave to mature for 1 month before use. Serve in liqueur glasses.

Pruneaux au vin rouge

Prunes in red wine

INGREDIENTS

- 13–14° proof red wine (Côtes-du-Rhône or Beaujolais)
- 175 g (6 oz) sugar
- 2 vanilla pods
- 150 ml (¼ pint) 65° proof rum
- 625 g (1¼ lb) large Californian prunes

A pleasant tidbit to serve after dinner is made with prunes and red wine.

In a large enamel-lined pan heat the wine, sugar and vanilla pods, slit down the centre. Heat very gently until the surface of the wine gathers a faint froth. Remove the pan immediately from the heat, add the rum, stir well and remove the vanilla pods. Wash, dry and reserve for future use.

Pierce the prunes right through by drawing a larding needle from one end to the other but do not stone. Place them in a large glass jar and pour the warm wine over to cover. Leave until cold and seal the jar hermetically either with a large cork or a ground-glass stopper, sealed with wax. Leave for at least 1 month before use, but the longer the prunes are left to macerate the better.

Serve one prune stuck with a cocktail stick in a small glass with just enough wine to cover the fruit.

Punch au vin blanc

White wine punch

TO SERVE EIGHT

INGREDIENTS

- 1 litre (1¾ pints) chilled white wine (Riesling or Moselle)
- 2 lemons
- 225 g (8 oz) castor sugar
- 1 sherry glass Kirsch
- 1 large bottle chilled soda water

Pour the wine into a large porcelain bowl, add 1 lemon, cut into very thin slices, the sugar and the Kirsch. Stir thoroughly with a wooden spoon to dissolve the sugar and crush the lemon against the sides of the bowl to extract the juice and the essential oils.

Pass the punch through a fine nylon sieve, add the soda water and serve with a slice of lemon and an ice cube in each glass. This is a very good summer thirst-quencher.

Boisson d'après-dîner

Summer after-dinner drink

TO SERVE SIX

INGREDIENTS

- 1 lemon
- 1 kg (2 lb) ripe peaches
- ½ bottle iced dry white wine such as Vouvray or Muscadet
- ½ bottle iced champagne or sparkling Blanc de blanc

Peel the lemon in one thin spiral with a vegetable peeler and put it into a punch bowl or a large china bowl. Add the strained juice of half the lemon.

Skin the peaches either by pouring boiling water over them and then plunging them into cold water, or by stroking the surface of the skin firmly with the blunt side of a knife blade before peeling. Cut the fruit into small slivers and turn them over immediately in the lemon juice to prevent discolouration. Add the white wine, mix well, cover and place in the refrigerator until required. Do this at least 2 hours before serving.

When ready to serve, add the iced champagne, mix well and serve in wide-topped glasses.

Boisson d'été

Non-alcoholic raspberry drink

TO SERVE SIX

INGREDIENTS
225 g (8 oz) raspberries
100 g (4 oz) lump sugar
1 lemon
1 litre ($1\frac{3}{4}$ pints) boiling water
a few strawberries for garnishing

Crush the raspberries and mash them with a wooden spoon through a fine nylon sieve into a bowl, collecting both the juice and the purée. Rub the sugar lumps on to the lemon peel to extract the oil, then squeeze and strain the juice. Mix together the raspberry juice, purée, sugar and lemon juice in a china bowl and pour the boiling water over the mixture. Stir well to dissolve the sugar and leave in the refrigerator until well chilled.

Place two or three small strawberries in each glass and fill three-quarters full with the iced raspberry drink.

Orange et citronnade

Non-alcoholic orange and lemon drink

TO SERVE SIX

INGREDIENTS
175 g (6 oz) lump sugar
2 lemons
4 oranges
1 litre ($1\frac{3}{4}$ pints) cold boiled water

Take a quarter of the sugar lumps and rub them over the peel of the lemons to absorb the oil. Rub the rest over the orange peel. Dissolve all the sugar lumps in the boiled water.

Squeeze the juice from both oranges and lemons and cut up the squeezed peel and pulp into small pieces. Add them both to the sugared water and leave to macerate for 1 hour. Pick out the lemon peel and leave the orange for another 2–3 hours. Place in the refrigerator until required.

Strain through a nylon sieve and serve with small ice cube in each glass. Made in this way and kept covered in the refrigerator this fruit drink keeps its fresh flavour for several days.

Top: pruneaux au vin rouge; punch au vin blanc; boisson d'été; *bottom:* boisson d'après-diner; orange et citronnade

Herbs, seasonings, tisanes and flavoured vinegars

In a country like France where hot sun and, in some areas, poor soil and low rainfall provide the ideal conditions in which herbs flourish wild, it is a natural consequence that their use should become firmly established in the nation's cooking.

Even in the largest cities, greengrocers throughout France provide, according to season, a plentiful supply of the most frequently used fresh herbs; chives, chervil, basil, tarragon, thyme, rosemary and, of course, parsley are to be found fresh all through the year.

Unfortunately this is not a facility we share in Britain, but in a country of gardeners it is a lack that is easily filled. The fresh herbs most currently used in French cooking and tisanes can be grown successfully in pots and window boxes by those who have no gardens and the seeds obtained from most garden centres.

Herbs and seasonings

The herbs most used in traditional French recipes, and taken in order of importance, are the following:

Tarragon is used fresh in salads and sauces and with vegetables, fish, chicken and veal. It is also used for making tarragon vinegar.

Chives and garlic are of the onion family. Chives can therefore be replaced in most cases by using the green tops of spring onions for salads, vegetables and egg dishes. Garlic must be used sparingly so that its flavour does not dominate.

Dill and fennel are both of the aniseed family and are used mainly for flavouring fish dishes. Bulb or Florence fennel is also grown as a vegetable.

Basil is most effective when used fresh with tomatoes and in company with olive oil, peppers and garlic. It loses its pungency when dried.

Bouquet garni is used in soups and casseroles. It is usually composed of 2 stalks of fresh parsley, 1 small sprig of thyme (fresh or dried) and a bayleaf.

A fifteenth-century herb garden in France

Bouquet aromatique is used when a more delicate flavouring must be imparted to bland meats such as veal, poached white meats, calf's head and chicken. It is composed of 1 sprig of summer or winter savory, 1 small sprig of rosemary or marjoram (fresh or dried), 1 stalk of tarragon, 1 stalk of chervil, basil and celery.

Bay is always used sparingly either fresh or dried. One leaf is sufficient to flavour the average dish. It is a versatile herb used in both savoury dishes and sweet dishes such as cooked fruit.

Chervil and parsley are of the same family and are used as a seasoning. Chervil has the more distinctive flavour which warrants its use as the chief ingredient of a popular soup named after it.

Sorrel is important as a flavouring in omelettes and soups and also as a main ingredient.

Rosemary, thyme, marjoram and savory (summer and winter variety) are all pungent herbs widely used in pâtés, meat dishes, soups, and sauces. They are, however, used sparingly as their flavour is over-riding and tends to dominate.

Juniper berries are used dried to flavour pâtés and game dishes. They must be used with discretion for they are pungent.

Bergamot, camomile, lime and mint are used either fresh or dried for making tisane or herb tea (*see page* 218).

All dried herbs should be stored in dark glass bottles to exclude light and well stoppered to preserve their aroma. Alternatively, line clear glass bottles with dark paper. Do not store herbs in tins.

The art of using herbs is one of the more important characteristics of French cooking. They are, in fact, used as a seasoning and therefore as a complement to the flavour of the main ingredients and must never dominate.

Black pepper is more frequently used than white since it is more aromatic, and always ground fresh from a pepper mill. Ordinary black peppercorns are often replaced by Jamaican pimento corns (allspice) for the same reason.
Orange peel, either fresh or dried, can be used to add a subtle flavour to meat recipes as well as sweet dishes. The dried variety can be prepared in advance by cutting the peel of a thin-skinned orange into finger-length pieces and drying them slowly in the bottom of the oven after it has been used and turned off. They should be left there until quite dry and hard and then stored in an airtight jar.
Tangerine peel can also be treated and used in the same way as orange peel.
Lemon peel is always used fresh.
Vanilla used for flavouring cakes and sweet dishes is best used in pod form. It has much more flavour than the liquid variety. The pod, about 10 cm (5 in) long, is dried after use and kept in an airtight tin, or wrapped in foil. It can be used up to four times again. After the first time it should be slit open and bent before use to increase the aroma.
Vanilla sugar is easily made by putting an opened pod into a screw-topped jar with 450 g (1 lb) castor sugar and leaving it there for a week before use.

Top row: English parsley, Continental parsley, chives, sorrel, pot marjoram, camomile, peppermint; *bottom row:* tarragon, bay, rosemary, common thyme, bronze fennel, winter savory, sage

Tisane or herb tea is the infusion of herbs used fresh in season and dried in the winter months, with which, at one time, countrywomen treated their family's minor ills. This medicinal connection has remained in the minds of some people as a prejudice, but the name tisane does do a great deal towards making them acceptable as a soothing after-dinner beverage, especially by those who cannot drink coffee late at night. Many of the more aromatic herbs such as camomile or lime flowers are looked upon as a pleasant alternative to sleeping pills. This could be nothing more than the effect of slowly-sipped hot water on a troubled digestion, but drinking tisane can become a very pleasant habit.

The dried varieties are sold in health food shops but gardeners will find a certain pride in producing their own.

The amount of herbs required varies but it is also a matter of taste and trial. The following quantities, to be increased or not as desired, will provide a general guide. As when making tea, always warm the pot first with boiling water.

Top : lime-flower tea being poured; *centre :* lime-flower, camomile; *bottom ;* peppermint, bergamot

Bergamot tea

This herb is used dried. Put 2 rounded teaspoons of herbs into a clean dry pot and pour 575 ml (1 pint) of fast-boiling water over them. Add 1 teaspoon of sugar to bring out the flavour, cover and allow to stand for 5 minutes before straining into the cups. More sugar can be added if desired. The dried leaves can also be used as a mixture with Indian tea in the proportion of a $\frac{1}{2}$ measure of bergamot to 1 measure of tea. This makes an economy in the amount of tea used and a refreshing tisane into the bargain.

Camomile tea

The flower heads used should be in the proportion of 16 fresh ones to 575 ml (1 pint) of boiling water. The quantity is doubled when dried flowers are used. Add 1 teaspoon of sugar to increase the flavour and for a very delicious aroma add 1 teaspoon of orange-flower water to each cup. Orange-flower water can be obtained at all health food shops.

Lime-flower tea

The dried sprigs of flower and leaves are used in the proportion of one large handful to 575 ml (1 pint) of boiling water. Add 1 teaspoon of sugar, stir well, cover and allow to stand 5 minutes before straining into the cups.

Mint tea

Peppermint (*Mentha piperata*) tea, when made with fresh mint requires a large handful of mint and stalks to 575 ml (1 pint) of boiling water and 1 teaspoon of sugar. Snip up the stalks and leaves finely with a pair of scissors before putting them into the pot or jug. Add boiling water, sugar, and cover. Leave for at least 5 minutes to infuse before straining into the cups. If dried peppermint is used allow 2 heaped teaspoons of herbs to 575 ml (1 pint) of boiling water and the same quantity of sugar.

Flavoured vinegars

The flavoured vinegar used in French cooking can be currently bought in Britain but it is much more economical to make one's own. Some French housewives still make the wine vinegar itself by simply pouring the dregs of their wine bottles into a wooden cask furnished with a *mère-de-vinaigre*. This is created by the acetic fermentation of the wine under the action of a fungus, *Mycoderma acati*. But to paraphrase Mrs Beeton, 'first obtain your fungus'.

A more simple procedure is to buy in bulk the wine vinegar sold in chemist's shops and flavour it with fresh herbs. This is more economical than buying it already prepared, and produces the same flavoured vinegar as that used in every French kitchen. Malt vinegar is never used for culinary purposes.

Tarragon vinegar

INGREDIENTS
- 1 litre (1¾ pints) white wine vinegar
- 2 stalks fresh tarragon, about 48 cm (15 in) long
- a 1-litre (2-pint) bottle

Wash the bottle in hot soapy water and rinse thoroughly in clear hot water. Place in a slow oven to warm the glass. Heat the vinegar in an enamel-lined pan until it feels quite warm to the touch of the little finger joint, but on no account should it boil. Meanwhile wash the stalks of tarragon in cold water and shake dry before bending them into halves. Insert them into the bottle and push them down below the neck. Pour in the warm vinegar, cork tightly and seal either with sealing wax or melted preserving wax. Leave to mature for at least one month before use.

When the bottle is opened the original tarragon can be removed and a fresh stalk inserted. This is not necessary but the action of the hot vinegar changes the colour of the herb and a fresh stalk improves the appearance.

This is the most popular flavour used by French cooks in meat dishes, salad dressings, and marinades.

Garlic vinegar

Substitute 2 cloves of garlic for the tarragon. Skin and lightly crush them. Place in the bottle and proceed as in the above recipe. (Use either white or red wine vinegar.)

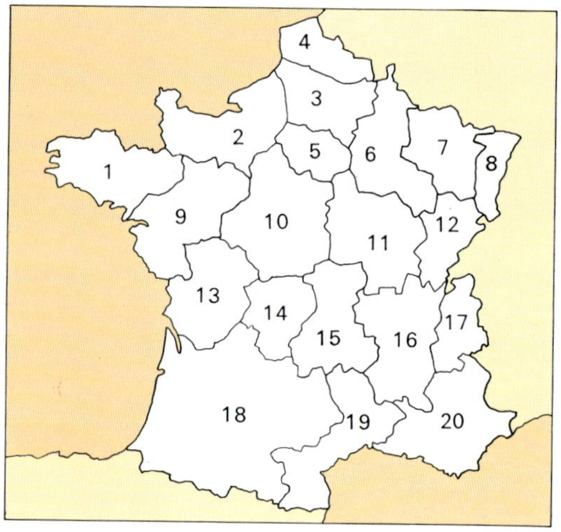

Each region of France is famous for certain food products (for details of Cheese *see pages* 174–9); the following list of regions gives those that are best known:

Bretagne (1)
Cheese. Mutton, pork, Nantes duckling, turkeys and game. Shellfish and freshwater fish. Cauliflowers, artichokes, onions and garlic. Strawberries and apples. Cider, Muscadet and eau-de-vie.

Normandie (2)
Dairy products. Fish and shellfish (ormers). Salt-meadow lamb and duck. Apples, cider and Calvados.

Picardie (3)
Cheese. Shell fish. Salt-meadow lamb, game, wild duck, teal and wild goose, also famous duck pâté. Vegetables. Cider and beer.

Artois (4)
Fish and freshwater fish. Beef, mutton and pork: sausages and black pudding. Pastries and caramels. Cider and beer.

Ile de France (5)
Cheese. Vegetables, particularly asparagus and mushrooms. Grapes: Chasselas de Fontainebleau, the King's vine arbour. Peaches and strawberries.

Champagne (6)
Cheese. Carp, pike, trout and salmon. Pork: andouillettes, ham and pigs' trotters. Game, thrush pâté and poultry. Snails. Honey and nougat. Pastries, gingerbread and macaroons. Wine, Champagne and brandy.

Lorraine (7)
Cheese. Crayfish, trout and pike. Foie gras. Pork: ham, black pudding and sausages. Pastries (mirabelle tart). Wine and fruit eau-de-vie (mirabelle and quetsch).

Alsace (8)
Crayfish, blue trout, pike and salmon. Sausages and black puddings. Geese (foie gras) and game. Wine and fruit brandy: quetsch, kirsch, mirabelle, sloe and raspberry. Pastries.

Pays de la Loire (9)
Goat cheese. Loire salmon and bream. Game and rillettes. Wine and Cointreau.

Orléannais (10)
Cheese. Freshwater fish. Poultry and game. Asparagus and fruit. Shortbread and pithiviers. Saffron. Honey, wine vinegar, cider and wine.

Bourgogne (11)
Cheese. Freshwater fish. Charolais beef cattle. Poulets de Bresse. Game: woodcock and game pâté. Snails. Vegetables and fruit, especially cherries and black currants. Mushrooms, truffles, and mustard. Wine and fruit liqueurs: cassis and prunelle. Marzipan, macaroons and nougatines.

Franche-Comté (12)
Cheese. Trout, pike, perch. Poulet de Bresse, game and wild boar. Saucisses fumées. Wine and liqueurs: kirsch, mirabelle and gentiane.

Poitou (13)
Cheese. Butter. Oysters, mussels and crayfish. Beef and pork. Poultry, ducks, foie gras and game. Artichokes, green peas and haricot beans. Chestnuts and walnuts. Biscuits, macaroons and caramels. Wine and angelica liqueur.

Limousin (14)
Cheese. Salmon, trout, crayfish, carp, perch and pike. Beef and pork. Game, especially hare. Mushrooms. Pastries, meringues, cherry tart.

Auvergne (15)
Cheese. Salmon trout, carp and tench. Pork, beef, mutton and game. Vegetables and fruit. Walnuts and chestnuts.

Rhône (16)
Freshwater fish. Truffles. Peaches, cherries, apricots and almonds. Wine.

Savoie (17)
Dairy products. Trout, char, burbot, eel, carp, crayfish, laveret and féra (the last two are unique to the province). Game, especially pâtés. Vegetables, especially cardoons. Honey. Chocolate. Gâteaux de Savoie. Wine and liqueurs: kirsch, eau-de-vie and vermouth.

Gascogne (18)
Cheese. Pork, charcuterie. Geese, duck (pâtés). Game: ortolans, thrush, woodcock and palombes. Honey, angelica, cassis liqueur and eau-de-coings (quince liqueur).

Languedoc (19)
Cheese. Spiny lobster, anchovy, eels, cod, cockles, lampreys, mussels, trout, bream, tench, crayfish and perch. Pork, lamb, poultry, geese, duck, snails, frogs' legs and truffles. Game. Tomatoes, aubergines and white beans. Fruit, crystallized fruits, honey. Wine.

Provence (20)
Cheese. Mullet, sardines, tuna fish, clams, octopus, sea urchins, sea perch and praires. Early vegetables and fruit. Truffles. Olive oil. Candied fruits, honey, herbs, nougat, almonds.

Index

Acknowledgments

The producers of this book would like to thank the following: Paul Kemp (photography); Christine Lloyd, Martin Newton (design and photography); Elaine Bastable, Caroline Ellwood, Carol Handslip, Joanna Percival (home economists); Vicki Robinson (index); Lighthorne Herbs, Moreton Morrell, Warwickshire (for supplying the herbs on page 217).

Also the following companies for the kind loan of accessories for the photography:
David Mellor, 4 Sloane Square, London SW1
Divertimenti, 68 Marylebone Lane, London W1
Elizabeth David, 46 Bourne Street, London SW1
John Lewis, Oxford Street, London W1
Liberty & Co. Ltd., Regent Street, London W1
Peter Jones, Sloane Square, London SW1

Black and white illustration acknowledgments
Mary Evans Picture Library **13**
Ann Ronan Picture Library **33**
The Mansell Collection **179**
The Mansell Collection **216**
The Rainbird Publishing Group Ltd **219**
Colour illustration acknowledgments
Spectrum Colour Library **44-5**
Spectrum Colour Library **72-3**
Picture Library (John Garrett) **122-3**